Praise

Whether you're debating a talk show host, co-worker, or "Fox addicted" Uncle Ralph at Thanksgiving, this book will teach you how to reach people's minds and hearts without wounding them in ways that produce the opposite result you wanted. Brilliant!

— Thom Hartmann, NY Times bestselling author
and America's #1 progressive talk show host

Read this book! Connection is the deep strategy for winning in politics… and in life. *Beyond Contempt* shows us ways to align our communication style with our values of inclusion, open-mindedness, and kindness.

— Joan Blades, co-founder, Living Room Conversations,
MomsRising, and MoveOn.org

Etelson channels her first-hand experience going door-to-door in this insightful exploration of how to connect with people, bridge divides, and communicate effectively across differences. She highlights the principles our canvassers practice every night: rather than tell voters what they believe is wrong, start by listening, treat people with respect, and introduce new information.

— Matt Morrison, executive director, Working America, AFL-CIO

Etelson's book is a true gem. It poignantly and compellingly captures the disdainful attitudes and counterproductive conversational strategies that many progressives employ when talking to conservative people. There are numerous clarifying examples provided to help support the sharp and probing analysis, as well as numerous gems of insight about the predicament we are in. The extremely illustrative and practical suggestions in the second half of the book about what folks can do is wonderful. The book helped improve both my thinking about the divide and the language that I will use when trying to nudge other progressives toward greater compassion and effectiveness. *Beyond Contempt* is an excellent resource for any liberal who wants to heal our divided nation or to pursue the goal of becoming more persuasive with conservatives.

— David Campt, principal, The White Ally Toolkit,
an initiative of The Dialogue Company

An extraordinary work, simultaneously sharply critical and brilliantly optimistic. *Beyond Contempt* makes the profound case that *style is content*, and the quality of our rhetoric matters. Here's a brilliant book that maintains that the goal for progressives is not merely recovery of leadership and power, but the creation of frameworks of logic and values that are consistent with our longer term goals. This is a revelatory work, positive and brilliant.

— Jerry Mander, founder, International Forum on Globalization,
and author, *The Capitalist Papers*, and *In the Absence of the Sacred*

Beyond Contempt carries a profound message that is beyond the scope of any brand of partisan politics. It is a map for how to create sustainable societal change from a place of integrity that aligns with the kind of world we want to create.

— Fareen Jamal, lawyer, accredited mediator,
past chair, Ontario Bar Association (OBA) Family Law Section,
2014 OBA Heather MacArthur Memorial Young Lawyers Award

Erica Etelson has the courage to hold up the mirror—first, to look at herself with unflinching honesty, and then to invite the rest of us to see how our disdain exacerbates the divide. She does not stop there, thankfully, but goes on to offer us a solution—a tool for changing our attitude so that we can be curious, direct, true to ourselves, and kinder to others. Erica Etelson can be our guide back to humanity. I hope you will take the mirror, and then follow her lead.

— Carolyn Wilkes Kaas, associate dean, Experiential Education,
co-director, Center on Dispute Resolution,
Quinnipiac University School of Law

In a political environment marred by Trump's extreme impropriety, it's easy for progressives to lose sight of our own role in deepening the divide. *Beyond Contempt* shows us why treating *all* people with respect is essential to our democracy and the key to building a winning coalition for 2020 and beyond.

— Karin Tamerius, MD, founder, Smart Politics

BEYOND
CONTEMPT

HOW LIBERALS CAN COMMUNICATE
ACROSS THE GREAT DIVIDE

ERICA ETELSON

new society
PUBLISHERS

Cover design by Diane McIntosh. Cover Image: iSock.

Printed in Canada. First printing November 2019.

Inquiries regarding requests to reprint all or part of *Beyond Contempt*
should be addressed to New Society Publishers at the address below.
To order directly from the publishers, please call toll-free (North America)
1-800-567-6772, or order online at www.newsociety.com

Any other inquiries can be directed by mail to:

New Society Publishers
P.O. Box 189, Gabriola Island, BC V0R 1X0, Canada
(250) 247-9737

Library and Archives Canada Cataloguing in Publication

Title: Beyond contempt : how liberals can communicate
across the great divide / Erica Etelson.

Names: Etelson, Erica, 1967– author.

Description: Includes bibliographical references and index.

Identifiers: Canadiana (print) 20190169958 | Canadiana (ebook) 20190169966 |
ISBN 9780865719170 (softcover) | ISBN 9781550927092 (PDF) |
ISBN 9781771423052 (EPUB)

Subjects: LCSH: Interpersonal communication. | LCSH: Political culture—
United States. | LCSH: United States—Politics and government.

Classification: LCC HM1166 .E84 2019 | DDC 302.2—dc23

Funded by the   Financé par le
Government   gouvernement
of Canada   du Canada

Canadä

New Society Publishers' mission is to publish books
that contribute in fundamental ways to building an ecologically
sustainable and just society, and to do so with the least possible impact
on the environment, in a manner that models this vision.

Certified

Ⓑ Corporation

MIX
Paper from
responsible sources
FSC
www.fsc.org
FSC® C016245

Note to Readers

The names and personal details of some people in this book have been changed to conceal their identity.

In writing this book, I've had to do something I try to avoid, which is to give unsolicited feedback concerning other people's speech. For every example I cite, there are hundreds more, including my own. The people whose speech I critique are not the villains of the story.

Book website: ericaetelson.com/beyondcontempt

Note to Conservative Readers

This book is written with a left-leaning readership in mind, and all of the analysis and examples stem from a left-wing perspective that takes for granted certain beliefs conservatives probably don't share. Powerful Non-Defensive Communication (PNDC), the technique used throughout this book to articulate political opinions, is itself nonpartisan. Sharon Strand Ellison's book, *Taking the War Out of Our Words*, teaches PNDC in a non-ideological context.

Contents

Acknowledgments xi

Introduction 1

1. Contempt and Its Discontents 17

2. Class-Based Contempt—Red with Shame 47

3. Why Not Everyone Is a Liberal 77

4. Curiosity—The Antidote to Contempt 105

5. Speaking Your Peace 125

6. Putting It All Together 153

Conclusion: To Bridge or to Break 169

Notes 181

Index 217

About the Author 227

About New Society Publishers 228

Only when you've
seen it all,
the depths and heights
and breadths of pain
inside yourself
and then begin
to recognize
it's really no different
in essence
from anyone else's,
anyone who hurts in mind
heart, body
who feels as you do—
angry, beaten, in despair—
that we all feel enough
in every breath—
whatever we needed,
did or didn't do

Only when you've
let it all,
this knowing, take residence
inside your heart, mind—
the loving thought, its evil twin,

petty, noble, sleazy, enlightened,
the beauty-filled or horror-ridden,
that the evil of the
torturer, murderer, or terrorist
is pain that can't be managed—
and realize it's all a part of you
and every other being,
that you and he or she are kin
same blood,
same breath

…

the worst not worse
than your worst,
the best not better
than your highest good

And only then
when you fall on your knees
before such Beauty,
can you apprehend
that a mighty kindness
is, in the end, your only Calling.

—Excerpt from "A Mighty Kindness" in forthcoming
collection, *Conscientious Objections,* by Dr. Monza Naff

Acknowledgments

I could not have written—or even conceived—of this book without the brilliant input of Sharon Strand Ellison, creator of Powerful Non-Defensive Communication (PNDC). Sharon's genius is the intellectual foundation underlying this book. Sharon, I'm so glad you got your chocolate in my peanut butter—thank you! And huge thanks as well to my extended PNDC family, whose unflagging support kept me afloat when waves of doubt were crashing down on me.

A big thank you to those who read early drafts and book proposals: Carrie Kaas, Don Moore, Ned Reifenstein, Marc Staton, and Karin Tamerius. Your validation that I was on the right track gave me the confidence to proceed.

Thank you, Monza Naff, for your beautiful poetry and spirit. And thanks for the 12 hugs a day and the oatmeal in Bend.

Muchas gracias to Jesse Combs for building out my website, to Simon Johnson for wrangling the voluminous endnotes into shape, and to Chris Cook for all manner of helpful advice and support.

I'm grateful to these people who gave generously of their time to share their thoughts and experiences with me: Michael Bell, Helena Brantley, Erica Buist, Ami Atkinson Combs, Anthony Fauci, Nell Fields, Dave Fleischer, Alex Gibson, Kaitlyn Harrold, John Hibbing, Paula Green, Gwen Johnson, Angela King, Luke Mahler, Marshall Mason, David Matsumoto, and Ira Roseman.

Thanks to the terrific crew at New Society Publishers—especially to Rob West for seeing the potential in this book and to Claire Anderson for top-notch copyediting. A round of applause, too, for the stellar services of the Berkeley Public Library and the National Writers Union, UAW Local 1981—solidarity forever.

I'm grateful for the efforts of Better Angels, Living Room Conversations, and SMART Politics in facilitating political discourse across lines of difference, and for visionaries and changemakers who never succumb to the nihilistic forces of apathy, cynicism, and despair.

To my family members, friends, and comrades: Thank you for listening to my endless ruminations and for tolerating my preoccupied state of mind these last two years. David and Liam, you're the best. I love you.

Introduction

Early in my first year of college, I got involved in the Nuclear Freeze movement. One night, I toiled into the wee hours stenciling a horrid little handmade poster that said: "We're not Communists and we're not homosexuals...We just want to prevent a nuclear holocaust."

The poster somehow succeeded in drawing a few dozen students to a meeting, after which a graduate student quietly took me aside and critiqued my poster's expressions of homophobia and red-baiting. The two concepts were unfamiliar to me, but I quickly learned that they were harmful and hurtful. The grad student's explanation was straightforward and casual—no shaming, no lecturing, no self-righteous indignation.

Had the grad student humiliated me, I might have withdrawn in shame or turned to a conservative campus group that would lick the wounds inflicted by the politically correct police. But thanks to her skill in teaching me something without putting me on the defensive, I was able to digest and accept the lesson.

I wish that the next chapter of the story was about how I modeled myself after her and sprinkled seeds of wisdom across America that blossomed into a progressive populist revolution. Not exactly.

One summer by the pool just after college graduation, my friend's boyfriend, upon learning that I was about to move to San Francisco, said he could never live in a place with "so many homos." I replied, "That's not a problem for men who are secure in their masculinity." It was a slam dunk by 1980s gender-binary standards, a sick burn on the deplorable homophobe. I showed him all right. But what did I show him? How to resent snarky liberals?

I carried on in a similar vein right up through the 2016 election, tuning in to Jon Stewart on an as-needed basis to remind myself how much smarter and superior my tribe of educated, mostly white liberals and progressives was. And then, the stuff of nightmares unfolded. A nihilistic demagogue had hijacked what was left of our democracy and turned it into the worst, most crass and dangerous reality TV show ever.

November 9 had barely dawned before my contempt level began registering in the ninetieth percentile, not just toward Trump but toward his supporters. As I binged on articles, blogs, and Facebook rants, my contempt was validated a hundredfold: Who *were* These People—these crazy, racist, misogynistic, gun-toting knuckleheads who voted for a self-aggrandizing, mono-syllabic, bilious, billionaire charlatan who would obviously stab them in the back as they sat in front of their TVs, being loboto-mized by Sean Hannity while swilling non-craft beer?

In fact, I knew nothing about These People and, at the same time, I knew all I needed to know—they were backward, brain-washed yokels who prefer cleavage to pantsuits and Ann Coulter's vicious racism to Stephen Colbert's satirical genius; rednecks who eat a lot of meat but not because they're following a Paleo diet. And they deserved to go down with their titanic mistake.

Where was Jon Stewart when I needed him most? Last I could recall he was having a mock orgasm as he thanked The Donald for descending from comedy heaven on a golden escalator to run as a vanity candidate.[1]

Who could blame us for berating and mocking half of the population? How could we *not* ridicule them? After all, our ad-versaries had long since become certifiably insane with their birtherism and their Benghazi hearings, their guns and their rage over Obamacare and transgender bathrooms. They were so dense and cognitively impaired, it was sad. Really, we might pity them if they weren't such a basket of deplorables.

Remember how George W. Bush didn't even know how to pronounce "nuclear"? Remember how we "mis-underestimated" him? Twice? Then we mis-underestimated those Tea Party nutters. And then we mis-underestimated The Donald. Acknowledgment of our hubris was in order, but instead we doubled down on condescension—the stupidity of those red-state rubes was once again destroying America.

Trump's election made many of us feel hurt, angry, and scared. Reeling from the daily shock and awe, we do our best to defend ourselves against his malevolence. Often, our defensiveness takes the form of contempt, a blend of anger, disgust, and superiority.

Faced with an increasingly oligarchical military-surveillance-prison-financial-industrial complex that varies little as Republican and Democratic administrations come and go, there's constant need to speak truth to—and about—power. But our truth-telling too often takes the form of what literary critic Tim Parks calls "failed" satire:

> [T]he criteria for assessing it [satire] are fairly simple: if it doesn't point toward positive change, or encourage people to think in a more enlightened way, it has failed. That doesn't mean it's not amusing and well-observed, or even, for some, hilarious, in the way, say, witty mockery of a political enemy can be hilarious and gratifying and can *intensify our sense of being morally superior.* But as satire it has failed. *The worst case is when satire reinforces the state of mind it purports to undercut, polarizes prejudices, and provokes the very behavior it condemns* [emphasis added].[2]

Parks was critiquing the French magazine *Charlie Hebdo*'s grotesque mockery of the Islamic prophet Muhammad, but he may as well have been writing about the ways in which the US liberal creative and political class has fostered a sense of moral and intellectual superiority that has thoroughly antagonized conservative Americans.

It's not just that we—liberals and progressives—vigorously disagree with their beliefs and are enraged by the brutality of militarism, corporatism, patriarchy, and white supremacy. We express our opposition in a condescending, self-righteous manner that invalidates their fears, questions their intelligence, and belittles values that are sacred to them—order, stability, religion, loyalty, individualism.

We *want* all Americans to be offended by all of the things that offend us but, when they aren't, instead of meeting them where *they're* at, we insult and shame them in an ill-fated effort to bring them around to where *we're* at. But from what I've observed and what social science tells us, hurling vitriolic truth bombs across the left–right divide only widens it.

Jodie Shokraifard, a working-class Obama voter who sat out the 2016 election, tells the story of being puzzled by a Facebook meme contrasting the migrant caravan with urban crime. When she asked her Facebook friends to explain the meme to her, they denounced her as an "idiotic Trump supporter." None would deign to explain the meme to her. Not one. "Why is it easier to call me racist and dumb than it is to answer the question?" Jodie asks.[3] Why, indeed. Here's a woman begging to learn something, but her supercilious "friends" are too cool for school. The pervasiveness of this attitude results in countless lost opportunities for learning and growth. Where will Jodie Shokraifard turn for understanding now that her liberal friends have cast her out?

A young man I'll call Todd told me that his aunt, whom he had always looked up to, began attacking him on Facebook when she learned he was a right-leaning Independent. She posted long rants decrying Republicanism, picked fights with his Facebook friends, and demanded to know if he supported Obama. When Todd said he didn't support Obama because of his positions on health care and other issues, she insisted that his reasons were invalid and that he must be a racist. Their relationship became estranged and never recovered, a turn of events that caused him great sadness.

American political culture grows ever more divisive, spiteful and abrasive, more cruel, more hateful. "Mainstream media," says Berkeley Graduate School of Journalism Dean Edward Wasserman, "have made a fortune teaching people the wrong ways to talk to each other."[4] Political discourse has become a hyperpartisan, vitriolic blood sport, terribly profitable for the corporate media and terribly terrible for society.[5]

Leftists are not the primary purveyors of cruelty and hate, but we're complicit in debasing the culture of political discourse. I draw no moral equivalency between (a) hateful rhetoric and actions against vulnerable groups of people and (b) abrasive, condescending, or spiteful words directed at those who promote or acquiesce in bigotry. But the epidemic of the former does not, in my mind, justify the epidemic of the latter, especially when the target is low-income whites whose American Dream has been smothered in its sleep.

Even participation *within* the Left can feel like a circular firing squad. During the 2016 primary, some angry Clinton supporters derided "Bernie bros," and some angry Bernie supporters denounced Clinton as a "corporate Democratic whore."[6]

Progressives may feel justified in being snide and impatient because we're losing ground on peace and social justice as fast as the ice sheets are losing mass. *How can our adversaries not see that Trump and the GOP (and, some believe, neoliberal Democrats) are driving us over a cliff?*

New Yorker satirist Andy Borowitz captures smug liberal weariness at having to enlighten ignoramuses:

> Many Americans are tired of explaining things to idiots, particularly when the things in question are so painfully obvious, a new poll indicates…According to the poll, conducted by the University of Minnesota's Opinion Research Institute, while millions have been vexed for some time by their failure to explain incredibly basic information to dolts, that frustration has now reached a breaking point.

Of the many obvious things that people are sick and tired of trying to get through the skulls of stupid people, the fact that climate change will cause catastrophic habitat destruction and devastating extinctions tops the list, with a majority saying that they will no longer bother trying to explain this to cretins.[7]

I'd like to think Borowitz was poking fun at liberal superiority, but I doubt we're his targets. Published online a week after Trump announced his candidacy, Borowitz was, like Stewart, cashing in on Trump's gift to satirists. But, like the failed *Charlie Hebdo* satire Parks critiques, it provokes the very behavior it condemns.

Humiliating one's adversaries is a dangerous business. It may be clever and gratifying, but it's not wise. The feeling of humiliation is a mixture of shame and anger. German social psychologist Evelin Lindner calls humiliation "the nuclear bomb of the emotions." By stripping away the other person's dignity, humiliation inflicts a mortal wound, leaving the humiliated mind to convince itself of the need to inflict even greater pain on the perpetrator. Lindner identifies horrific spirals of humiliation in the genocidal histories of Germany, Somalia, Rwanda, and Serbia, where she learned the Somali proverb, "Humiliation is worse than death; in times of war, words of humiliation hurt more than bullets."[8]

Most Trump supporters have views that liberals loathe. The trouble comes when we go beyond challenging the views to humiliating, denigrating, and "othering" the people themselves, the "deplorables" who are afflicted not only with contemptible belief systems but with bad taste, low intelligence, and gullibility. We treat them like cardboard cutouts of stereotypical redneck bigots or brainwashed evangelicals who have no valid cause for complaining.

We deny Trump supporters the legitimacy of their grievances because we don't look beyond the white nationalist demagoguery that has hijacked said grievances. But as Lindner cautions, "For our own sake and safety, we must give serious study and attention to all feelings of humiliation, because *even if the injury is imaginary, the revenge is just as real* [emphasis added]."[9] When we dehumanize others, we invite them to dehumanize us. A vicious cycle starts spinning—one with enough centrifugal force to jettison the altruistic impulses that hold society together.

Trump is the king of contempt. Lacking a positive vision for our country, he fills the void by insulting his enemies. Instead of focusing relentlessly on crafting and communicating a strong progressive agenda, the Left strikes back with caustic tweets and YouTube smackdowns wherein a liberal hero "utterly destroys" or "owns" some conservative or another. Nancy Pelosi was approvingly dubbed the Queen of Condescension when she mockingly clapped back at Trump during the 2018 State of the Union address, her smile an unmistakable smirk.[10] This, after questioning Trump's "manhood" and comparing him to a skunk during the standoff over border-wall funding.[11]

No matter how abusive and crass Trump is, we can choose our style of expression, our path toward what writer Charles Eisenstein calls "the more beautiful world our hearts know is possible." Every time we express ourselves, we can consider: Will a stinging counterattack make me feel less hurt and afraid? For how long? Will it touch someone's heart or stir up their bitterness, cause them to see me as more or less of a fellow human being?

Some believe that we must always fight fire with fire and see a call for respectful communication as an objectionable form of tone policing that protects the oppressors. Others, including the Dream Corps' #LoveArmy, the Revolutionary Love Project, and Reverend William Barber's Repairers of the Breach movement, assert that unity and respect for the humanity of all people are the preconditions for enduring social justice. #LoveArmy's mission is to "win without deepening divides." It asks members to commit to guiding principles like "Turn to each other, not on each other," "Call each other up—not out," and "Heal divides."[12]

In a 1959 speech to the War Resisters League, Martin Luther King, Jr., said that the civil rights struggle was against evil *forces*, not evil *doers*, and that the end goal is redemption, reconciliation, and the creation of a beloved community. "To retaliate [with hate and bitterness] would do nothing but intensify the existence of hate in the universe...someone must have sense enough and morality enough to cut off the chain of hate."[13]

In an echo across the decades, I heard the same sentiment articulated at the 2019 Othering & Belonging Conference. There, Reverend Ben McBride, whose Operation Ceasefire initiative led to a 40 percent drop in Oakland, California's homicide rate, called on the audience to be "hard on structures, soft on people" and to stop "othering" our adversaries: "What's the point of getting to the Promised Land if you become the pharaoh in the process?" His organization, PICO California, is focusing on "bridging" rather than "breaking."[14]

Alicia Garza, cofounder of the Black Lives Matter movement, struck a similar chord in a powerful talk she gave in Detroit in 2017. Garza reflected on the need to not only build power but to *transform* it, to "call us back to our humanity" by organizing movements across lines of difference and eschewing the desire for revenge. Though her talk concerned the role of white women *within* social justice movements, I believe the principles she articulates can be applied to conservatives as well.

> A movement that rejects the potential of liberatory relationships is a movement that is destined to fail. A movement that believes that change is not possible will not succeed. Not everyone will pursue change, even when given the opportunity. But many will, and it's our job to be the alternative that is more attractive than the status quo. Colonization, capitalism, imperialism, white supremacy, heteronormativity, patriarchy—all of these systems function to break the bonds of relationship between us. Our movement must be a different one. One that seeks to forge many different kinds of relationships that reject the systems that tear us apart, reject the fear and hatred, and that reject power *over* in favor of power *with*...We are here to examine how we can bring about the world we desire while dismantling the one we don't.[15]

Not everyone shares the philosophy of radical inclusivity. Some may agree with it in theory but aren't able or willing to abide it. As Reverend Jennifer Bailey, founder of the Faith Matters Network, compassionately explains, some people are in too much pain to engage openheartedly in building bridges across lines of difference, an endeavor that requires a degree of vulnerability that may not be possible for those who have been hurt by white supremacy, heteropatriarchy, or classism.[16]

Beyond Contempt represents my personal choice in how to communicate with people whose beliefs I view as harmful, dangerous, or irrational. As an able-bodied, white, straight, financially secure, native-born, Jewish, cisgender woman, I'm safe from many of the threats Trump has ramped up and don't want to criticize the choices oppressed people make about how best to protect themselves or express their grief, fear, and rage; hence, this book is an invitation, not a prescription.

∼

Beyond Contempt is for liberals and progressives who want to be able to communicate with the tens of millions of Americans who approve of Donald Trump and some or all of the views he represents. Some of them may be your family members, friends, or neighbors. Some of them are the voters whose doors you'll be knocking on in the summer and fall of 2020, or who will see your tweets, blogs, and Facebook posts, your letters to the editor, your campaign ads and speeches. If you've been avoiding Trump supporters since 2016 or have an outrage hangover, this book is for you.

The first half delves into the dynamics of contempt, how and why it arises, and how people respond (poorly) to being treated with contempt. I survey the cultural landscape, showing how media and politics are rife with contempt, much of it class-based. And I show how contempt toward Trump voters often goes hand in hand with indifference toward the well-being of faltering white working-class communities.

We can be passionate and angry, we can hold wrongdoers accountable, we can even be confrontational and disruptive; but if we lace our speech with vitriol, if we engage in caustic Twitter feuds, if we express our beliefs in a snide or self-righteous manner that deprecates those who disagree, I believe that we do our cause a disservice. When we spice up our speech with snark, only the choir savors the taste.

If, after reading the first three chapters, you believe that scorning and scolding Trump supporters is counterproductive, then the second half of the book invites you to try a different mode of expression.

Several years ago, I chanced upon the work of Sharon Strand Ellison, creator of a novel communication approach called Powerful Non-Defensive Communication (PNDC™). Ellison has trained thousands of educators, attorneys, government officials, and corporate and nonprofit leaders, and was credited with turning around the trailing campaign of Barbara Roberts, Oregon's first woman governor, by training Roberts in PNDC. She also trained activists who successfully defeated an Oregon ballot initiative that would have legalized discrimination against gay and lesbian public school teachers.

I've worked extensively with Ellison to apply PNDC to the current political divide, enabling liberals and progressives to engage with conservatives in ways that defuse hostility and create the possibility of finding common ground or, at least, do not cause them to become defensively entrenched in their position. Much of the material in the second half comes courtesy of Ellison's genius in phrasing questions and statements in ways that can open hearts and minds or, at least, not seal them shut. After decades of work as a public interest attorney and activist, I've had to unlearn several adversarial and self-righteous communication pitfalls. My skill with PNDC is a work in progress; there are times when I revert to convincing, judging, or withdrawing in disgust. Rest assured that you can rely on Ellison's expertise to guide you past my weak spots in chapters four, five, and six. (Apart from communication techniques, the views expressed in this book are my own, not hers).

For the most part, the communication guidance in this book applies to one-on-one conversations with ordinary people with whom you'd like to be able to talk without blowing your stack. It can also be helpful in interactions with people in positions of power (and their staff) when your strategy includes dialogue or negotiation. Lastly, there are some takeaways for media commentators and activists writing or speaking on divisive topics.

Beyond Contempt is not a call for genteel manners or meekness. It's an invitation to reclaim and reimagine a democratic notion of civility that facilitates public discourse through listening, understanding, and deliberating. Canadian philosopher Mark Kingwell put it best: "A society guided by civility will allow a political debate that is vigorous, even fractious, while retaining a goal we should consider binding: the possibility that minds can be changed."[17] So long as the United States is a democracy, we will share it with conservatives—our choice is whether to communicate with them in a manner that fosters understanding and goodwill, or that stirs up hatred.

PNDC doesn't call for being nicey-nice, feigning respect for hateful or dangerous beliefs, or subordinating justice to civility. It's not about adhering to norms of decorum that, some have argued, have been established by the powerful to insulate themselves from public accountability. It's not about being conciliatory or compromising—unless that's the chosen strategy for a reformist agenda. Rather, it's about listening to adversaries and articulating your position, passionately and compassionately, modeling the more beautiful world you want to live in. In *my* more beautiful world, there's accountability but not shame, reconciliation but not punishment, anger but not cruelty, authentic rage but not performative outrage, and passionate commitment to my beliefs, alongside compassion for the vulnerability of those who feel threatened by my beliefs.

What I value so deeply about PNDC is that it empowers people to speak their truth without blaming, denigrating, and gratuitously antagonizing others. We can stand up, sit in, speak up, shut down; we can march, strike, and boycott. We can disrupt institutions that treat human and ecological crises with indifference. We have an array of tactics at our disposal, and if we wield them not as weapons of war but as tools for promoting understanding and prompting action, they'll be of greater value.

In my communication, I can *choose* not to be cruel to the cruel. When I speak, it's to express my pain, fear, or anger, not to blame or punish those who have done wrong by me, or demonstrate my intellectual or moral superiority. I can speak my mind without degrading someone else in the process.

To a certain extent, antagonism is unavoidable in the social justice struggle. When Martin Luther King, Jr., led civil rights protestors in nonviolent civil disobedience, many disapproved of their disruptive, confrontational tactics, yet their disapproval didn't dampen public support for the civil rights legislation enacted during that tumultuous era. I believe that's because King eschewed gratuitous personal attacks and demonization of the movement's racist foes. As King said in praise of the early civil rights leader W.E.B. Du Bois, "He did not content himself with hurling invectives for emotional release and then to retire into smug, passive satisfaction."[18]

For King, the social justice struggle was rooted in beloved community, and conflicts reconciled in ways that turn opponents into friends and "bring about miracles in the hearts of men."[19] I might not be spiritually capable of going so far as King did to befriend or love my opponents, but I do recognize the futility—and danger—of inflaming their hatred of me.

Trump is the anti-King. In a 1990 interview, Trump said of then-President Bush, "I disagree with him when he talks of a kinder, gentler America. I think if this country gets any kinder or gentler, it's literally going to cease to exist."[20] Trump sees compassion as the enemy. Do we?

Among the many factors that made Trump's rise possible is the toxic state of our political culture, brimming with vitriol and bereft of empathy. Opinion leaders and political figures have increasingly adopted a combative, nasty, self-righteous style. Both sides do it in different ways and to different degrees. There are plenty of books you can read about the mean-spirited, dishonest, and divisive antics of right-wing ne'er-do-wells. This book is about our bad, not theirs.

The majority of Americans are exhausted by tribal divisiveness and say that the outrage culture has led them to tune out politics altogether.[21] When people disengage, they're more apt to make uninformed decisions at the voting booth or stay home, which leaves elections in the hands of voters who are disproportionately wealthy, evangelical, and/or NRA members.[22] The Left has its own faithful base, but we need the increasingly apathetic blue-collar swing voters of all races to show up, too.

As the 2020 election gets underway, scorn for Heartland and Appalachian voters is not what the doctor ordered. Pulitzer-prize winning writer and progressive populist Art Cullen, who publishes a local newspaper in Storm Lake, Iowa, criticizes Democrats like the Clintons for whom Iowa is flyover country…that is, until the Iowa caucuses roll around, and then suddenly they touch down to express dismay over rural hard knocks.[23] As I recount in chapter two, somewhere along the way, the Heartland became Dumfuckistan, its troubles written off as the self-inflicted wounds of racist old white fools—never mind the fact that those fools wield 159 out of 538 electoral votes.

Many leftists believe our efforts are better spent mobilizing young and minority voters than wasting time with Cullen's Midwestern swing voters. I favor a both/and approach to voter turnout. Droves of working-class voters of all races in swing states chose not to vote in 2016, in far greater numbers than the margin of Clinton's loss.[24] In addition, substantial numbers of economically populist Obama voters turned to Trump, enough in key electoral states to tip the election.[25] Democratic success in the 2018 midterm elections was a function of *both* high base turnout *and* Trump voters who flipped blue (and who, political scientists believe, could swing either way in 2020).[26]

According to Republican strategist Ari Fleischer, Trump's re-election strategy again hinges on flipping white working-class swing voters.[27] But alas for Trump, Working America, the political organizing arm of the AFL-CIO, has surveyed thousands of swing-state voters and found that many of them are ambivalent about Trump's performance—and open to ditching him in 2020.[28] We won't win back blue collar whites with disdain.

Consider a young white Pennsylvanian swing voter like Kaitlyn Harrold, who quickly came to regret her vote for Trump. Harrold grew up in a conservative white suburb of Pittsburgh and has family members on both sides of the aisle. She didn't like either candidate but was influenced by several Haitian-American coworkers who were voting for Trump because they believed that the Clinton Foundation misappropriated monies it had raised for Haitian earthquake victims. She also figured that being so rich, Trump wouldn't be an "establishment puppet."[29]

Harrold didn't approve of Trump's bigotry, but it wasn't until she moved to Pittsburgh and "met people who watched their best friends get shot on the street" that she began to understand systemic racism. "My hometown was all I knew, and I was very influenced by my community and didn't see the big picture," she explains. Once she began empathizing with victims of racism and poverty, her moral compass shifted, and she switched her party registration to Democrat. Harrold didn't jump ship because her coworkers hectored her. She shifted because they shared their stories with her. Even her vote for Trump was motivated by compassion for Haitian-Americans she believed Clinton had wronged.

How many other Kaitlyn Harrolds are out there, decent people who are not entrenched in reactionary ideologies but whose parochial upbringing steered them toward Trump? And how many are we surrendering to Trump when we treat them with contempt?

～

In *Rules for Resistance*, seasoned opponents of autocracies from around the globe beseech Americans not to make the same mistake they did of feeding tribal polarization by scorning their adversaries as stupid, gullible, and racist. "Don't hate people for voting for Trump," writes Indian journalist and Narendra Modi critic Satyen Bordoloi. "Understand them, engage with them today…Don't force fence-sitters to jump on the side of the bigots by you calling them so."[30] In my research for this book, I heard American conservatives saying much the same: that they value loyalty dearly, and liberal contempt makes them *more loyal* to Trump and unifies them in hatred of their enemy (us). "Donald Trump may be a fool," notes conservative journalist Rod Dreher, "but he's their fool."[31]

No matter who occupies the halls of power after 2020, the struggle for peace, and social and environmental justice never ends. Many of us will forever be lobbying, rallying, writing, speaking, filmmaking, artmaking, litigating, teaching, and tweeting to bend the arc of the future toward justice. In every one of these endeavors, we can accelerate change, defuse backlash, and increase cohesiveness by communicating respectfully—or, at least, neutrally—with those who are animated by a different set of values, hopes, fears, and, yes, heavy sigh, "facts."

The radical premise at the heart of this book is that asserting our own humanity does not require the degradation of other people's humanity—that we can honor the dignity of every person, *even if the other side doesn't*. The belief that we *should* humiliate and belittle our opponents is rooted in what Ellison calls "the war model of communication," in which dialogue is a battle with a winner and a loser, and it's our soldierly duty to browbeat our opponent with force. In war, that force is lethal; in communication, it creates and maintains the great divide.

Washington Post columnist Margaret Sullivan has sage advice for journalists laboring in the age of Trump: "Lose the smugness. Keep the mission." Her advice to journalists (which many *Post* writers have ignored) applies equally to activists, elected officials, influence leaders, and the rest of us. Holding the powerful accountable is more important than ever and is best achieved with a measure of humility.[32] *Beyond Contempt* is an invitation to learn how to communicate across the great divide with integrity, passion, and compassion. It will show you how to imbue your words with the power to defuse hostility, build connection, and, just maybe, discover that somewhere in the great divide there exists an island of common ground where we can break bread together as fallible, complicated, sad, joyful humans.

1

Contempt and Its Discontents

*If we write off half of society as deplorable,
we forfeit claims on their attention.*

—Edward Luce, *The Retreat of Western Liberalism*

Psychologist John Gottman can watch a married couple talk for a few minutes and predict with 94 percent accuracy whether that couple will still be together in 15 years. The number one predictor of divorce? Contempt.[1]

Out of a pool of 56 couples, it was the seven who harshly criticized each other, rolled their eyes, and made snide remarks who didn't make it to their sixth anniversary. Had Gottman randomly guessed which couples were destined for divorce court, he would have had a 0.0000000004 percent chance of correctly identifying all seven. Gottman isn't psychic, but he understands contempt's power to destroy relationships. If contempt can erode the love between two adults who had planned to spend their lives together, imagine what it can do to political adversaries.

If you can't imagine, watch a two-minute video called "Man Gets Schooled by Anti-Fascism Sign."[2] The video is from a 2018 May Day rally in Seattle, where 21-year-old Luke Mahler, dressed in a Patriot Prayer t-shirt, tried unsuccessfully to rip up a discarded sign reading, "In the Name of Humanity, We REFUSE to Accept a Fascist America" while onlookers heckled him. (Patriot Prayer is an "alt-right" group. Although not considered a hate group by the Southern Poverty Law Center as of this writing, Patriot Prayer rallies alongside hate groups and provokes violent clashes with antifascist protestors.)[3]

The hecklers mocked Mahler's strength and intelligence, suggesting that "educated engineers" at the nearby Amazon office could help him out. "You need a liberal to help you with that, dude. You're too fucking stupid to figure it out on your own," said one of them. A video of the encounter went viral, providing an online forum for a barrage of taunts. There were hundreds of hateful comments posted by people on both sides: those who saw him as a Nazi who deserved to be ridiculed and "alt-rightists" furious that he had embarrassed them.

Online hecklers reveled sadistically in Mahler's humiliation, calling him a "dumbfuck," "human garbage," and "soy boy." Several said they were trying to get him fired from his job at a local restaurant. Others mocked his "manboobs" and weak hands, speculated that he was a virgin, and wished he would be beaten to death.

As I scanned the nasty comments, I couldn't always tell the two sides apart:

"Hey you, out of the gene pool."
"He should use his teeth before someone knocks them out of his stupid head one day soon."
"Nothing better than watching pathetic Nazis get humiliated."
"You can tell how miserable and dumb he is…what a waste of a life."

Occasionally, a commenter expressed concern that the verbal abuse had gone too far, especially since Mahler is autistic. Such heresy was quickly stamped out as fascist apologism. When one person suggested that "mocking someone for being weak is against liberal values," another responded, "Mocking people is against liberal values. Lucky for us, conservatives and alt-right aren't people."

Mahler says he tried to destroy the sign not because of what it said but because it was created by Refuse Fascism, a group he claims had glitter-bombed and assaulted members of his group (an obscure offshoot of Patriot Prayer) months earlier.[4] (He provided me with video footage of the glitter bomb.) When I asked him how he felt about the public shaming he was experiencing, he showed no emotion and said his autism makes it hard to recognize sarcasm.

I don't know what to make of Mahler. He could be a full-fledged white nationalist. He could be, as he insisted to me, a defender of free speech who counts Muslims, gays, and Latinos among his friends and group members. He could be a college junior dabbling in the "alt-lite," trying to find himself. He could be all or none of the above. But for the hecklers, he was a cardboard cutout of a white nationalist, devoid of humanity, worthy only of venomous contempt.

One astute commenter predicted that if Mahler weren't already "incel," he would be now. (*Incel* refers to the online community of involuntarily celibate misogynists.)[5] The alt-right actively targets autistic, depressed, and socially anxious individuals in online discussion forums and gaming sites.[6] Whatever loneliness, angst, or anger led this young man to Patriot Prayer could only have been magnified by the public humiliation.

The hecklers may have believed themselves to be doing the right thing in ruthlessly shaming a racist. But feeling as though we're doing the right thing doesn't necessarily mean we are.

The Contempt Reflex

Contempt is a complex sentiment produced by a blend of anger, disgust, and, frequently, superiority. It's a feeling of scorn toward someone we hold in low esteem and wish to reject or punish. We display contempt through facial expressions and vocalizations, such as sneering, eye-rolling, snorting, sighing, and tsk-tsk tongue clicking.[7] Next time you catch yourself rolling your eyes at someone, ask yourself what you're feeling. (If that someone is your significant other, make an appointment with Dr. Gottman.)

Contempt is often leveled by a higher-status individual looking down upon a lower-status other, as suggested by the common term "beneath contempt." In the act of displaying contempt, we assert our superiority and social dominance over the contemptuous other.[8]

In a split second, the brain can appraise another as morally or intellectually inferior and, therefore, unworthy of one's attention.[9] Often, we treat the entire person's character as contemptuous rather than homing in on a specific offensive behavior or trait. If I hold someone in contempt, there's little reason to engage them in dialogue—a casual sneer or snide comment will generally suffice to dismiss the contemptuous other.

Trump dispatched his 2016 rivals with crude displays of contempt—"Lyin' Ted," "Little Marco," and "Low-Energy Jeb;" he is gearing up for 2020 with "Sleepy Joe" and "Crazy Bernie." A TV or radio personality looking to fill airtime and delight their partisan audience might go beyond a snarky put-down and indulge in a lengthier reverie on the idiocy, lunacy, and moral reprehensibility of the object of their contempt.

The "emotional goal" of contempt is to exclude or punish the inferior other. By showing contempt, I inflict shame on the transgressor and then remove them from consideration.[10] I might not even trouble myself with explaining the basis for my views—it's so *obvious* that I'm superior and anyone who doesn't recognize this is hopelessly clueless. In other words, I write the person off as irredeemable or, as Hillary Clinton classified half of Trump supporters, "deplorables."

Clinton's supporters saw the blowback against her "deplorables" gaffe as unfair. Perhaps. It's true that, in the next and underreported part of her speech, she spoke empathetically about the other half of Trump's base, people who felt that the government and economy had let them down and that no one cared about them.[11] But in 2018, she was still dissing the Heartland and blaming its washed-up residents for her defeat:

> If you look at the map of the United States, there's all that
> red in the middle where Trump won. I win the coasts. But

what the map doesn't show you is that I won the places that represent two-thirds of America's gross domestic product. So I won the places that are optimistic, diverse, dynamic, moving forward.[12]

If, as Clinton claims, her base of coastal elites is optimistic, diverse, dynamic, and moving forward, the implication is that red-state voters represent pessimism, white ethnocentrism, lethargy, and backwardness.

In politics, perception is reality. If a voting block perceives Hillary as disdainful toward them, then she is. And because she tossed out the unsubstantiated charge that "half" of Trump voters belong in the basket of deplorables, that left *all* Trump supporters wondering if she was referring to them. With a 50-50 chance that they were being placed in the basket of deplorables, they were incensed, just like they were when Obama made the following comment on the 2008 campaign trail: "They get bitter, they cling to guns or religion, or [have] antipathy to people who aren't like them, or [use] anti-immigrant sentiment or anti-trade sentiment as a way to explain their frustrations." Eight years later, Iowan Dennis Schminke cited Obama's comment as part of his rationale for voting for Trump: "His comment, the whole thing, it's been worn out to death, that clinging to God and guns, God and guns, and afraid of people who don't look like them, blah, blah, blah. Just quit talking down to me."[13]

Contempt rankles, and the alienation it engenders has a long half-life.

Contempt Toward Trump and His Base

Several times a day, Americans are subjected to Trump's latest outburst of Islamophobia, bellicosity, misogyny, white supremacy, narcissism, mendacity, ineptitude, and/or ignorance. For the first year or so, I lapped it up. I loved to hate it. Watching Trump act despicably or butcher the English language made me feel vastly superior. Alongside my revulsion and rage, what really fueled my horrified fascination with Donald J. Trump was my contempt for him.

Princeton psychologist Susan Fiske has observed that, when someone is in a scornful frame of mind, their brain's reward center lights up in the same way as when they are praised.[14] In other words, contempt feels good; when we unleash it on an adversary, it can serve as a fleeting emotional pick-me-up, like those who delighted in the man-versus-sign heckling. When I deem Trump—or one of his supporters—to be reactionary and stupid, then I'm quite the stable genius by comparison. If they're racists, then I'm morally superior. If they're gullible "fake news" consumers, then I'm a savvy freethinker. If they're ruled by fear and anger, then I'm a rational actor with a complex inner life. And if These People—these know-nothing, fearful bigots—are controlling the levers of power, then I have a strong urge to assert my dominance over them by displaying my disdain.

When, oh when, will those racist old white guys just die off?

Contempt is junk food for the soul. And for Lefties whose souls have been battered daily since 2016, it's an irresistibly gratifying treat, and one that can feel like a necessary form of emotional self-regulation and protection. Trump's hairstyle, physique, and incessant bluster provide an all-you-can-eat smorgasbord of contemptible delicacies. From the moment he announced his candidacy, we mocked him, fat-shamed him, grammar-policed him, and pathologized him, and we laughed, oh how we laughed, right up until about 10:30 p.m. EST on Election Day, and then we cried.

We were chastened, but not for long. Hardly a day has gone by without my coming across a reference to the crazed, obese, orange Cheeto. On July 4, 2019, activists floated a giant diaper-clad Trump blimp at the National Mall. When he insisted on the border wall, Nancy Pelosi questioned his manhood. In defiance of the legitimacy of his election, I took to referring to him exclusively as BLOTUS (Biggest Liar of the United States).

We liberals and progressives indulge in cheap gratification by deriding conservatives in ways that violate our own values—we fat-shame Chris Christie, slut-shame Megyn Kelly, gay-bait the Trump–Putin "bromance," and IQ-shame too many to mention here. We disparage the "fever dreams" of "rabid right-wing nut-jobs" and, in so doing, denigrate those who suffer mental illness as well as conservatives. We refer to rural states as "flyover" country and its inhabitants as rednecks or, as Silicon Valley CEO Melinda Byerley put it, "shithole[s] with stupid people."[15] We lament that the simple-minded "Joe Six-Pack" just doesn't get it. None of this goes unnoticed by working- and middle-class conservatives and, just in case a snide remark slips by, there's a squadron of right-wing commentators standing by to make sure These People feel the sting of liberal condescension.

Weeks before the 2016 election, political comedian Bill Maher expressed exasperation at the number of states that Trump looked certain to win: "What the fuck does it take in this country to have being a human being supersede being a Republican?"[16] Maher's shock and horror are understandable, but when he contemptuously suggested that Republicans are subhuman, he did Trump a favor by playing the role of the sneering liberal elite. (Maher's classist contempt is notorious: In 1998, he mocked the death of seven workers in a Kansas grain elevator, one of whose bodies was still missing, saying that the community should check their loaves of Wonder Bread.)[17]

Maher's snipe echoed actor Julia Roberts' gibe during a 2000 Democratic National Committee (DNC) fundraiser: "Republican comes in the dictionary just after reptile and just above repugnant...I looked up Democrat. It's of the people, by the people, for the people."[18] Roberts' wisecrack smacks of snobbish superiority—just picture the room full of wealthy DNC donors who smugly see themselves as warm-blooded pillars of virtue. Rinse and repeat at the 2017 Golden Globes, where Meryl Streep knocked football as inferior to "arts," and again during the 2018 Tony Awards, where Robert DeNiro waved his fists in the air and bellowed, "Fuck Trump" to a standing ovation of tuxedo-clad glitterati.[19] Feeling superior feels good. In fact, I'm feeling a tad superior in denouncing their superiority right now in case you didn't notice. (The contempt reflex is hard to restrain.)

A week after Maher's doozy, filmmaker Michael Moore said that anyone who voted for Trump was a "legal terrorist" and added:

> It's like somebody went to Dr. Frankenstein last year and said, "I need a candidate who is the embodiment of every awful male trait, every awful white-man trait, and every awful rich guy trait and roll that all into one candidate"... He literally is a representative for each of these things that we've been seeing a gradual end to...The days of these dinosaurs are over. It's got to be hard on them. Nobody likes to give up power. We've been in charge for about 10,000 years, so it's a long run. We had a great streak.[20]

However accurate Moore's diagnosis may be, the way he articulates it conveys an existential degree of contempt: Your days are numbered, deplorable white dinosaurs, and good riddance.

As his movie *Fahrenheit 11/9* attests, Michael Moore understood better than anyone how white blue-collar voters' feelings of resentment and alienation fueled Trump's rise. Yet he's been provoking These People since 2001, when he published *Stupid White Men*. The title alone speaks volumes, and the book relentlessly and gratuitously stereotypes and derogates the "stupid white men" who voted for George W. Bush, the stupidest white man of them all.

Moore satirically speculates that male birth rates are decreasing because Mother Earth is wisely rendering extinct pot-bellied boneheads whose purpose can be better served by a test tube and turkey baster.[21] Put yourself in the shoes of the people Moore lambasts. What greater shame is there than being told you're so worthless you shouldn't even exist? The guys in your Swing Left chapter might not bridle at being called "stupid white men," but most white American males do, so what's to be gained by turning whiteness and maleness into epithets?

Contempt and condescension, rather than investigative reporting, fill the cable news airwaves. Watch CNN and MSNBC hosts and guests smirk knowingly at Trump's latest abomination. Notice when they cross the line from zealous reportage to sarcastic bloviating. Do we really need to watch Chris Cuomo and Kellyanne Conway go at it for the umpteenth time on CNN? Cuomo knows she's going to lie and spin, so what's the purpose in hosting her, other than to create a combative spectacle?

I cheered for CNN's Anderson Cooper when he demolished Trump's Orwellian assertion, days after calling Nicaragua and Haiti "shithole" countries, that he was the "least racist person you will ever interview."[22] But after my contempt-high wore off and I watched the clip again, I began noticing Cooper's sarcasm and eye squinting, and his use of repetition to cast Trump in an even more unflattering light. Cooper wasn't merely furious with Trump; he was, I suspect, gratifying his desire to show how much he despised and disdained Trump. It was appropriate—indeed, necessary—for Cooper to report Trump's overt racism, but the condescending manner in which he packaged the presentation undermined its power. In the eyes of Trump supporters, I suspect Cooper's report came across as a haughty harangue, its meaning lost on them as they mentally deflected the implication that they were racist for voting for him.

Morning Joe cohosts and political moderates Joe Scarborough and Mika Brzezinski, whose show MSNBC teases with the tagline "brutal honesty," are notorious for their excoriations of Trump, his administration, and his base. Brzezinski, for example, called Secretary of State Mike Pompeo a "butt boy" for the crown prince of Saudi Arabia, and Scarborough has castigated as "stupid" anyone who believes there's a crisis at the southern border.[23] Meanwhile, liberal talk-radio host Mike Malloy fills the airwaves with fantasies of right-wing adversaries suffering gruesome deaths.[24]

Not all TV and radio personalities act superior, but enough of the 24/7 news cycle is replete with contempt to keep These

People convinced of "elite liberal media bias." Rather than subject themselves to scorn, they tune in to Fox.

Just to be sure I wasn't imagining things, I contacted David Matsumoto, a psychologist at San Francisco State University and a renowned expert in the fields of both micro-expressions and contempt. Matsumoto says contempt is "rampant" in the media. Though he usually examines frame-by-frame footage fastidiously to detect subtle, fleeting expressions of contempt, in today's polarized political arena, Matsumoto requires no such high-tech scrutiny to recognize it.[25]

Political scientist Jeffrey Berry and sociologist Sarah Sobieraj, two Tufts professors, mapped ten weeks of right and left cable TV, commentary shows, talk radio, political blogs, and newspaper columns to determine the prevalence of what they call "outrage discourse"—speech that intentionally provokes an emotional response through the use of tactics such as belittling, mockery, insults, misrepresentations, and ideologically extreme language.[26] They documented outrage discourse in *100 percent* of TV episodes, 99 percent of talk radio, and the vast majority of blogs and columns surveyed. While they found considerably more overall outrage speech on right-wing media, the Left holds its own when it comes to mockery and belittling.[27] Rod Dreher, a conservative who reports drifting right in reaction to liberal disdain, observes, "There is animosity and polarization on both sides, but…most of the organic *disdain* comes from educated liberals…Motives are impugned *constantly*. These people just know they have the magic answers for society, and the only reason anyone would disagree with them is because they are stupid bigots."[28]

On late-night comedy shows, many of which serve as *de facto* news programs, contempt is daily fare. Satirists perform a public service when they help us see contradictions and hypocrisies we might otherwise have missed. However, as Caitlin Flanagan, a moderately conservative contributing editor at *The Atlantic* notes, they don't always punch up. Flanagan concedes that Trump's grotesqueness invites disparagement, but chastises comedians who go after his supporters. She cites Samantha Bee's takedown of a young, Trump-admiring Christian boy as "Jerry Falwell in blond, larval form."[29] That's not comedy, that's cruelty.

Flanagan describes shows like Bee's and John Oliver's as "imbued with the conviction that they and their fans are intellectually and morally superior to those who espouse any of the beliefs of the political right." She goes on to make a disturbing observation:

> Though aimed at blue-state sophisticates, these shows are an unintended but powerful form of propaganda for conservatives. When Republicans see these harsh jokes—which echo down through the morning news shows and the chattering day's worth of viral clips, along with those of Jimmy Kimmel, Stephen Colbert, and Seth Meyers—they don't just see a handful of comics mocking them...they see exactly what Donald Trump has taught them: that the entire media landscape loathes them, their values, their family, and their religion...No wonder so many of Trump's followers are inclined to believe only the things that he or his spokespeople tell them directly—everyone else on the tube thinks they're a bunch of trailer-park, Oxy-snorting halfwits who divide their time between retweeting Alex Jones' fantasies and ironing their Klan hoods.

I understand the longing for satire in times like these—it's the spoonful of sugar to make the very bad news go down. But perhaps such news *shouldn't* go down. Perhaps comedians are inadvertently lulling us into a hubristic stupor in which we somehow think that virtuous consumption of comic irreverence (the hilarity of which only superior beings such as ourselves can appreciate) renders us invincible against proto-fascist buffoonery. John Oliver sarcastically begged Trump to run and offered to donate to his campaign.[30] Like nearly all liberals, Oliver radically—and contemptuously—underestimated "the Donald," goading him on from Trump Tower to the White House.

Whatever comedians' contribution to—or neutralization of—resistance to Trumpism, the problem is that everyone's trying to act like John Oliver these days. Even newscasters like Anderson

Cooper and everyday people in casual conversation jeer at Trump and his supporters, and forget the bipartisan, pre-Trump origins of crises like climate disruption and poverty.

This brand of "corporatized outrage" is, as writer Charles Duhigg astutely observes, "fundamentally manipulative and tends to further the interests of the already rich and powerful."[31] It takes the heat off the corporate advertisers and obscures their role in creating the mess we're in. And it's probably one of the reasons why public confidence in the press has sunk to 44 percent.[32]

CNN and MSNBC decry Trump's refusal to disclose his tax returns every day, but how many stories have they done on how the IRS has moved from auditing billionaires to auditing low-income households that claim the paltry earned income tax credit?[33] How many exposés of corporate tax avoidance? Anti-Trump "corporatized outrage" is cheap when there's no budget for investigative journalism; plus, there are no uncomfortable sit-downs with corporate sponsors required.

Mainstream journalists lace their prose with vitriol. *New York Times* columnist Charles Blow doubled down on Clinton's infamous "basket of deplorables" gaffe.[34] After conceding that, as a candidate, Clinton shouldn't have insulted voters, he went on to say that "deplorable" was too charitable a description of Trump and his supporters. I agree with Blow that actively supporting Trump reflects support for or indifference to Trump's bigotry, but castigating those millions of Americans as deplorable was a gift to Trump that keeps on giving.

After the election, *New York Times* columnist Paul Krugman pilloried the "chumps" and "losers" who "shot themselves in the face" and "basically destroyed their own lives" by voting for someone who would take away their health insurance.[35] *Daily Kos* founder Markos Moulitsas was more blatant in his schaden-freude, publishing this blog post after the election: "Be Happy for Coal Miners Losing Their Health Insurance. They're Getting Exactly What They Voted For."[36] Other political blogs like *Wonkette*, *Crooks and Liars*, and, yes, *Contemptor*, seethe with scorn.

The *New York Times* and *Washington Post* have full complements of columnists who gleefully bash Trump and his supporters to the exclusion of vitally important non-Trump news analyses. Their contempt is contagious. In January 2018, when the *New York Times* published letters to the editor from voters explaining their reasons for supporting Trump, other *Times* readers excoriated the paper: "Why do you keep asking questions of Trump voters? Who cares what they think?" wrote one reader. "Please don't ever do that again," said another reader victimized by exposure to the thoughts of 14 Trump voters.[37]

Accusations of stupidity are the leading form of denigration of Trump and his supporters. *Gawker*'s Hamilton Nolan specialized in trashing the "fucking dolts" and "dumbass hicks" who supported Trump during the primaries.[38] *Salon* chimed in with articles about the "idiots" who voted for Trump when they weren't too busy killing themselves with tobacco and fried food, and called for readers to shame "dumb Trump fans."[39] At a 2017 Make America Great Again (MAGA) rally, I saw a counterprotester jeer at a man for not knowing the meaning of "hegemony."

Here's a smattering of headlines from 2017 and 2018:

"We're with Stupid" (with a photo of Trump), *The New York Times*.[40]
"Why Republicans Love Dumb Presidents," *New York*.[41]
"Donald Trump's Biggest Flaw: He's Not That Bright," *Chicago Tribune*.[42]
"Trump Wants a Big Parade (For Himself). It's a Surpassingly Dumb Idea," *The Washington Post*.[43]
"Seriously, How Dumb Is Trump?" *Huffington Post*.[44]
"Too Stupid to Know They're Stupid," *Cache Valley Daily*.[45]
"Are American Voters Actually Just Stupid?" *Salon*.[46]
"Trump Is Hoping You're Too Stupid to Notice," *The Washington Post*.[47]
"How Republicans Got So Mean and Clueless," *The Washington Post*.[48]
"Linguistics Expert: Trump Sounds Like Your Beer-Swilling Uncle," MSNBC.[49]

So, too, is my email inbox filled with subject headers insulting the intelligence of Trump and his appointees. But as Jonathan Chait notes in the *New York Magazine* article cited above, Trump's base doesn't care about his intelligence. What they care about is feeling scorned. They hate it.

Hell Hath No Fury Like a Political Adversary Scorned

An established body of social psychology research shows that people get defensive and closed-minded when their status, self-worth, and political or religious beliefs are threatened.[50] If I tell you that Albert Einstein wasn't such a great physicist after all, your brain will probably remain calm; you may even believe me and change your mind. But, as at least one brain-imaging experiment has shown, if I tell you something that contradicts your beliefs about abortion or gun control, the areas of the brain related to fear and identity light up like a pinball machine, and there is little possibility you will change your mind.[51] The difference? Your identity and self-worth are bound up in your ideological beliefs, but you probably don't have an emotional stake in preserving Einstein's reputation.

Karin Tamerius, a former psychiatrist and founder of the non-profit SMART Politics, explains, "Our political attitudes and beliefs are intertwined with our most basic human needs—needs for safety, belonging, identity, self-esteem, and purpose—and when they're threatened, we're biologically wired to respond as if we're in physical peril."[52] Any challenge to self-worth can be threatening, and when the challenge is laced with scorn, defensiveness intensifies. When someone is scorned, the amygdala (the brain's fear center) lights up and issues a fight-or-flight command. As far as the amygdala is concerned, a threat to one's beliefs or status is equivalent to a growling tiger getting ready to pounce, and it must protect the self from attack.[53]

When we get defensive, cognition, and the parts of the brain responsible for empathy and reason, shut down. We become so preoccupied with defending ourselves that learning something new becomes nearly impossible. As any teacher will tell you, safety is a prerequisite for learning. Sometimes, people who are scorned become so agitated and frustrated that they wish for bad things to befall the scorner.[54]

An experiment at the University of Pennsylvania intentionally subjected students to scorn and evaluated their responses. The researchers showed students high-tech alarm clocks and asked them to assess their viability as new products. Each student had a virtual partner (who was, in fact, a confederate of the research team) who provided one of four types of feedback on the students' assessments—contemptuous, angry, neutral, or failure. Failure feedback was expressed simply as a low score (e.g., "Your score is four out of 10"). Angry feedback was, "I'm getting really pissed off at your work." Contemptuous feedback included statements like "Okay, whatever, as a U. Penn. student, I'm surprised by the low quality of your performance."

Students who received contemptuous feedback responded with significantly more verbal aggression than did students who received the other three types of feedback. The contempt recipients often returned the contempt, saying things like, "I think you're off base—you have nothing to contribute," whereas the other students (who were not scorned) offered apologies like, "I'm sorry, please forgive me."[55]

The Pennsylvania study corroborates an enormous body of research showing that feelings of shame damage people's self-worth, disrupt their ability to feel empathy, and prompt them to externalize the blame and lash out aggressively at convenient scapegoats.[56] In other words, shame makes people feel like a worthless pile of shit, and so they find someone to blame and attack for making them feel bad, but the shame creeps back in right away and with it the need to lash out again and again. This dynamic is particularly strong among people with an inegalitarian, dominate-or-be-dominated "social dominance orientation" when they feel that their status is being threatened.[57]

As we'll see in the next chapter, many Trump supporters are experiencing a perceived loss of status and honor. If Trump supporters are anything like the University of Pennsylvania students, being treated with contempt is likely to elicit an aggressive or vindictive reaction like donning "Proud Member of the Basket of Deplorables" t-shirts or calling you a "snowflake" or a "lib-tard."

When *New York Times* columnist Nicholas Kristof interviewed Oklahoma Trump supporters in 2017, they said they were dismayed by Trump's cuts to programs they rely on but were still loyal to him. Why? Because of resentment toward Democrats who mocked them as stupid racists, among other things.[58] Kristof's article elicited the wrath of liberal readers incensed that he was seeking to humanize Trump-supporting monsters. "I'm just going to say it: I hate these people. They are stupid and selfish. Screw them. Lose your jobs, sit home, and die," wrote one reader.[59]

Conservative author David Blankenhorn says a tribal backlash is occurring among Trump supporters—many were ambivalent in 2016 but have become more entrenched in reaction to being derided as racists.[60] Blankenhorn was so alarmed by this dynamic that he founded Better Angels, an organization that helps foster dialogue across lines of difference.

Liberal writer Thomas Frank remarked on the same dynamic when he breakfasted with the Macon, Missouri, Lions Club in December 2016. Many of the Lions had voted apprehensively for Trump out of "disgust with the perceived moral haughtiness of liberals."[61] "Disgust"—they knew they were the butt of liberal contempt and returned it with a vengeance in the form of a vindictive blowhard, a Bully-in-Chief who would bring liberals down a peg. We make it easy for Trump to satisfy his base merely by returning our contempt.

A commentary that appeared in *The American Conservative* just after Trump was elected provides another case study of returned contempt. A white, 46-year-old man named Andrew wrote a comment addressed to the publication's liberal readers:

> I don't believe I'm actually a racist, but you're going to label me that way anyway, so I'll just accept it…On one issue after another, the response to my opinion is some variation of "You're a racist!" (Or sexist, or homophobic,

or bigoted, or guilty of white privilege—the whole litany.)
I get it. My opinions are not to be valued, or even considered. I'm a bad person! If only I were educated (but I
am). If only I was enlightened…Dear liberals, Democrats,
progressives, leftists: Your use of the word "racist" doesn't
work anymore. We get it. You're superior. You're enlightened and we're not…We have given up trying to talk you
out of your presumptions, or trying to earn your approval.
We no longer consider it worth our while to reassure you
that we're not "that kind" of Republican.

    …[I]f there's one thing Trump has done, he's given us
some backbone to make our voices heard…I cast my vote
for Trump reluctantly. Now, I couldn't be prouder.[62]

Andrew may be guilty of asserting white male victimhood as a
defense against being held accountable for bigotry. At the same
time, if liberals rely on contempt to administer accountability,
then there will inevitably be blowback from the Andrews of the
world. Indeed, a few months after Andrew's post, two more white
men chimed in with eerily similar and self-aware observations.
Zapollo wrote:

I'm a white guy. I'm a well-educated intellectual who enjoys
small arthouse movies, coffeehouses and classic blues…

    And yet. I find [that] some of the alt-right stuff exerts
a pull even on me. Even though I'm smart and informed
enough to see through it. It's seductive because I am not a
person with any power or privilege, and yet I am constantly
bombarded with messages telling me that I'm a cancer, I'm
a problem, everything is my fault.

    I am very lower-middle class. I've never owned a new
car, and do my own home repairs as much as I can to save
money. I cut my own grass, wash my own dishes, buy my
clothes from Walmart. I have no clue how I will ever be
able to retire. But oh, brother, to hear the media tell it, I
am just drowning in unearned power and privilege, and

America will be a much brighter, more loving, more peaceful nation when I finally just keel over and die.

Trust me: After all that, some of the alt-right stuff feels like a warm, soothing bath. A "safe space," if you will. I recoil from the uglier stuff, but some of it—the "hey, white guys are actually okay, you know! Be proud of yourself, white man!" stuff is really VERY seductive, and it is only with some intellectual effort that I can resist the pull…

It baffles me that more people on the left can't understand this, can't see how they're just feeding, feeding, feeding the growth of this stuff…

An anonymous white man echoed Zapollo:

What the left doesn't get is it's turning people like me—reasonably moderate, go-along-to-get-along types—into full-blown reactionary radicals. Ideas that I once would've rolled my eyes at I'm now willing to give a hearing. I don't think I'm some paragon of rational thought and self-control by any means, but it concerns me that if I'm willing at least to entertain some of these ideas (critically and deliberately), what about the people who embrace them more impetuously or because their circumstances seemingly leave them no other option?…What follows from all of this cannot bode well.[63]

Liberal disdain was a recurring complaint of many Trump supporters interviewed by blogger Sam Altman: "Stop calling us racists. Stop calling us idiots. We aren't. Listen to us when we try to tell you why we aren't. Oh, and stop making fun of us."[64]

Tufts professors Berry and Sobieraj note that the fear of being perceived as racist looms large in the minds of conservatives, and this fear has two consequences: They avoid talking politics with liberals and they seek refuge in right-wing outrage media.[65] The problem extends even beyond conservatives: A whopping *80 percent* of Americans view "political correctness" as a problem. I believe much of that has to do not with *what* liberals say but *how* we say it—the self-righteous "call-out culture" that even some leftists find irksome.[66]

Four white men at a red–blue dialogue I attended said they used to be liberal but got tired of being lectured to and scolded. None of them liked Trump, but they did find his hostility to liberal finger-wagging highly appealing. One of them said he hated Trump but less so every time the Left attacks his supporters: *He may be a fool but he's our fool.*

The backlash isn't confined to men. Cindy Kiser, an unemployed mom in Arkansas who voted for Obama and then, with reservations, Trump, says that she's become desensitized to and alienated by "the labels [misogynist, Islamophobic] thrown around." The feeling Cindy gets from Democrats is, "We don't even want to be in a democracy with you because you've made such a bad choice."[67] Ditto Madonna Massey, a Louisiana Republican who says she likes Rush Limbaugh because he defends people like her against liberals who insult them as fat, racist, ignorant losers.[68] Double-ditto University of North Carolina student Maggie Horzempa who said being called a bitch by liberal students and a "disgrace to womanhood" deepened her commitment to conservatism.[69]

These are the voices of ordinary conservatives, not right-wing operatives, and they are beaming us a very urgent message. Whether it's labeling them bigots or denigrating their lifestyle, religion or intelligence, liberal contempt is helping to bring the long-simmering culture war to a rolling boil and pushing conservatives deeper into Trump's corner. It's a curious irony, this defensive reflex to more deeply embrace whatever it is one is condemned for embracing. It's harmful and ignoble, but it's real.

Christina H., a latent liberal *Cracked* magazine columnist raised in a climate of parochial bigotry, wrote a hilarious essay about her ideological transformation—and how it could have been expedited if liberals had acknowledged that she came by her beliefs honestly. "It would probably be a more appealing journey if it was known to be a super common and chill one, and not a daredevil Evel Knievel jump across a chasm that only one man is known to have survived, and that man eats his meals through a straw now."[70] Christina wants liberals to know that potentially open-minded conservatives are quietly lurking on social media— and that they are capable of inching in a progressive direction if they aren't attacked as "moralistic morons" when they express discomfort with values that contradict their religious beliefs.

She urges liberals to acknowledge that conservatives hold their beliefs sincerely: "I know it's hard to believe a member of the dominant race and/or religion of the country could honestly consider themselves a besieged underdog but people really believe this. It's not a pretend tactic to fool outside observers…It's actually very easy to believe your own small town or local religious community is an isolated pocket of 'sanity' in a hedonistic, liberal world."

No one wants to think of themselves as a bad or stupid person; therefore, no conservative is going to say, "You know, you're right, my beliefs are stupid and selfish and racist, and I hereby disavow them. Thank you for showing me the error of my ways. I can see now how superior liberals are, and I want to become one."

Backlash Contempt

Right-wing media are well aware of what makes conservatives bristle. Michelle Malkin, Laura Ingraham, and Todd Starnes of Fox News have devoted entire books to the subject of "liberal elite" derision of middle-class Americans' intellect and lifestyles.[71] (Ingraham gives as good as she gets with chapter titles such as "Flower Power Take a Shower.") They have observed a degree of alienation and have done their utmost to intensify and weaponize it.

At the 2018 Conservative Political Action Conference, Wayne LaPierre, CEO of the National Rifle Association, took aim at liberal Democrats who, he bellowed, were putting the United States on a fast-track to socialist totalitarianism. Absent evidence of the socialist menace, he instead relied on the tried-and-true trope of the "intellectual elites" who, he said, "think that they are smarter than the rest of us, and think they are better than us. They truly believe it, and you know it." LaPierre warned the audience that they should be very frightened of these elites, who "ridicule" and "disrespect" core American values and, given a chance, will erase constitutional rights and freedoms, and install a socialist dystopia. "That's why the Second Amendment is of supreme importance."[72]

Note LaPierre's rhetorical progression: Elitists think they're superior; therefore, they won't hesitate to trample your rights and impose their will; therefore, you need guns to protect yourself from their tyranny. Right-wing propagandists like LaPierre weaponize intimations of liberal contempt to great effect, and every time we say something condescending or snide, we unwittingly effectuate their playbook. The last thing Wayne LaPierre needs is more ammo.

Trump has a unique brand of demonizing the liberal elite menace. He uses the media as a proxy because, as he well knows, his supporters have for decades been conditioned to view the media as bastions of liberal elitism. Trump skipped White House correspondents' dinners not merely because he's thin-skinned, but because snubbing the media reinforces its enemy-of-the-people status. Instead of attending the glitzy affair, he held rallies in swing states during which he trashed the fourth estate; told the crowd that media "hate your guts"; and later tweeted a split image showing (a) the black-tie-clad dinner guests and (b) himself touring a tool factory.

At a 2017 rally in Phoenix, Arizona, Trump told the crowd, "I always hear about the elite. You know, the elite. They're elite? I went to better schools than they did. I was a better student than they were. I live in a bigger, more beautiful apartment, and I live in the White House, too, which is really great. I think, you know what? I think we're the elite. They're not the elites." He reassured the crowd that they were "smart" before resuming his attack on the enemy of the American people, saying, "The media can attack me. But where I draw the line is when they attack you, which is what they do. When they attack the decency of our supporters."[73]

Trump stands up against those mean lib-tards who aren't as smart as they think they are or else why is Trump in the White House and they're not. The failing *New York Times* and anyone who believes a word it prints is a Loser. Trump is a Winner and, by extension, so are his loyal followers. They're willing to overlook the gold-plated spoon in the so-called populist billionaire's mouth because the words coming out of that mouth do not judge, insult, and shame them.

The merging of the strongman and his followers is a staple of demagogic propaganda. When liberals engage in behavior that resembles the role Trump has scripted for them, they strengthen his hand. I suspect Trump would have been delighted to see a counterprotester at a MAGA rally ridiculing a white man for not knowing what hegemony means and having "no culture." As one West Virginian Trump voter explained, "As the hit pieces [against Trump] kept coming, it seemed to many that Trump was being unfairly victimized by the media. Perhaps we sympathized with him because, as people from the hills who have also been rejected by the establishment, we know what it feels like."[74] What this voter expressed is a profound truth about human behavior—we bond with those who are attacked by the same group of people attacking us.

If you were a conservative-leaning American with the choice between someone who made you feel ashamed of your politically incorrect views and unsophisticated lifestyle, or someone who defended your right to think and feel whatever you want, who would you pick?

Why Liberals Scorn "Trumpkins"

Psychologist Susan Fiske views scorn as a form of self-defense. When we as a group feel we are losing ground—and, oh, how we're losing ground—our contempt helps reassure us that, despite our loss of control, we're still better than the "other" group.[75]

Contempt also helps us create psychological distance between ourselves and the object of our contempt. If someone makes a sexist comment, for example, the contemptor can hide her vulnerability and shield herself from further damage by psychologically distancing herself from the "sexist pig."[76]

The 2016 election disturbed my homeostatic balance and sent me reeling into a contemptuous tailspin. Every day another gut-punch landed, and my contempt reared up to reestablish some illusory sense of balance and control.

Today's hyperpartisan environment is a breeding ground for contempt. Partisans often make negative assumptions about the other side's beliefs and values, withholding the benefit of the doubt in favor of instant condemnation and guilt by association. A Trump voter is presumed to be a bigot, a moron, and/or a dupe entitled to the same treatment as a certified neo-Nazi. A Trump resister, by contrast, is a morally superior hero entitled to lampoon the enemy and justified in their schadenfreude. Expressing contempt against Trump supporters feels like a public service announcement: "These people will be the end of us."

When abortion foes were incensed by the passage of a late-term abortion law in Virginia in 2019, *Salon* writer Amanda Marcotte immediately pronounced their outrage "phony." In an article entitled, "Festival of Phony Outrage: No, Conservatives Don't Actually Care about Late-Term Abortion," Marcotte was adamant that anti-abortion activists' professed love of fetal life is inauthentic.[77] Her proof? According to Marcotte, a Republican legislator slandered abortion-seeking women by, in her words, "painting the tiny number of women who get late-term abortions as lazy sluts" and feeding a sexist stereotype that views such women as "stupid" and "careless" "bimbos." Well yes, that does sound pretty bad, except that he never uttered or implied anything of the kind and was never anything less than polite and straightforward in his questioning of the bill's pro-choice author.[78] Even if he were a jerk, to jump from there to the conclusion that all anti-abortion activists are disingenuous misogynists is unfounded, unfair, and enormously contemptuous. If I told a conservative that I support a law making it illegal to spank a child because it breaks my heart to see the harm spanking does to little children and they said, "You don't give a damn about kids, you just want to undercut parental authority," I would be mighty peeved. What Marcotte did in her article was just that—a maddeningly unfounded accusation of disingenuousness, or worse, a condescending implication that she knows better than they do why they're against abortion.

Liberal contempt is frequently triggered by Trump himself, the king of contempt, with his pithy putdowns ("crooked Hillary," the "failing *New York Times*"); demagogic tirades at rallies; and giving the proverbial finger to democratic norms. When he derides us, we retaliate. But Trump is also a master conjurer of *backlash* contempt: You're calling us stupid and crooked? No, you're stupider and crookeder. He's an incubator for viral contempt between partisan tribes whose ability to engage in productive discourse has all but collapsed.

According to Fiske, acting superior to another group bolsters our sense of belonging in our own "in-group."[79] Registering our collective outrage is certainly appropriate, even vital, especially for groups who are directly threatened by Trump. If I didn't have people with whom I could commiserate, the rankness and bedlam would threaten my sanity. It's when group cohesion becomes tribal arrogance that problems arise. Anger and disgust blend to form contempt; from there, it's less than a half-step to dehumanizing the objects of our scorn. Whoever sent an email to the wife of Supreme Court Justice and accused sex offender Brett Kavanaugh that said, "May you, your husband, and your kids burn in hell" took that half-step.[80]

New York University social psychologist Jonathan Haidt is an expert in what he calls "the psychology of self-righteousness." Haidt believes that what's destructive about contempt is its alienating quality of cool indifference toward people we view as morally inferior. "Contempt," writes Haidt, "paints its victims as buffoons worthy of mockery, or as non-persons worthy of complete disregard. It therefore weakens other emotions, such as compassion."[81] Think about Haidt's admonition in the context of the dehumanizing mockery of the autistic man who couldn't destroy the antifascist sign—the hecklers (and their admirers) were so walled in by their moral superiority that their capacity for empathy was impaired.

Though I didn't send Kavanaugh's wife a death threat, I was unable to muster an ounce of empathy for him during his nomination hearings. I was aware that Kavanaugh could *conceivably* have been innocent. I was aware that sex offenders were often victims before they became perpetrators, and I assume that most people who abuse alcohol have experienced trauma or emotional neglect. I was also aware that Kavanaugh came of age in a culture of toxic masculinity that wounds men, too. As the mother of a teenaged boy (and someone who did plenty at that age I'm not proud of), I could have empathized with Kavanaugh at the same time that I unequivocally rejected his fitness for the Supreme Court. But Kavanaugh's belligerence, entitlement, and remorselessness—and the GOP's determination to "plow right through," as Senator Mitch McConnell put it—so utterly enraged me that my ability to see Kavanaugh as a human being lay submerged under a thick blanket of contempt. I found myself wishing that he'd drink himself to an early death.

Contempt is a first step on the path to dehumanizing the other tribe. If the "contemptible other" is worthless, then I can safely disregard their hopes and fears. As the distance between us grows, I might become so indifferent as to ignore their suffering or even go to war against them, as Matsumoto and others have documented.[82]

Contempt toward moral transgressions like bigotry and deceitfulness does arguably serve a social purpose, much in the way that Puritanical shaming attempted to suppress then-unacceptable behaviors like blasphemy and fornication. But there's evidence that disparaging and stigmatizing wrongdoers interferes with their ability to change—so many psychological resources are marshaled to defend against stigma, there's little left to respond constructively.[83]

I see contempt operating in discourse the way I see punishment functioning in the criminal justice system—as revenge against people we see as moral transgressors. It's a quick fix, but not necessarily a humane, just, or efficacious one.

In Matsumoto's view, the only situation in which treating evildoers with contempt could be constructive is when there's an overwhelming consensus that the behavior in question is utterly taboo, for example, terrorism. Otherwise, Matsumoto says, directing scorn toward the offender precludes productive discussion.

As the 2016 election made painfully clear, many forms of bigotry aren't quite the taboo many of us assumed them to be. That's not to say that there should be no consequences for expressions of bigotry—accountability and boundary-setting are crucial. But there are effective accountability mechanisms that do not involve contempt, which I'll detail in chapters four and five.

Rutgers University psychologist Ira Roseman suggests that it's possible that contempt toward Trump could be fueling the resistance and/or could help mobilize disgusted voters in 2020.[84] Researchers have barely begun to study the impact of contempt-laden messaging on electoral outcomes, and the preliminary findings are fuzzy.[85] There's scant evidence that contempt is a winning message for left-leaning candidates and there's a significant risk of alienating swing voters made to feel deplorable. We will never out-contempt Trump and, should we try, I fear we will lose our way in a wilderness of hurt. Trump is his own negative campaign ad. There's little to be gained by obsessing over his awfulness but much to be gained by emphasizing the virtues of his challenger.

Hillary Clinton tried to parlay contempt into victory. Days after Trump clinched the GOP nomination, she gave a speech in San Diego excoriating Trump's ideas as "dangerously incoherent" and suggesting that his self-proclaimed "very good brain" warranted psychiatric evaluation. Cue audience laughter.[86] Toward the end of the speech, she expressed confidence that she would win because Americans with common sense, Americans who know that America is already great, would "make the right decision." I doubt the specter of a smug blue-state audience laughing gleefully at Clinton's jibes played well with fence sitters whose common sense had been called into question.

Though the upsides to contempt are, in my opinion, heavily outweighed by the toxic downsides, I recognize that contempt may be a particularly important form of protection for members of oppressed groups who feel acutely threatened and demoralized by Trump's reign and, hence, have a greater need for contempt's in-group cohesion and mood- and esteem-boosting properties. Given what people of color, Muslims, and LGBTQ communities have had to endure, I'm not about to contempt-shame them but, instead, invite them—and everyone—to consider the alternative means of communicating their feelings and beliefs, discussed in chapter five.

Contempt Spirals

Contempt antagonizes, shames, and infuriates people. They often respond with aggression and hostility, sometimes in the form of boomerang contempt. At its worst, contempt derogates and dehumanizes the "other" and can be the first step on the path to the kind of vilification that results in interpersonal or intergroup violence or genocide.

Dishing out contempt has an addictive quality. There's a fleeting feeling of gratification at having put the deplorable in their place. But when the contempt high wears off, there's an emptiness or sometimes an icky, shameful feeling that comes with not representing one's best self. Our self-esteem takes a hit and, all too often, we compensate by finding another opportunity to derogate someone.

When feeling good about oneself is achieved at the expense of another person's self-esteem, a vicious cycle begins spinning. It's gratifying to watch a *Crossfire* clip like "Jon Stewart Wrecks CNN to Pieces" until I notice that the very same clip exists in a parallel universe of right-wing click bait entitled, "Tucker Brutally Exposes Hypocritical Stewart."[87] A cliché about things going 'round and coming 'round comes to mind, with each side lashing out with more intensity the more they feel that their tribe's dignity has been assaulted.[88]

The Trumpist worldview divides the population into us-versus-them tribes. When we, too, indulge in "othering" of our adversaries, we help erase nuance, harden tribal divisions, and inspire backlash political movements.

We blame Trump supporters for the mess our country is in and train our wrath on them accordingly. This keeps us from seeing our part in the slide toward oligarchy, kleptocracy, and authoritarianism. Trump exploited political vulnerabilities made possible by the decades-long erosion of public infrastructure; data mining and psychographic targeting; atrophying of civic and democratic institutions; transfer of wealth to war profiteers and the 1 percent; corporate consolidation of media; and disenfranchisement of voters of color.

Contempt plays into the right-wing strategy of deflecting attention away from these substantive issues. When Samantha Bee apologized for calling Ivanka Trump a "feckless cunt," she lamented that the brouhaha her remark had generated was drawing attention away from the very issue Bee was upset about: the hundreds of immigrant children being separated from their parents.[89] When contempt enters the scene, it becomes the story, and the real problems fueling Trump's rise to power get buried under the avalanche of snark.

When liberals heap scorn on These People, right-wing propagandists are able to create a linkage between liberal values and liberal elitism in their audience's minds. They say, in effect, "Look at how those liberal snobs look down on you and don't care about you and maybe even hate you. It's safe to assume that anything they propose will be bad for you. *They* are your enemies and, therefore, *we* are your friends." This elitist taint takes the shine off everything liberals promote, from solar panels to healthy food to gun safety—it all somehow becomes a sinister plot to inflict elitist values on red-blooded Americans who know better than to believe that clean air and fresh vegetables and gun-free public spaces are healthy and wholesome. We must stop enacting the right-wing populist playbook or surrender These People to right-wing populism for the long term.

People have a long memory for how unpleasant it is to be on the receiving end of contempt.[90] Even if we dial down our scorn now, it could be many years before the hurt and distrust wear off. While that's unfortunate, it only underscores the urgency of doing so. Contempt is like greenhouse gases that linger in the atmosphere for years—the sooner eliminated, the better.

2

Class-Based Contempt—
Red with Shame

We're the smart ones. Remember, I say it all the time:
You hear, "the elite," you're smarter than they are...
let them have the word "elite." You're the super-elite.

—Donald Trump, West Virginia, 2018[1]

For decades, the GOP has appealed to working-class whites' ethnocultural identities and social conservatism to gain their allegiance to a party that represents upper-class and corporate economic interests.[2] By the time Trump descended the golden escalator, many middle Americans saw the GOP as the "working people's party," and Trump capitalized on that chicanery at every podium he mounted.

Trump's election was the crowning achievement of the cultural wedge strategy, but what was once a wedge is now a stake through the heart of democracy. Every time we treat Trump supporters with contempt for their identities or indifference toward their real or perceived economic anxiety, we strengthen Trump's hand as it pushes the stake deeper. In his uniquely brash (and, I'm fairly certain, insincere) way, Trump *empathizes* with the dishonorable loss of status—real or imagined—that white middle Americans are experiencing. He takes the shame and/or resentment they feel and projects it onto oppressed social groups and establishment politicians.

Trump provides his supporters with an *emotional* service. He licks their wounded pride: "We are Americans," he bellows, "and the future belongs to us. The future belongs to all of you... every forgotten man and woman and child in America."[3] The rally goers cheer the loudest and longest when he hails them as courageous, hard-working Americans.[4]

When liberals mock Trump's intelligence or inarticulate speaking style, it's a thumb in the eye of blue-collar voters who are drawn to Trump precisely *because* he talks like them.[5] His pathological boastfulness, so vexing to his detractors, lifts the spirits of ardent supporters whose pride has, like Trump's, been wounded by scornful liberals. Thus does the indignity of being looked down upon resonate with Trump's base, empowering Trump to play the absurd role of the "populist billionaire" who drains the swamp not of capitalist cronies but of liberal elites who denigrate middle Americans. *He may be a fool but he's our fool.*

Trump praises rally goers, telling them how incredible and great they are, and berates the networks for training their cameras on him instead of the crowd in all its wonderfulness. "It's up to you, folks. You have the power with your vote to defend your family, your country, your values, your faith, and to defend your dignity...and we are going to win, win, win...because we are Americans."[6]

Trump has a strong hold on those who feel insecure about their status in a rapidly changing world. Many long for the good old days, when being white, male, and Christian conferred un-questioned status. Others long to once again feel proud of mas-tering their trade or launching their own small business, proud of their hometown, proud of putting food on the table. Trump stokes their pride, liberals extinguish it, and they go back to Trump and their tribe of Trump supporters to refuel. As Penn-sylvanian coal miner Paul Hela, speaking to documentary film-maker Alexandra Pelosi inside an abandoned mine shaft, said, "I just respected somebody that actually took us into consideration about coal mining and how important we are to the world and our country...he gave us a voice."[7]

Delving into the class-based dynamics of Trump's appeal is complicated by the fact that the majority of his supporters are *not* working class.[8] Nonetheless, liberals *perceive* his base as working class, perhaps because most Trump voters don't live in large coastal cities and have, on the whole, lower educational attainment than Clinton voters.[9]

Highly educated liberals too often come across as condescending know-it-alls. "These people just know they have the magic answers for society, and the only reason anyone would disagree with them is because they are stupid bigots," notes one anonymous conservative raised in rural poverty.[10]

Liberals lace their anti-Trump rhetoric with class-based contempt, and Trump leverages that contempt to turn working-class whites against those mean, snotty liberals and their elite political party. "Today," Trump pronounced at his final campaign rally in Michigan, "the American working class is going to strike back. Finally."[11]

Right-wing backlash propagandists like Ann Coulter and Rush Limbaugh have been training white middle-American wrath against the so-called "liberal elite" for decades. By the time Trump was surfing the backlash wave, it had become a tsunami of pent-up resentment. Liberals unwittingly facilitate this strategy when we look down on white working-class Americans and offer them little that will materially improve their lives or make them feel more financially secure. Said one Trump voter, "I'm angry that they're so outraged now, but were never outraged over an existing terrible system."[12]

Indianapolis mayor Pete Buttigieg raised the hackles of establishment Democrats when he noted that blue-collar Midwesterners have noticed that the rising tide didn't lift their boats as promised and that they find it condescending when coastal liberals accuse them of voting against their economic interests.[13] Whatever you may think of Buttigieg and his political prospects, he's put his finger on a hugely important class dynamic that Democrats ignore at their peril. Ohio Senator Sherrod Brown tells a story with the same takeaway: Campaigning for Al Gore at a factory, some of the workers grumbled about Gore's stance on gun control and gay rights. When Brown pointed out that he agreed with Gore on those issues and had a lifetime "F" from the National Rifle Association, they said, "Well, yeah, we know that, but you're on our side."[14] As a pro-union, anti-NAFTA, anti-war member of Congress who frequently invoked the "dignity of work," Brown had burnished his pro-worker bona fides. His constituents were confident enough of this to reelect him by six points at the same time that they cast their ballots for Trump.

Working-class whites have been steadily abandoning the Democratic Party for decades, and their voting strength in swing states has propelled more than one Republican presidential candidate to victory. This trend reached its apex in 2016 with 61 percent of white working-class women and 71 percent of white working-class men voting for Trump. Two years later, millions of those same voters rebuked Trump, voting blue in the 2018 midterms and leading political scientists to ponder whether a white working-class *re*-realignment will contribute to a Democratic sweep in 2020.[15] It could, but not if all of the Democratic entrées are served with a side of scorn.

Class in America has racial, gender, economic, educational, occupational, geographic, and cultural dimensions. In her book, *White Working Class*, University of California, Hastings law professor Joan Williams outlines a three-tier class structure dominated by a professional–managerial elite who are college educated and have incomes in the top 20 percent. At the bottom are poor people with median incomes of $22,500 (in 2015). Williams places everyone else in a hybrid "working-middle-class," by virtue either of their income or lack of college education. This middle, Williams notes, has seen their financial prospects and social status tank in recent years.[16]

Many middle Americans live in fear of sliding into financial ruin. Sixty-one percent of Americans don't have $1,000 on hand to handle an emergency.[17]

Distinct from middle Americans, upper-middle and upper-class professionals are known as the "creative class," the "knowledge class," or the "technocracy," terms that implicitly subordinate the supposedly noncreative, ignorant, and backward folks who perform menial jobs. This professional–managerial class creates and markets cultural fads for the benefit of corporate shareholders. They determine what's hot and what's not. They cast Homer Simpson as a fat, dopey, working-class stooge worthy of mockery. They castigate poor whites as "trailer trash." They discriminate against job candidates who say they like country music in favor of candidates who play water polo.[18] They hate Trump, quip about the feeble-minded parochialism of his white working-class dupes, and ponder whether IQ tests should be administered at the voting booth.[19]

Trump attracted whites from up and down the ladder, but it was working-class whites who bore the brunt of liberal wrath. These voters were held uniquely responsible for Trump's victory, and the punditry's focus on them obscured from view the sinister forces that have corrupted electoral politics and mass culture for decades. These poxes on our house include voter suppression and gerrymandering; corporate campaign spending; the right-wing disinformation machine created and funded by super-wealthy, highly educated ideologues and cynics; and the misogyny, violence, and racism that infect mass culture. But the mainstream media paid scant attention to the movers, shakers, and culture creators, opting time and again to blame the working-class rubes who somehow failed to recognize that America is, as Hillary Clinton insisted, already great.

Classist scorn entrenches working-class Trump sympathizers who, while not the biggest segment of Trump's base, are still substantial in numbers and capable of swinging left. It also turns off the millions of disillusioned working-class voters who increasingly stay home on Election Day.[20] In Michigan alone, which went to Trump by a margin of 10,704 votes, more than 87,810 voters, most of them Democrats, saw fit to mark their ballots all the way down to Drain Commissioner—but didn't vote for President.[21]

Classism is the final frontier of socially acceptable bigotry. It creates cultural polarization between liberals and working-class whites, and Republicans have capitalized on this chasm to great effect.

Right-wing propagandists are experts at weaponizing liberal disdain. They direct their aggrieved audience's attention toward mean-spirited lib-tards and away from the tax breaks they've bestowed upon the 1 percent; away from workplace exploitation; away from the ways in which the system is rigged to protect corporations and banks. And since liberals often ignore these issues, too, there's no counterforce against the rightward tug. In the absence of progressive populism, right-wing populists strip the class out of class resentment and replace it with cultural stand-ins (guns, religiosity, heterosexist masculinity, patriotic/nativist pride) and with scapegoats, namely immigrants, people of color, and their liberal handmaidens. Absent a class struggle of haves versus have-nots, socially conservative, white blue-collar Americans and their historic antagonists (the rich) huddle together under the Republican tent. (Class struggle does not mean bashing rich people, as I explain in chapter five.)

The liberal bogey refrain goes like this: "Those big-city latté liberal elites hate you and think you're stupid and racist. They belittle you, your religion, and your way of life, and aim to take away what's rightfully yours and give it to the black and brown people they like better." It's a powerful trope because it resonates with something their audience feels: contempt. Absent contempt, working-class voters might be more dubious of the narrative, but since the first half rings true, maybe the second half is true, too. We need to start making these propagandists' jobs a whole lot harder.

Sarah Smarsh, author of *Heartland*, a memoir of growing up poor in Kansas, suggests that societal contempt toward poor people "becomes the poor person's contempt for herself." She recounts a culture of shame in which complaining about one's economic struggles was frowned upon, and "no one loathed the concept of 'handouts' more than the people who needed them."[22] When liberals mock the gullibility of working-class people duped into voting against their class interests, it's worth remembering that they've been conditioned to do so for centuries. Disdaining them for it may deepen their self-contempt.

Because of the slippery nature of class, classist statements can often be made with plausible deniability. For example, one local newspaper columnist coined the term "Trumpkin," blending Trump and bumpkin. Get it? Ha! After gracing his readers with explicit put-downs of "gullible goobers" whose stupidity brought us Trump, he laments Trumpkins' inability to enjoy Mozart.[23] Nowhere in the article did the author mention class or income, but his meaning is clear: Trumpkins are white trash.

The Patch was more explicitly classist, publishing an article on 100 California cities deemed "the most redneck." The post is devoid of journalistic value, its sole purpose to mock "good ol' boys" who enjoy fishing, tobacco, and barbecue. When those "good ol' boys" hear Trump lambast the media as "the enemy of the people," they may think back to articles like this one that caricature them as yokels "shootin' their guns, driving their needlessly large trucks around, crushing cases of Coors Lights till the light of day."[24]

Satirist Alexandra Petri of *The Washington Post* leaned heavily into classist stereotypes in a 2017 piece that was a mockery of downwardly mobile Trump supporters dressed up as a satire of her fellow journalists' sudden interest in the Rust Belt.[25] She begins:

> In the shadow of the old flag factory, Craig Slabornik sits whittling away on a rusty nail, his only hobby since the plant shut down. He is an American like millions of Americans, and he has no regrets about pulling the lever for Donald Trump in November—twice, in fact, which Craig says is just more evidence of the voter fraud plaguing the country. Craig is a contradiction, but he does not know it.

The article is packed with classist jabs and mockery of the grief that her fictitious characters feel about plant closures and the decline of their rural towns:

> Lydia Borkle lives in an old shoe in the tiny town of Tempe Work Only, Ariz., where the factory has just rusted away into a pile of gears and dust. The jobs were replaced by robots, not shipped overseas, but try telling Lydia that. (I did, very slowly and patiently…) She says she has had just enough of the "coastal elitist media who keep showing up to write mean things about my town and my life…"

Petri is aware that blue-collar conservatives feel demeaned by journalists yet proceeds to lampoon them. She was in good company with former MSNBC host and multimillionaire Keith Olberman, who derided Sarah Palin and Ted Nugent as "trailer-park trash" when they visited Trump at the White House.[26]

Trailer trash, white trash, rednecks, hillbillies, hicks, country bumpkins, the underclass—these are classist slurs. There's much to dislike in Palin and Nugent, but none of it in any way is connected to the character of trailer-park residents.

James Fallows, who spent years interviewing residents of Trump country for *The Atlantic*, says that rural Americans, from California's Central Valley to the Rust Belt to Maine, share "an acute awareness of being looked down on or condescended to by big-city fashionable America."[27] Sociologist Arlie Hochschild reports much the same resentful and defensive attitude on the part of Louisiana Tea Party members fed up with the "easy potshots" directed against them by liberal TV pundits.[28]

Fallows and Hochschild aren't alone in their observation of class resentment. A series of *Washington Post* articles in 2018 attributed Trump loyalism to profound feelings of resentment toward coastal elites whose scorn soundtrack is stuck on replay. Iowa farmer Dan Smicker, for instance, said he felt hurt by assumptions equating conservatism with racism and homophobia: "I have a lifetime friend, and our friendship will end when one of us dies. This is a gay gentleman whom I have admired for 40 years. I mean, I would cut both wrists and bleed out for this guy, and it hurts me badly to be called a homophobic. Okay?" Smicker, who chairs his county's Republican party, went on to speculate that labeling conservatives as bigots further alienates the discontented "common man" who then gravitates to Trump because he feels like no one else is listening to him.[29]

Like the Midwest, Appalachia has long been ignored and belittled. Only belatedly did environmentalists acknowledge that catastrophic job loss in coal country is a legitimate concern, and that laid-off coal miners need and deserve an alternative livelihood. West Virginia, a state that had been solidly blue for decades, bled red for George W. Bush in 2000, in no small part because of the coal industry's devastatingly steep decline throughout the 1990s.

Many former Democrats in coal country nourished the hope that Trump would turn things around economically. A resident of the poverty-stricken rural county of McDowell explained, "Politicians have failed us, and it can't get much worse, so why not give a successful businessman a chance to run things differently?... Trump seemed to be a person who would break up the champagne party in Washington and look out for us little people."[30]

Imagine that you live in a town that has been dominated by coal for 100 years. Everyone you know works in the mines or for the service sectors that support mining. During Obama's tenure, the mines close, unemployment tops 17 percent, and garbage piles up on the streets due to the loss of tax revenue. Unemployed miners, once the charitable backbone of the community, are no longer in a position to give back, and opioid and meth epidemics rip through the community. To top it off, electricity rates shoot up when the utility has to start procuring coal-fired power from another state. Along comes Hillary Clinton, warning that "a lot of coal miners and coal companies [would be put] out of business."[31] But then there's Trump, promising a coal comeback. Who would you vote for? (Clinton had expressed her support for unemployed coal miners, but many right-wing media outlets broadcast her quote out of context. Without hearing her quote in its entirety, it makes some sense that coal miners reacted to this by voting for Trump.)[32]

"Voting for Clinton would have been a betrayal of my people," says Kentucky career counselor Gwen Johnson who, in between fleeting fits of tears and rage, mapped out for me precisely the devastation recounted above. Johnson says she supports women in government and would have voted for Clinton, except for her comment about coal. "We were in a place of despair," says Johnson. "I'd rather vote for a groper of women than a woman who says she'll put coal miners out of work."[33]

Johnson also interpreted Clinton's "basket of deplorables" gaffe as a classist slur against poor rural folk. Coming as it did a few months after Clinton's coal gaffe, it makes perfect sense that Appalachians would see the comment through the lens of class, write off Clinton as an establishment elitist, and embrace and defend Trump.

Alex Gibson, the executive director of the Appalshop media-and-arts nonprofit in eastern Kentucky, notes that Trump speaks the language of respect. Trump saw that Appalachian communities were despondent, and he told them, it's not your fault—it's NAFTA's fault, immigrants' fault, Obama's fault, the EPA's fault—you worked hard, and they screwed you over. Gibson says outsiders treat Appalachia like a used-up resource colony whose troubles are of no concern now that the region no longer serves the capitalist regime. One of a handful of African-Americans in his community, Gibson feels doubly alienated from the American Dream, as a black man and an Appalachian.[34]

Aware of Trump's "respect" charade, Democratic West Virginia state senator Richard Ojeda ran for a congressional seat in 2018 in a district that Trump had carried by 49 points. Though Ojeda lost by 12 points, his multiracial, pro-union working-class coalition closed the gap by an astonishing 35 points compared to 2016. The final words of Ojeda's final 2018 campaign spot? "We deserve respect."[35]

Like Appalachians, Southerners have long endured ridicule. For some coastal liberals, the South is the land of lowbrow culture inhabited by obese rednecks who talk funny. The Deep South, wrote a *Chicago Sun-Times* columnist, is a "Yahoo Nation" that "contains not one major city, nor one primary center of creative and intellectual density."[36] After Trump's infamous slander of Nicaragua and Haiti as "shitholes," I saw the following Facebook post:

> All I see is hypocrisy. I live in the South and I'm used to liberals calling our states shitholes and worse. Maybe that's why I don't care too much if the President calls third-world countries shitholes. I've got a new theory. Maybe y'all don't like Trump because you see too much of what you don't like about yourselves in him.

Liberal superiority assaults the dignity of working-class Americans. From Appalachia to the Rust Belt to the Gulf Coast, they all evince genuine hurt. It's a grievance that is voiced too often to ignore or to dismiss as a phantom conjured by right-wing propagandists.

Was It the Economy, Stupid, or the Racism?

The biggest 2016 postmortem controversy was whether Trump voters were "left-behind Americans" motivated by economic angst or bigots trying to forestall the end of white, straight, Christian male dominance. A significant amount of evidence points to bigotry as the primary driver of many voters, but…it's complicated.[37]

Political scientist Diana Mutz, one of many researchers who concluded that racial resentment trumped economic anxiety in the 2016 election, notes that her results belie something a little different from commonplace racism. She found that most white Trump supporters don't see people of color as inferior; rather, they perceive people of color to be doing well, thereby threatening their dominant status in society.[38] *White Identity Politics*, an important book by political scientist Ashley Jardina, parses white identity and racism. Jardina's data shows that significant numbers of whites who are proud of "white" or "Anglo-Saxon" culture do *not* look down on other cultures but do see them as competing with the dominant white culture.[39]

My point isn't to defend white-status anxiety and tribalism as more-acceptable variants of racism, but to suggest that the more nuanced we liberals are in understanding what gives rise to the brand of racism some Trump supporters embrace, the better we can tailor our responses.[40] And the more we can honestly acknowledge that white Americans of *all* classes and regions are afflicted with some degree of racism, the less apt we are to come across as smugly superior.

While *most* white Trump voters found Trump's white nationalism reassuring, this shouldn't eclipse from consideration those who were motivated by economic anxiety or by a toxic blend of economic and racial anxiety and resentment. White voters who are oppressed by classism have had their fear and resentment misdirected toward people of color and immigrants. It's the oldest trick in the white supremacist handbook. As long as there are unequal classes, there will be class resentment; as long as there is class resentment, it will get misdirected against people of color. A capitalist economy requires an exploited underclass, and working- and middle-class whites sure as heck don't want to populate it.

"The language of class has become deprecated, while that of culture and identity has taken center stage," observes writer Kenan Malik in an article in *The Guardian* about Great Britain that applies equally to the United States. "As a result, many in the working class have come to see their economic and political marginalization as a cultural loss. Many have redefined their interests in ethnic rather than in class terms."[41]

In exit polls, most Trump voters named immigration and terrorism as their top issues, but a lot of them fingered the economy.[42] Only 13 percent of Trump voters believe their children will achieve a better standard of living than they have.[43] These were the people who voted for Obama but then came to believe that the Democratic Party was disconnected from the needs of working-class whites.[44] An astonishing 57 percent of voters who blamed Wall Street, rather than Obama or George W. Bush, for the recession, voted for *Republicans* in 2010 House races. As liberal *Washington Post* columnist E.J. Dionne quipped, "When critics of Wall Street vote overwhelmingly for the Republicans, something is badly awry in the Democrats' approach."[45]

Though they may be a minority of Trump's base, it's important to pay attention to them, not just because they're the prized "swingable" voters in 2020, but because they're hurting—not as much as working folks of color—but hurting, nonetheless. Unemployment, poverty, and disability are higher in rural than in urban areas, and rural areas have experienced comparatively little economic recovery since 2008.[46] Automation and offshoring will only continue to make a bad situation worse.

Even those who support Trump because of his promise to seal the border aren't *necessarily* xenophobic. They may be legitimately fearful of immigrants' willingness to work for substandard wages and resentful of how the corporate demand for cheap labor drives immigration policy. (There is mixed evidence of the extent to which immigrant workers drive down wages, but the perception and fear are real.) It's tempting to deny the legitimacy of white working-class grievance when it comes wrapped in racism, but people can be two things at once—prejudiced *and* victims of decades of militarism; automation; austerity-driven budget cuts; and regressive trade, anti-union, deregulatory, and taxation policies.

Photographer Chris Arnade got to know many of the (supposed) meritocracy's losers during a two-year photojournalism road trip. His takeaway? They live in disintegrating, opioid-flooded factory towns, suffer constant anxiety, and feel humiliated by the sad condition of their lives and their collapsing communities.[47]

British journalist Gary Younge offered a similar montage in a series of articles for *The Guardian*, concluding that "the link between economic anxiety and right-wing nationalism" may be overstated but is undeniable: "...Trump's victory cannot be explained by racism alone—and the efforts to understand race and class separately result in one misunderstanding them both entirely."[48] He cites, for example, Jamie Walsh, a 35-year-old white working-class Trump voter from Indiana, who says that poor whites resent being accused of having privilege. Walsh also says they resent being made to feel stupid and politically incorrect for wanting someone to have their backs the way they perceive liberals supporting women and minorities: "White privilege pisses poor white people off because they've never experienced it on a level that they understand. You hear 'privilege' and you think money and opportunity and they don't have it."

A 2019 study found that liberals who learn about white privilege become less sympathetic toward poor whites.[49] Many assume that, if poor whites were unable to leverage their racial privilege, they have only themselves to blame for their plight. This kind of either/or thinking—racism *or* classism—leaves low-income whites with nowhere to turn to other than white nationalism or self-blame.

Like Younge and Arnade, investigative journalist Alexander Zaitchik suspected that something more complex than straight-up bigotry was fueling Trump's success during the GOP primaries. His book, *The Gilded Rage*, portrays the complex and sometimes contradictory beliefs and motivations of Trump voters. "Human beings are complicated," says Zaitchik. "If you try to reduce them to something, in almost every case you'll be proven wrong."[50]

Zaitchik encountered bigotry, "but almost never was that at the top of people's lists about why they supported Trump. I gave people plenty of time to reveal themselves, and they most wanted to talk about cratering economies, lost industries, elite condescension, and betrayal." They were, Zaitchik concluded, far more resentful of "condescending elites" than of people of color.[51]

Many of the Trump supporters Zaitchik interviewed harbored progressive populist leanings and were sorely tempted to vote for Bernie Sanders but for the antisocialist fulminations of their favorite talk-radio red-baiters. Echoing Zaitchik, former Secretary of Labor Robert Reich also found enormous support for Sanders among Rust Belt voters who, during the 2015 primaries, praised

Trump and Sanders as the only candidates who would give the system a badly needed shakeup.[52]

In 2018, a team of journalists from *The Washington Post* interviewed Trump supporters in Midwestern districts that had been solidly Democratic for decades but swung wildly for Trump in 2016. Downward mobility and the erosion of the American Dream were recurring themes frequently offered as the basis for their vote.[53] Several complained that coastal media and politicians had ignored the Midwest. Some blamed their declining quality of life on people of color and immigrants. While some were exuberantly loyal to Trump, others regretted their vote.

According to some studies, working-class whites and Republicans are, as a class, more racist by certain measures, but this doesn't create a license to overgeneralize. Twenty-eight percent of Democrats (and 75 percent of Republicans) attribute blacks' inability to get ahead to their personal failure, not to discrimination.[54] Racism is embedded in the minds of *all* white Americans to some degree—including among aerospace engineers who beat black people at Unite the Right rallies; among Stanford-educated chemical engineers who sic the police on black people barbecuing at a public park in Oakland; and among professionals who pick "Greg" over "Jamal," even when the two fictitious candidates have identical résumés.[55] White-power groups actively recruit on college campuses, and many of its spokespeople are college educated.[56]

For educated liberals to suggest that *they're* racist and *we're* not is not only polarizing, it's untrue. Gibson, whose insights concerning Trump's appeal in Appalachia were discussed earlier, says he's experienced no overt racism in his rural Kentucky town. Is there a black man in San Francisco, Los Angeles, or New York who would say the same?

Trump's base includes voters from all classes and ethnicities—even a smattering of poor people, Muslims, and blacks. Twenty-eight percent of Latinx Americans voted for Trump.[57] There's no one-size-fits-all explanation that preempts the need to explore any given individual's motivations. When we overgeneralize, we risk alienating the very people we need to reach. The Right has successfully driven a wedge between working-class whites and people of color. When we call out racism without acknowledging that the winner-take-all system is rigged to favor the wealthy,[58] we facilitate this divide-and-conquer strategy.

For a significant number of voters, Trump was a desperate and/or pissed off Hail Mary motivated by something more multi-dimensional than racism. Voters like Ed Harry, a union organizer, who was a lifelong Democrat until "blue-collar America essentially had the door shut in its face" by establishment Democrats. Harry then hitched his wagon to the only outsider in the race, the one who called out the "rigged system."[59] Voters like Connie Knox, a Democrat who lost faith in Obama when he championed the Trans-Pacific Partnership.[60] These anecdotal reports may only reflect a narrow margin of Americans, the ones who are experiencing economic dislocation and have given up hope that the Democrats will ever do anything about it. But elections are won and lost based on such margins.

Before and after the 2016 election, Working America interviewed a thousand working-class swing voters in Ohio and Pennsylvania. It found that roughly half were "searchers" open to swinging left after having a conversation about health care, jobs, or social security.[61] For working-class voters, the divide isn't Democrat versus Republican: It's working Americans versus the elite, says Working America Director Matt Morrison.[62]

Brookings Institution Senior Fellow William Galston warns against the folly of writing off rural America: "Think through the political consequences of saying to a substantial portion of Americans, which is even more substantial in political terms, 'We think you're toast.'"[63] Three months before the 2016 election, Senator Chuck Schumer did just that, proclaiming, "For every blue-collar Democrat we lose in western Pennsylvania, we will pick up two moderate Republicans in the suburbs in Philadelphia, and you can repeat that in Ohio and Illinois and Wisconsin."[64] Schumer assumed Democrats could relinquish a segment of its base and still win. That segment now belongs to Trump, and a Democratic win in 2020 will require some portion of Schumer's discounted working-class voters in swing states to abandon Trump and some portion of disaffected Democrats to get back to the polls.

Schumer's hubris brings to mind another Democratic axiom— that when nonwhites become a majority of the population in 2040, the Republicans will have to fold up their little tent once and for all. It strikes me as the height of arrogance to presume that a nonwhite majority will usher in electoral utopia. That year is a long way off, and hard-right politicians, especially if they're autocrats like Trump, are capable of doing irreversible damage between now and then, including an intensified effort to dis- enfranchise a coming nonwhite majority whose loyalty toward Democrats is, in any event, waning. To the extent that conserva- tive whites fear Democratic predictions of a political realignment, they will support whatever it takes to vitiate that realignment. Reassurance, rather than anticipatory gloating, would go a long way toward defusing the white-angst time bomb.

This is not to suggest pandering to the narrative that whites are a beleaguered minority. But it doesn't cost anything for white liberals to hear what it *feels* like for whites whose vulnerability is, *in their minds*, tied to the fact that their numbers and cultural status are washing away. Instead of extending an empathy life vest, we try to drown them in shame, and back to Trump they go for affirmation of their once-and-future greatness. Trump-brand white nationalism will be far less contagious when there is a bet- ter diagnosis and prescription for what ails middle America.

Briahna Joy Gray, Bernie Sanders' press secretary (as of this writing) and a former editor at *The Intercept*, wrestles with the moral and strategic dimensions of shaming racist Trump sup- porters, drawing on research showing that shame-prone individ- uals try to preserve their self-esteem by lashing out at convenient scapegoats. She comes to the following conclusion:

> Of course, the responsibility for bigotry lies squarely on the shoulders of bigots, but it's worth considering whether the language we use might influence whether whites see

the future as one to be afraid of, or as an inclusive one in which equality benefits them, too. There are humanistic reasons for that: Everyone, regardless of race, should be able to feel a sense of community, belonging, and individual pride in an egalitarian future. But it is also in the self-interest of racial justice movements to think about the social factors that help drive the discontented in one direction or another. If a particular method is found to actually fuel the growth of the alt-right, it needs to be examined critically, because nothing is more liable to hurt people of color than a flood of angry young men joining white supremacist groups.

As disturbing as it is to hear people voice antipathy toward or discomfort with the emerging nonwhite majority, Gray believes that berating them inhibits their capacity for redemption:

> [A] shaming approach can make us indifferent to the complex human factors that underlie decisions we detest…Applying shame to an entire category of people, rather than conducting a more nuanced assessment of why people feel the way they do and did what they did, means we might miss those among the blameworthy who might be identified as something more mutable, more persuadable than a "deplorable"—someone who might be convinced to join our side next time around.[65]

I don't think there's a singular explanation for what animates every racist mind in America. What's important is that we not presume any given Trump voter to have been motivated by racism and, if they do show themselves to be racist, that we peel back the layers and respond to whatever we find at the core.

Most white Americans are aware that racial disparities exist, but many don't understand why this is so. Progressive communications expert Anat Shenker-Osorio is part of a research team testing how progressive candidates can effectively frame issues of race and class. As of this writing, the team's preliminary finding among Minnesota voters is that a message that explicitly addresses both race and class is the most effective way to counteract GOP dog whistles. The following message flipped 57 percent of white Minnesotans, who had previously received a xenophobic GOP flyer, to the progressive candidate:

> Whether white, black, or brown, 5th generation or newcomer, we all want to build a better future for our children. My opponent says some families have value, while others don't count. He wants to pit us against each other in order to gain power for himself and kickbacks for his donors.[66]

What Shenker-Osorio's research demonstrates is that many whites will defy the dog whistle when they are given a narrative that promotes solidarity with, rather than resentment of, people of color. Shenker-Osorio says that it's crucial to "help white people understand why it is that these severe racial disparities exist, rather than just naming the disparities, which leaves people to fill in the causal relationship for themselves."[67] In other words, dismissing them all as incorrigible racists is political suicide. Psychiatrist Jonathan Metzl, author of *Dying of Whiteness: How The Politics of Racial Resentment is Killing America's Heartland*, has a similar take: Immunizing white working-class voters against Trump's brand of racial resentment-mongering requires deep conversations about white privilege *and* the honorable values and traditions of conservative white communities so that they can see how white nationalism *contradicts* conservative values.[68]

Documentary filmmaker Whitney Dow recorded the oral histories of 100 white Americans and observed that white men are struggling to adjust to the "deconstruction of the white-male archetype...They are struggling to construct a just narrative for themselves as new information comes in, and they are having to restructure and refashion their own narratives—and coming up short."[69] It's a work in progress, one that is hindered by shaming and blaming.

CNN commentator Van Jones said in a 2017 talk describing his travels through Trump country, "I've met straight, white, cisgendered, heterosexual Trump voters who are some of the best people in this country...I've seen it, and I can't unsee that. I can't unknow that, and then participate in all of this bashing and all of this trashing that has become so popular and has become so easy."[70]

It was Jones who, on Election Night, coined the term "white-lash" to explain and bemoan Trump's victory. But in his book, *Beyond the Messy Truth*, he says that viewers misunderstood him. He did not mean to suggest that all Trump voters are racists. Noting that 70,000 Rust Belt residents voted for Obama and then for Trump, Jones believes that Trump voters had mixed motives, including resentment toward corporate globalization that Steve Bannon and the alt-right parlayed into nativism and white supremacy.[71]

The expression of contempt toward middle-American Trump voters fails to acknowledge the real pain some of them have experienced as market capitalism wreaks havoc. It also overlooks middle-class voters' very valid grudge about having to pay for social welfare benefits for people just a little worse off than they are. Because wealthy Americans and corporations haven't paid their fair share of taxes in decades, the middle class bears the burden. They're legitimately ticked off about it, even if the object of their resentment is misplaced.

People are more complex than yard signs. But for many leftists, Trump's open embrace of white supremacy is all we need to know about what animates his supporters. Our fear and loathing of bigotry eclipse other dynamics that could coexist in the hearts and minds of some of Trump's base. And those other dynamics—anti-establishment sentiment, distrust of globalization and automation, genuine religious faith, and an attachment to familial and communal bonds—are inroads that we should travel upon more often. The fact that, in 2016, 68 percent of voters agreed that "traditional parties and politicians don't care about people like me" speaks volumes about the intensity of populist discontent.[72]

There are 23 million white working-class Americans thought

to be potential swing voters in 2020.[73] As of March 2018, 18 percent of Trump voters reported feeling lukewarm or cold toward Trump.[74] That's too many to write off as deplorable.

Listen

Katherine Cramer's book, *The Politics of Resentment*, is chockablock with rural Wisconsinites' bitter resentment of cultural elitism. Over and over, Cramer's subjects complain that urbanites (by which they mean residents of Madison!) disregard commonsense wisdom and practical, hands-on skills, and denigrate cherished rural values and ways of life. When Obama became the breakout candidate in 2008, they preferred him to Hillary because they saw him as "down-to-earth" (a perception that wore off over time).

Cramer visited with 27 groups over five years. What she learned from these hundreds of "listening sessions" was that, according to some rural Wisconsinites, the "haves" are not necessarily rich—they're cultural elitists who ignore the needs of rural folk, and see rural values and lifestyles as inferior. While Cramer documented a fair amount of racism, at the same time, she is adamant that rural pride and racist white pride are not the same.

Back in 2005, Jean Hardisty, founder of Political Research Associates, a social justice think tank, observed that the Right's success was, among other things, a function of their skill in doing something the Left, Katherine Cramer aside, doesn't bother much with…listening:

> Their genius was that they first engaged in a practice of active listening and found a core of resentment among large numbers of Americans—about race, class, gender, and sexuality—that could provide the emotional base for a new intellectual paradigm. They did this in the 1970s, at precisely the time when liberals stopped listening, presuming that the reactionary ideas of the old Right were so far out of favor that only the most uninformed and backward voters supported them.[75]

Hardisty's contemporaries maintain that the key to defusing the reactionary Right is extending empathy to white middle-Americans.[76] This strategy is the polar opposite of contempt.

Listening empathetically to a racist is a tall order but when we fail to do so, or when we presume people to be bigots, we pay a steep price. If we don't hold open the possibility of redemption, there will be none.

The legendary Highlander Center, a Tennessee social justice leadership institute, modeled a blend of empathy and account-ability in reaction to a white supremacist arson attack that burned down its main office in 2019. Its press release explained that the white-power movement has "targeted working-class and cash-poor white communities' search to find a sense of belonging, dividing them from people who support efforts to improve the material conditions of all people." The press release went on to discuss the impact of the white-power movement on blacks, Muslims, Jews, and immigrants.[77]

In a brilliant TED Talk after the election, African-American poet and racial-justice activist Theo E.J. Wilson, who spent months lurking in online "alt-right" echo chambers to better understand what animates white nationalists, resurrected Hardisty's long-ignored advice: "It is time that we start seeing people as people and not simply the ideas that we project onto them or react to...There is no way out of each other. Stop trying to find one." Wilson criticizes liberals for having "wide acceptance for everybody, except for those who have honestly held conservative viewpoints" and for their "wholesale demonization of everything white and male," a habit that he believes fuels white nationalists' momentum.[78] (Wilson must have been reading the mind of this Trump supporter who said, "There is something hypocritical about the Left saying they are uniters, not dividers; they are inclusive and then excluding half the population with comments on intelligence and irrelevance in the modern world.")[79]

Wilson concludes that humanity requires an upgrade, an evolution in consciousness that enables us to have empathy for one another and bring about a renaissance of human connection.

This may sound naive, but the capacity for a nuanced under-standing of human foibles is a core progressive value. When people damage themselves with drugs or alcohol, we recognize the conditions that led them to self-medicate. When they steal, we see poverty and the culture of materialism at play. When they kill, we want to know whether they suffered childhood abuse. We try to understand what causes people to hurt themselves and others, not for the sake of condoning their behavior, but because only by understanding what motivates pathology can we hope to unwind it. The same principle applies to bigotry.

If we swallow Wilson's prescription, contempt is contraindi-cated.

Post-Industrial Mayhem

Bill Clinton's Treasury Secretary, Lawrence Summers, admits that he never visited Rust Belt cities devastated by NAFTA. Displaced white workers "weren't heavily on our radar screen," he said, not-ing that the Democratic Party base is a "coalition of cosmopolitan elite and diversity."[80]

Summers' "cosmopolitan elite" are highly educated, affluent people who travel the world, live in ethnically diverse cities, and are in constant global communication. For them, the benefits of globalization are myriad, and the downsides invisible. But for those whose idea of the good life is more slow-paced and pa-rochial, global economic and communication networks are a threat to their livelihoods, their way of life, and their commu-nities, which have been ravaged by foreclosures, offshoring, and automation.

Our economy is being rocked by hugely disruptive enterprises that have reduced many workers to precarious, underpaid piece-work in the gig economy and Amazon fulfillment centers. Ar-tificial intelligence breakthroughs will only elevate the level of disruption.

Successful technocrats sometimes sneer at others' failure to get with the program. Though many affluent liberals have compas-sion for poor folks, others lean into the myth of the meritocracy to rationalize their wealth, glossing over the intrinsic inequality of a meritocracy in which, by definition, there are winners and losers. "You're all fucking welfare cases!" a protestor yelled at Trump rally goers in Albuquerque. "You just don't want anyone else getting any!"[81] A heartwarming moment of working-class solidarity it was not.

Fewer than half of Americans born in 1980 will earn as much as their parents, compared to 79 percent of those born in 1950 and 92 percent of those born in 1940.[82] Low-wage white workers have seen their pay stagnate or decrease for decades. (Black and Latinx workers' wages have risen but still lag far behind whites'.)[83] Since 1971, the percentage of middle-class households has fallen by 10 percent—half of those households joined the upper class and half the lower.[84] Little wonder then that the middle class looks with hopeful anticipation upon the rich and with anxious dread upon the poor.

In *The Limousine Liberal*, historian Steve Fraser traces the rise of right-wing populism to the Nixon presidency when blue-collar whites realized that "their social contract with New Deal liberalism was expiring." Structural unemployment and wage stagnation were taking their toll, but the Democrats offered no solutions. Nixon offered no help to the working class either; instead, he celebrated their folkways, initiating a culture war steeped in noble traditions like hard work and humility and pernicious ones like patriarchy and white supremacy. Reagan and George W. Bush carried on in this vein, with Bush going so far with the plutocratic populist ruse as to provide hard hats to the corporate lobbyists who populated his campaign rallies.[85]

Nixon voters' discontent was not only financial. They bemoaned the atomistic quality of modern life writ large.[86] On that score, the situation has only deteriorated. The social fabric is weak, civic participation is anemic, and poor people are regarded as losers, when they're regarded at all. The bipartisan myth of the meritocracy has effectively displaced altruistic values of community and care, resulting in social conditions shitty enough to impel nearly 5 percent of Americans to try to take their own lives.[87]

Coincident with economic precarity and incohesion are several significant demographic and cultural shifts: The proportion of whites in America has decreased from 88 percent in 1970 to 72 percent in 2010.[88] Today, women compete with men in the workplace, gender identities are in flux, multiculturalism is the norm, marriage equality is the law of the land, and there's a new lexicon for discussing race and gender—and impatience toward those who aren't yet hip to it. Whites are, on the whole, overrepresented in higher education, politics, corporate management, and prestigious professions like law, medicine, and journalism. But not working-class whites.[89] While people of color and middle-class white women are slowly gaining representation, poor whites' stars are not rising. On the contrary, their well-being, as measured by life expectancy, health, educational attainment, and income, is declining.[90]

These deteriorating social conditions set the stage for race hustlers to forge a counterfeit bond between rich and nonrich whites—a bond that tends to suppress any claims the have-nots might make on the wealth of the haves. As Briahna Joy Gray astutely argues, absent a class analysis, calling out Trump's racism can perversely bolster his position as the great white savior who has the best interests of white Americans at heart (thereby obscuring his avaricious allegiance to crony capitalism).[91]

Racist precepts were constructed to justify the slave trade and have served handily ever since to pit poor whites against blacks in the capitalist rat race.[92] As economic inequality hits new extremes, oligarchs are more than happy to have nonrich whites blame immigrants and people of color for their inability to get ahead. Those who are down-and-out have one of three explanations for their circumstances—the system is flawed; they're losers who have only themselves to blame; or it's the fault of scapegoats and their liberal coddlers. To the extent that economic elites seal off door No. 1, our democracy is imperiled by the temptation to enter door No. 3.

Most liberals understand that gender equality, and racial and ethnic diversity are not the cause of economic decline, but put yourself in the shoes of a white conservative living in an area undergoing rapid diversification. Ku Klux Klan leader Rachel Pendergraft says that hate groups' numbers are swelling with new members who feel like "strangers in their own country."[93] Even if one isn't experiencing downward mobility themselves, seeing others in their community struggle—and mistakenly linking those struggles to racial diversity and liberal immigration policy—makes them worry about what the future holds for them as the white minority.

Liberal professionals look upon nationalism with unmitigated horror, because all they see is the racist aspect. What they're missing is how nationalism is a reaction to the detrimental impacts of globalization. Two-thirds of working-class whites and three-quarters of Trump primary voters see trade deals as harmful to American workers, and there's plenty of evidence that they're right (and that foreign laborers are being exploited in the bargain as well).[94] When Trump tells them he will bring back their jobs by shredding unpopular trade and climate deals, that sounds pretty damn good.

After NAFTA passed, the president of the electrical workers' union vowed revenge: "Clinton screwed us and we won't forget it."[95] Twenty-four years and a few dozen Trump anti-NAFTA jeremiads later, rank-and-file electrical union members welcomed Trump to their Philadelphia job site.[96] Minnesota iron and steel workers, too, say they've never forgiven President Clinton for NAFTA and that Trump won them over with his outspoken commitment to killing the Trans-Pacific Partnership. Trade deals, they say, are their *No. 1 issue* and the reason the once-solidly blue North Star state is turning red.[97]

Liberal Democrats are right: We're not going back to the closeted, corseted, Jim Crow 1950s. But we're not going back to the Clintonian 1990s, either. That much was made evident in 2016.

City University of New York sociologist Charlie Post summed up the 2016 debacle like this: "Traditionally Democratic working-class voters were faced with the choice between a neoliberal who disdained working people and a right-wing populist who promised to bring back well-paying manufacturing jobs. Many stayed home, and a tiny minority shifted their allegiances from the first African-American president to an open racist and xenophobe."[98] Or, to put it in Michael Moore's less academic terms, Trump's victory was "the biggest fuck you ever recorded in human history."[99]

Post's conclusion aligns with the views of Trump voters in blue-collar Howard County, Iowa, which Obama won by 20 points and Trump won by a staggering 41. Pat Murray, a press-brake operator and Democratic member of the county Board of Supervisors, said, "Democrats always say we're going to fight for the working people. The last few elections, we haven't shown that at all." Murray didn't vote for Trump, but his brethren did. And in interview after interview, the reason they gave was Clinton's elitism. They caucused for Sanders and, when he lost the primary, turned a desperate eye on Trump.[100]

Blue-collar whites weren't Clinton's only detractors. Civil rights scholar Michelle Alexander argued during the primary that Clinton didn't deserve black people's vote; evidently, she wasn't alone. Eleven percent of black 2012 Obama voters stayed home in 2016, representing a loss of 1.6 million votes, many of them in swing states that Trump won by razor-thin margins.[101] Some black Milwaukee residents told reporters they were disillusioned with how little their lives had improved after eight years of Obama and couldn't bring themselves to vote for Clinton.[102] As pollster and strategist Stanley Greenberg notes, "The Democrats don't have a 'white working-class problem.' They have a 'working-class problem,'" borne of decades of alignment with the economic interests of the elite.[103]

To hear political analyst Thomas Frank tell it in *Listen, Liberal*, too many Democrats have stood by and watched—if not cheerleaded—as the invisible hand of the market grabbed black, brown, and white middle-Americans' wealth and handed it over to oligarchs.[104] Democrats in the Clinton mold have, as Open Markets Institute Policy Director Matt Stoller puts it, "replaced a New Deal-era understanding of economic and political democracy with an ideology that justified the pillaging of working-class

Americans by a new group of political and economic elites."[105] The Democratic Party has moved so far to the right on economic issues that Bernie Sanders' 2016 platform looked like Dwight Eisenhower's![106] Having hewed to a centrism that has skewed so far to the right, and having made little effort to reposition the center further to the left, Democrats' working-class mantle was, by 2016, threadbare.

In becoming the party of upper-middle-class professionals that, as Frank puts it, "no longer speaks to the people on the losing end of a free-market system that is becoming more brutal and more arrogant by the day," an opening has been created for the right-wing to co-opt class and for Trump to disingenuously inveigh against the establishment.[107] What's more, Frank laments, "…the task of deploring and denouncing the would-be dictator Trump has entirely crowded out the equally important task of assessing where the Democratic Party went wrong…They don't need to persuade anyone. They need only to let their virtue shine bright for all to see."[108]

You may not agree that neoliberal economic free trade and deregulatory policies are to blame for our country's economic woes, and my task here isn't to convince you to reject market capitalism or to see the meritocracy as mythical and arbitrary. I'm suggesting that there are social and political conditions, other than or in addition to bigotry, that make many working- and lower-middle-class people feel "left behind." If they hired Trump to blow up a system they see as rigged, campaigns that promise to return to the good ol' days of 2015—before Trump ruined everything—will not inspire, nor will conversations that refuse to acknowledge how the good ol' days were rife with cynicism and despair. Trump's solutions to complex problems are dangerous, simplistic, and cruel, but the problems are real.

Something Is Wrong

Many Americans suffer not only from financial anxiety but from a deepening crisis of uncertainty about what the future holds. The old order is disintegrating before a coherent new way of understanding the world has taken hold.

Contemporary society can feel disorienting and empty. We live in an age in which the very notion of observable reality is collapsing. Technologies that allow for fabricated photos and videos to be produced and disseminated have given rise to the business of concocting a dizzying array of alt-realities. The proliferation of online content created by anonymous individuals and bots adds to the unaccountable, hateful, carnival-like atmosphere of social media. As virtual reality entertainment and infotainment options mushroom, the blurring of fantasy and reality will only become more destabilizing, and our minds more vulnerable to being colonized by bad actors.

The human mind has not evolved to parse reality. It feels to me like we're living in a state of "future shock" foretold by futurist and author Alvin Toffler in 1970, in which exponential change, population growth, new technologies, and information overload come at us faster than we can absorb. Some people are adept at handling these changes and rise to the top of the technocracy, while others seek outlets in mood alteration, shopping, gaming, and other forms of escapism. Those most rocked by future shock are easy prey for demagogues who replace complex realities with faulty syllogisms.

"Something is wrong, the common person feels, correctly," mused writer George Saunders as he road-tripped across the country trying to understand why Trump supporters feel so aggrieved. Zipping past the "bland, bright spaces, spaces constructed to suit the purposes of distant profit," Saunders saw how a cynical materialist like Trump can fill the void left when chain-store employees' hopes and dreams wither away under the fluorescent glare of corporate America.[109] Making America great again sounds preferable to sinking into despair.

Until the Democrats or a viable third party offers an explanation and a solution for Americans subsumed by the cognitive dissonance that lives at the intersection of the American Dream and the American reality, many of them (mostly the white ones) will take comfort in Trump's nationalist fairy tale. Trumpism might not wind up materially improving their lives, but at least it casts them as heroes rather than zeroes.

Many Americans feel threatened and disoriented by a storm of cultural, technological, occupational, and social change, some of it progressive, some of it nihilistic. Change—even when it's for the better—can be stressful and disorienting. And when demographic change coincides with the overall deterioration of the social fabric, it's easy to confuse correlation with causation (and Fox News is there to muddy the waters).

As author Charles Eisenstein writes, "Hate and blame are convenient ways of making meaning out of a bewildering situation."[110] In the disorienting, dehumanizing condition that is modern capitalism, people's lives are stripped of meaning and purpose. Reduced to serving as cogs in a machine that is ready to discard them the moment their net productive value trails a Honduran's or a robot's, people seek solace in grand narratives that cast them as victims whose honor will be aggressively restored by a no-nonsense, rule-breaking strongman.

Trump's ability to mobilize fear and resentment is terrifyingly impressive and has left many on the Left counting the days until the gullible, racist morons who voted for him get their comeuppance. We can either continue deriding and antagonizing middle Americans or we can see their humanity and show them ours. As our nation dips its toes into fascist waters, classist contempt is, I fear, a reckless shove.

3

Why Not Everyone Is a Liberal

If we could read the secret histories of our enemies,
we would find in each person's life
sorrow and suffering enough to disarm all hostility.

—Henry Wadsworth Longfellow

Would you feel warmer toward conservatives if you knew that they can't help being conservative any more than you can help being liberal, that they came by their beliefs honestly, just like you did, and hold them dear, just like you do? Would you feel less inclined to look down on them if you understood the moral and cognitive foundations of conservative ideologies?

There's a tendency among liberals to see well-heeled Trump supporters as selfish wealth hoarders and non-wealthy ones as hapless dupes who don't know what's good for them—why aren't they tax-and-spend liberals, for God's sake? I've found my own thought process skidding toward such condescension numerous times.

As discussed in the last chapter, some of Trump's base are "Trump triers" who felt betrayed by Democrats and scorned by liberals. They were willing to place their bets on someone who promised to bring their jobs back or, at least, do them the honor of paying lip service to their plight. But apart from Trump's unique ability to leverage class-based contempt, there's an underlying belief structure that many Trump supporters and conservatives generally adhere to. This chapter examines those belief structures, how they form, and why they're resistant to revision.

There is no single explanation for every one of the almost 63 million Americans who voted for Trump, and most have more nuanced and ambivalent beliefs than liberals generally presume. In 2018, a group of social scientists studying political polarization conducted in-depth interviews with Americans across the political spectrum. Contrary to their expectation, most of the people had far more complicated views than "absurdly inaccurate" partisan media caricatures had led them to believe. Even when speaking with people who held very different beliefs from their own, they were surprised by how often they were able to find common ground.[1] I experienced much the same at a Better Angels' red–blue workshop where conservatives expressed great concern over issues like economic inequality, corporate power, gun control, and unrestrained profit maximization.

Who do you suppose said this about Trump's stance on immigration?

> He has basically called them all criminals and said they're not coming in here. It seems that there's been this group stereotype. But what about those who have come here for reasons of need?...What about the fathers, the mothers, the children, who have come here and are willing to go through the process to apply for asylum so they can come into this country and benefit from not having to be oppressed continually by criminals?...It's all fear-based, and frankly it's based upon selfishness—"I'm going to lose something by them coming in."[2]

Nancy Pelosi? Corey Booker? Nope. It was Ammon Bundy, the Mormon militia leader of the armed 2016 Malheur National Wildlife Refuge occupation. He went on to sever his ties with the militia movement, warning that Trumpist nationalism resembled Nazi Germany. We all contain multitudes.

Political beliefs stem from how we see the world and our role in it. By adulthood, everyone lives inside of what sociologist Hochschild calls a "deep story" that helps us make sense of a complex world. The story, etched in emotional memory, is subjectively true.

Chief among the building blocks of the deep story are biology and upbringing. There is some evidence that up to 40 percent of political views are inherited genetically, and the rest are functions of environmental influences, namely parenting.[3] Over a lifetime—bit by bit, experience by experience, broadcast by broadcast, meme by meme—we all come to believe certain things.

The way our parents nurtured and disciplined us makes a profound impact on our psyches, our sense of right and wrong, our expectations of ourselves and others, and our attitudes toward authority. Four out of five people vote like their parents. There's no bigger predictor of political ideology than that of one's parents.[4] If your worldview is very different from your parents or siblings, you're the exception.

How did your parents expect you to behave, and what did they do when you violated their rules? Did they use bribes, time-outs, spankings, silent treatment, shame, lectures, yelling, punishment, or reason? Did they demand obedience or were family rules subject to negotiation? Did they make a virtue of independence, and did they inculcate it through shaming your dependency or rewarding your precocity? Did they limit the range of acceptable emotions that could be expressed in the home? Did they hold you to a higher or lower standard than they held themselves? Did they listen to you? Did they ever apologize or admit making mistakes? Were they abusive or neglectful? When they said they were doing something "for your own good," did you believe them? Did you idealize them?

How you answered the above questions strongly predicts how you'll answer these: Do you presume people to be trustworthy or untrustworthy, good or bad? Do you see life as a zero-sum game in which the strongest or smartest deservedly dominate others, or do you feel that your fate is interconnected and that all beings have equal worth? Do you believe that people in power are justified in pursuing their self-interest, or do you believe that the purpose of holding power is to lift up everyone? Do you submit to or question authority? Do you idealize authority figures or see them as nuanced, flawed humans? Do you feel vengeful toward people who do wrong, or are you more interested in making the victim whole and preventing further injury? Do you think people who do bad things were born bad and cannot change, or do you think circumstances caused them to make poor choices and that they are capable of change? When you're in need, are you comfortable asking for help or does doing so feel shameful? Is your morality guided by an internal sense of right and wrong, or by the prospect of an external punishment or reward?

Childhood experiences, together with biologic predispositions, provide the material with which our ideological set point is calibrated. Our genetic makeup predisposes us to certain psychological and physiological traits, which, in turn, correlate strongly with political orientation. Once that orientation is established, it's highly resistant to modification.[5]

A trio of political physiologists who literally wrote the book on biopolitics note that people whose propensities run counter to yours *literally* "do not see what you see, fear what you fear, love what you love, smell what you smell, remember what you remember, taste what you taste, want what you want, or think what you think."[6] Among the most important of these propensities are fear and disgust.

Fear and Disgust

Conservatives tend to be more fearful than liberals, so much so that their amygdalas are larger and more active. The more fearful one is at age four, the more conservative one is 20 years later.[7]

Neuroscientist Daniela Schiller explains that the human brain encodes fear when observing scary incidents or being told to be afraid of certain things or people.[8] Repetition is key. If you watch footage of the World Trade Center crumbling over and over or, if you tune in daily to a show that barrages you with inflated, inaccurate, and/or hysterical stories about all the bad hombres who are out to get you, you develop a fear of and bias against those people. Fox News knows this. That's why they hit the panic button every few minutes, reminding people of their mortality—and the vulnerability of white hegemony—which motivates them to defend against such existential threats.

A field experiment conducted in the months following 9/11

reveals just how damaged the national psyche was on the heels of such a massive trauma: A random sample of Americans was asked what chance they thought the average American had of being hurt in a terrorist attack in the next year. The mean response was 48 percent.[9] Let that sink in for a moment. They predicted that 138 *million Americans*—nearly half of the population—would be attacked by terrorists.

After 9/11, even many liberals signed off on the notion that Iraq would have to be invaded and civil liberties curtailed to make us safer. The Senate vote in favor of the Patriot Act was 98 to one. Trillions of dollars, hundreds of thousands of lives, and an extensive erosion of civil liberties later, it's pretty clear that allowing fear to guide policy was catastrophic.

Jumping at Shadows, journalist Sasha Abramsky's exploration of the fear epidemic gripping the United States, makes sense of what I believe supercharges the belief structures of many Trump supporters. Our culture is awash in fearmongering, though seldom concerning the things we should rationally be afraid of. Sensationalized crime and terrorism coverage is riveting, but the recitation of the much larger numbers of people killed by air pollution, car crashes, workplace accidents, diabetes, prescription-drug fatalities, and suicide, not so riveting. People's ability to accurately calibrate risk—and to support reasonable policy measures that correspond to the level of risk—is subverted by overactivation of the brain's fear center.

Chronic anxiety can cause a host of mental and physical ailments.[10] Many Americans are, as the saying goes, sick with fear. Only 14 percent (most of them progressives) see the world as basically safe and nonthreatening.[11] Knowing this makes me feel more sympathetic toward someone whose panic button is on a hair trigger—the consequences of living in a state of chronic anxiety are as unpleasant and unhealthy for the individual as for society as a whole.

There are people in my life who I know to have good hearts, but whose fear and anxiety makes them gravitate toward command-and-control solutions or wealth hoarding. Sometimes, I, too, find my mind wandering in that direction: After the latest school shooting, maybe my son's school *should* have a metal detector. Maybe such thoughts have crossed your mind, too.

A propensity to experience intense disgust is even more predictive of conservatism than fear. Scientists can predict with 95 percent accuracy whether someone is liberal or conservative based on brain scans showing how their neural networks react to pictures of disgusting images.[12] (Fun fact: Trump is a self-described germophobe known for ordering his steaks well done.)

Disgust is the most visceral of emotions, and our sensitivity to it is largely hardwired.[13] As with fear, the disgust reflex can lead conservatives to bypass reason and endorse policies that protect them from perceived contaminants. Doing otherwise is a super-human feat requiring one to override powerful physiological danger and distress signals.

When we ran out of hamburger buns and my low-disgust-sensitivity husband shaped our burgers into logs to fit inside hot-dog buns (take a moment to conjure up that image), I had to force myself to eat the poop log, telling him—between unpleasant bites—to never do that again! Taking a more consequential scenario, when Ebola broke out in Africa in 2015, Republicans were significantly more worried about becoming infected, and far more supportive of quarantines and travel bans.[14]

Evolutionary biologists believe that fear of foreigners may be rooted in an instinct to defend against pathogens that the local population has no immunity to. Indeed, anti-immigrant sentiment is strongest in states with the highest incidence of infectious diseases. People who are wary of immigrants also tend to be suspicious of strangers in general, perhaps because having a smaller social circle reduces the risk of contagion.[15] Though modern medicine diminishes the rationale for germophobia, our premodern neurobiology hasn't gotten the memo.

Disgust sensitivity also predicts homophobia. In one study, college students, including liberals, exposed in a lab setting to the smell of vomit, moved to the right when surveyed about their views on gay marriage.[16] I would guess that a predisposition toward disgust and fear also plays a significant role in some people's aversion to homeless residents and endorsement of harsh policies toward them.

I don't like where fear and disgust propensities lead (to distrust and hostility toward foreigners, indigents, and gays), but understanding the role they play in political orientation—and the fact that they didn't consciously choose these propensities—helps me empathize. Empathy enables me to understand conservative opinions better while leaving me free to continue opposing and resisting any that I deem harmful.

Authoritarianism

Right-wing authoritarianism centers around the notion that safety and stability are best maintained when people defer to a strong leader who does whatever is necessary to maintain order. In an authoritarian worldview, hierarchy is the natural order; those in power (God, parents, bosses, whites, males) have the right and responsibility to punish their inferiors when they threaten to disrupt the order or transgress the moral precepts established by authority figures.

When parents are authoritarians, the child learns early on that the authority figures' needs come first. If they don't obey, they're bad and have only themselves to blame for whatever punishment, failure, or unhappiness ensues. Parents, teachers, bosses, and religious and political leaders are infallible by dint of their position. Systemic injustice cannot be recognized because its existence implicates authority figures. When individuals fail, it's either their fault or the fault of a despised "other" fingered by the authority figure.

Order is of paramount importance, although the authoritarian leader is allowed to break rules and norms, and sow temporary chaos, so long as the endgame is restoring order. Take Trump supporters' justification for harsh immigration crackdowns, even on tiny children. Most are not sadists who enjoy seeing families torn apart. What I've heard them say is that crossing the border illegally is an unacceptable violation of law and order. On the "Make America Relate Again" podcast, one interviewee noted that border separations are sad, but as long as they're "within the letter of the law" (they aren't), she's okay with them.[17] Another said:

> I struggle between that core belief in the rule of law versus a heart that says, "We have to help people. We can't turn people away after they've come through terrible circumstances." That's the moral dilemma because my heart and my belief system go one way, which is in favor of taking care of people, and then the other side of me says, "But there's [sic] laws, and laws have to be followed or you don't have an ordered society."[18]

Even some Mexican-American citizens oppose a pathway to citizenship for those who crossed illegally—they're probably not racist; rather, they likely value order.

I believe that the need for strict law and order stems from a person's biological fear sensitivity and from being raised with strong external controls on their behavior—if coercion and the threat of punishment are what kept them in line, then they might assume that, in the absence of external controls, people will go wild. There's a lack of trust that people are intrinsically decent. They might be decent people, but they may have some doubts about how they would have turned out absent the rod.

Authoritarian sympathies intensify when people feel afraid.[19] That's why right-wing propagandists lean so heavily into fear-mongering. Specifically, they stoke the fears that trouble authoritarians the most, things that threaten the social order—the coming minority majority, Muslim terrorism, illegal immigration, feminism. The take-home message is that everything will be okay if you rally behind a domineering leader. Such use of fear is, in the words of one GOP strategist, a "standard tactic."[20]

Trump supporters are, on the whole, more authoritarian than the general public.[21] His primary voters believed society had become "too soft and feminine" and that the country was so far off track that it needed a leader who would break the rules to set things right. A narrow majority agreed that the government had paid too much attention to the problems of people of color; half favored the concept of a Muslim ban.[22] More than half believe Trump should be able to overturn judicial decisions and would support postponing the 2020 election on Trump's say-so.[23]

Tribalism

In a multicultural society, right-wing authoritarianism has a strong tribal component. The strong leader represents one tribe, the "in-group," against the invalid claims of the "other" tribe. Members of the tribe are expected to be loyal, especially when the tribe is under attack.

Tribalism exerts a strong force because it satisfies some basic human needs. Psychologist Abraham Maslow's famous "hierarchy of needs" pyramid ranks physiological necessities like food and shelter as the most important; followed by safety; belonging and intimacy; esteem and self-actualization. Tribal membership potentially serves to meet all of these needs and can be positive and healthy—look at indigenous nations or hometown pride. But it can also be dangerous, like when soccer fans beat up rivals or when white supremacists wield torches.

Humans are evolutionarily wired to categorize people and favor those we've sorted into our "in-group."[24] This likely explains why people in most countries, including the United States, significantly overestimate the percentage of the population who are immigrants—they're on the alert to spot difference.[25]

If you feel a kinship with people of your ethnicity, religion, or gender, or have an affinity for your alma mater or sports team, these are forms of tribalism. Tribal loyalty to political party can be very strong, particularly when it's bound up with pride of place. Southern whites maintained their tribal allegiance to the Democratic Party for a century, voting for fellow Southerners Lyndon Johnson and Jimmy Carter despite these candidates' support of civil rights. In fact, when people look at images of their party's candidate, the area of the brain associated with emotional identification lights up—yay, that's my team captain, I feel good![26] No surprise then that 92 percent of registered Republicans voted for Trump.[27]

Tribal partisanship is so intense that partisans tend to overlook the moral transgressions of their own party's leaders and double down in condemnation when the transgressor is from the other party. Evangelicals voting for a serial adulterer comes to mind, but rest assured that Democrats have double standards, too.[28]

Even when it comes to utterly trivial distinctions, people show an irrational preference for people who are like them. In one experiment, children consistently wore red or blue T-shirts to school for three weeks. Though the teachers said nothing about the T-shirts, the kids, when asked, said that kids with the same color T-shirt as their own were smarter and better.[29] What's more, in a related experiment, kids at summer camp who suffered social anxiety themselves were less able to feel empathetic toward kids wearing the "other" color T-shirt who also had experienced an incident of social exclusion.[30] They saw themselves and members of their tribe as victims but didn't see or care much about the suffering of others outside their tribe.

In an even more stunning expression of irrational tribal behavior, test subjects were brought, one by one, into a lab and told they had been randomly assigned to a group they would never meet. They were then asked to allocate rewards to members of their group and members of the "other" group. Behind Door No. 1, all members of both groups would get the maximum reward. Behind Door No. 2, their group would get *less* than the maximum, and the other group would get *even less* than that. Darned if they didn't choose Door No. 2. So strong was their tribal allegiance to an imaginary group that they were willing to shoot themselves in the foot to win out over the other group![31] They wanted to be, as Trump would (and frequently does) put it, "winners."

Conservatives tend to be more tribal than liberals. I believe this stems from the high value they place on loyalty and safety. They're equally compassionate, but their compassion tends to extend to a smaller circle of people.[32]

For far-right conservatives, their ethic of care is often of secondary importance to loyalty and authority.[33] Their news sources are more partisan, and they are more inclined to trust information from a member of their tribe and distrust information from the opposing tribe or nonpartisans.[34] GOP leadership has moved to the far right over the past 30 years and has vilified liberals and Democrats, "othering" the opposition to reinforce tribal loyalty. The rank and file have moved to the right with them.[35] They assume that what's good for the tribe as a whole (or what they're told is good for the tribe as a whole) is good for them personally, though this is often far from true.

When people's natural tribal instincts marinate in racist ideas and misinformation, white nationalism flourishes. In a white-nationalist tribe, no one will berate members for being politically incorrect, stupid, or parochial; no one will call into question American exceptionalism; no one will dwell on America's genocidal history. It's a safe space, a place where they can lick their wounds, bolster their self-esteem, and be accepted for merely being a member of the tribe. If the tribe is under attack, there's safety in numbers, and the tribe can wall itself in against the threat. The tribe can retaliate. The tribe can seek revenge. It feels safe. It feels stable. It feels good.

Some Trump voters see themselves as members of a white-nationalist tribe. White Republicans, in general, hold more racist views than white Democrats, according to 2016 General Social Survey data.[36] But as crucial as it is to recognize Trump's racist appeal, so, too, is it crucial not to presume an individual Trump supporter to be any more racist than the average white American. Half of Trump supporters agree with the following endorsement of multiculturalism: "By accepting diverse cultures and lifestyles, our country is steadily improving."[37]

From the outside looking in, Trumpist white-nationalist tribalism is delusional and toxic. Inside the tribe, however, primal needs are being fulfilled. Denigrating the tribe only serves to strengthen it. Self-defense is what tribes do when they're under attack—that is their essential function. This, I believe, is why Brett Kavanaugh delivered such an aggressively hyperpartisan performance to the Senate Judiciary Committee in response to accusations of sexual assault. He was rallying the troops, mobilizing the base, entrenching the loyalists. At the moment when Christine Blasey Ford's testimony was so authentic that even Trump admitted it was "very compelling," that moment when it looked as though a few Republicans might break ranks, Kavanaugh reminded them of their tribal obligations.

When the scandal first broke, Republican voters' support for Kavanaugh polled at 74 percent; it shot up to 89 percent by the end. Senator McConnell's approval rating among Republicans also rose massively in response to his hyperpartisan performance.[38]

Trump has held an 87 percent approval rating among Republicans, convincing the majority of them to set aside their quaint belief that candidates who commit immoral acts in their private lives cannot be trusted to act ethically in office. Several Trump voters told *The New York Times* that, while they know he's no angel, media attacks against Trump made them want to defend him.[39] This is why it's counterproductive to attack and belittle political opponents—doing so makes them defensive, and they seek the protection of their leader and the affirmation of their tribe.

Deep Stories

By the time we're young adults, most of us have strong, rigid moral values and tribal affiliations. We have a sense of who we are, who's on our team, what's important to us, and what's right and wrong. We have beliefs about human nature and the existence of a higher power. We've internalized an ethical hierarchy that tells us how to prioritize harm reduction, fairness, loyalty, authority, and liberty.[40] And we have a strong belief in the degree to which individuals are personally responsible for their lot in life. All of this together weaves the subjective deep story inside of which we live, love, and vote.

There is no single deep story that animates all Trump supporters, but there is one that seems to resonate for many. In *Strangers in Their Own Land*, Hochschild maps out a deep story of white grievance, lost honor, and wounded pride that rings true to most of the Louisiana Tea Party Republicans she met and one that I've seen articulated by Trump supporters in other parts of the country as well.[41]

In this story, working- and middle-class whites see themselves as having spent their lives patiently standing in line, working hard, playing by the rules—waiting for their turn to achieve the American Dream of prosperity and security. But it's starting to seem like the line isn't moving anymore, and they're stuck in the middle, with poor and mostly nonwhite people behind them. They see people cutting in line—people of color, immigrants, government employees—and liberals escorting these people to the front of the line, via affirmative action and taxpayer-funded programs. When they object, the liberals reprimand them for not having enough empathy for the line cutters. Adding insult to injury, these same liberals disdain their cherished beliefs in patriotism and Christian morality, call them rednecks, and count the days until they die off. These folks have come to feel like strangers in their own land. There's a tribe of people who feel the same way, and they're wearing MAGA hats.

The deep story *feels* true: It has elements of objective truths like wage stagnation, declining life expectancy, and the shredding of the social contract, blended with emotional truths like wounded pride. This is coupled with stereotypes and ignorance regarding why whites are in the middle and nonwhites are in the back of the line to begin with.

For liberals and people of color, hearing a deep story premised, in large part, on white supremacy can be triggering, to say the least. When I began reading *Strangers in Their Own Land*, frustration and judgment eclipsed my ability to empathize. The title alone made me bristle—what do they mean *their* own land? I couldn't climb over what Hochschild calls the "empathy wall," which prevents one tribe from understanding the other.

Eventually, I was able to develop curiosity about what the book's subjects had to say and consider upbringings and experiences that were different from my own. Looking beyond white supremacy, I got curious about a remarkable paradox at the heart of their deep story—their persistent faith in a laissez-faire, survival-of-the-fittest capitalist system that (as I see it) has made Louisiana one of the poorest, most polluted, and cancer-ridden states in the nation. Why, I began to wonder, have they submissively stood in line while profiteers (dating back to slavery) have exploited them and polluted their backyards?

Hochschild suggests that their submissiveness could be rooted in a centuries-old, paternalistic white-planter culture, in which desperately poor whites were grateful to ruling-class patrons who allowed them to sharecrop on their land. The planter class encouraged landless whites' aspirations of joining the "landed" class—they were *white*, after all, and their whiteness conferred the possibility of a rags-to-riches dream come true.[42] Freedom from indentured servitude—compared to a lifetime of chattel slavery— was colonial America's foundational white privilege.

The specter of planter-class paternalism continues to haunt contemporary white Southerners and even conservatives in other regions. They take pride in stoically and uncomplainingly enduring pollution and bravely accepting risk—to do otherwise, they believe, will cause innovation and productivity to stagnate. Some of them sincerely believe that capitalism maximizes liberty and prosperity, and they are willing to make sacrifices (such as their health) to keep it unfettered. They worry that government assistance erodes community bonds, rewards sloth, undermines personal responsibility, and puts an unfair burden on hard-working taxpayers. They worry that too many free-riders can damage the economy. There is a certain honor in aspects of their worldview that I can acknowledge—without losing sight of how their narcissistic grievance narrative is rooted in the poisoned soil of white supremacy and nourished by a paradoxically class-free form of right-wing populism that sometimes disparages, but never confronts, financial centers of power.

Mistakes Are Made

The deep story outlined above, like any deep story, contains some truths and some fallacies that arise due to cognitive errors. A cognitive error is faulty reasoning that *feels* correct because it fits inside our deep story. A cognitive error can also be random, a spontaneous mental glitch unrelated to ideology.[43]

Cognitive errors arise innocently and are unrelated to intelligence. In many cases, cognitive errors are our intuition gone awry. While intuition often serves us well in daily life, in complex situations that call for slow, careful deliberation and reasoning, relying on intuition alone can lead to the wrong conclusion.[44]

We *all* make cognitive errors, though, depending on our media choices and deep story, we may be more prone to some types of errors than others. I'm not aware of any studies that show conservatives making more overall cognitive errors than liberals or vice versa. Cognitive errors come in dozens of flavors, only a few of which I'll discuss below. While it can be helpful to learn how to spot cognitive errors, I wouldn't go around accusing people of making them. One person's cognitive error is another person's common sense, and disparaging someone's rationality is condescending and unfair, given that everyone whose name isn't Spock is fallible.

Headwind–tailwind asymmetry. The human brain is Velcro for negative experiences. It makes sense from an evolutionary perspective—you definitely want to remember which plant made you puke. But in the modern version, people tend to be more in touch with all of the hard knocks that life has dealt them and forget about how good luck or help from others has benefited them.[45] This can make them resent paying taxes while they're oblivious to how they benefit from government services. It can keep them from recognizing whatever form of privilege they might enjoy. This cognitive error is fertile ground for the politics of white-male grievance. It can also blind rich people to the advantages of an upper-class upbringing.

Correlation versus causation. If there are 20 percent more Latinxs in my city than there were 20 years ago and crime has risen 20 percent during that period, then Latinxs are responsible, right? Of course not, but many people don't know the difference between correlation and causation, and even those who do sometimes conveniently forget it.

Future discount/present bias. Although it doesn't always seem like it when we sit and try to meditate, we are preoccupied with the present: We want good health, security, and creature comforts, and we want them now. What's happening right now is viscerally real compared to imagining a remote future. Present bias leads people to undersave for retirement and to neglect good nutrition and exercise.[46] It also shows up in contemplation—or lack thereof—of the long-term impacts of burning fossil fuels.

Conformity bias. Were you ever 14 years old? Good, then I don't have to explain this one, but here's a jaw-dropping experiment that shows how strongly conformity bias affects even adults: The subjects examined drawings of 3D objects and identified whether the objects were the same or different. When actors in the room gave intentionally wrong answers, the subjects gave the wrong answer 41 percent of the time—even though the correct answer was obvious. When people overrode the group and gave the correct answer, brain scans showed their amygdalas lighting up.[47] Nonconformity is *scary*, even in a no-stakes situation with people you'll likely never see again.

One fascinating manifestation of conformity bias is when someone consciously says prejudiced things they don't truly believe for the sake of fitting in. Conversely, sometimes people *refrain* from expressing their prejudices for the sake of fitting in. Many researchers believe that people's attitudes toward "other" groups have less to do with their experiences with members of those groups than with the prevailing attitudes among members of their *own* social group. When the group norm shifts, the individual's behavior and beliefs shift accordingly. In one experiment, researchers were able to increase or decrease people's stereotypes of African-Americans by simply telling them (falsely) that their level of stereotypic thinking was lesser or greater than their peers![48]

Conformity bias is also, I believe, at play in climate denialism. The weight of evidence regarding climate disruption is so overwhelming that to deny it is akin to denying that the Earth is round. But if the leaders of your tribe are adamant that it's a hoax, then it requires a modicum of bravery and self-confidence to contradict them. Climate denialism is strongly predicted by political affiliation and, contrary to popular belief, not connected to knowledge of science.[49]

Progressive activists are more susceptible to conformity bias than other Americans, including very conservative Americans. Forty-two percent report feeling pressured by other progressives to think and talk a certain way.[50] Once I became aware of this, I began to take note of how often I adopt the progressive consensus without fully and rigorously thinking it through for myself.

Attribution error is the tendency to overemphasize personal characteristics and to ignore situational factors when judging someone's behavior or success in the world. The thinking is: When I do something wrong, I can't help it, but if someone else does the same thing, it's because they're a bad person (or inferior race/religion/gender). If I'm broke, it's due to circumstances beyond my control, but when someone else is poor, it's because they've made bad choices. I believe attribution error plays a role in conservatives' emphasis on "personal responsibility" and their skepticism of social welfare programs.

Attribution error is often implicated in stereotyping—if a white person is on welfare, it's because they're down on their luck, whereas a black welfare recipient must be lazy. Tucker Carlson of Fox News owned up to attribution error during a surprising rant against market capitalism. For years, Carlson has blamed black poverty on the supposed black "culture of poverty." Now that he sees poverty decimating *white* families and communities, he realizes that there's something wrong with the economic system.[51] (Hopefully, his epiphany will stick.)

Author David Campt, creator of the *White Ally Toolkit*, notes that attribution error can also show up when a person of color, who has suffered innumerable incidents of actual discrimination, mistakenly believes they are being treated poorly because of their race.[52] Some cynically refer to this as "playing the race card," ignoring the pervasively racist cultural context that gives rise to the error.

Ascribing offensive beliefs to Trump supporters' bad character is an attribution error that disregards all of the experiences, information sources, emotional needs, and cognitive errors that have shaped and influenced their belief structure. If you had the same genes, parents, teachers, religion, experiences, and news sources, your fears, hopes, and dreams would likely resemble theirs.

Confirmation bias. Humans look for evidence that confirms their beliefs, ignoring or discounting evidence that does not. Countless experiments have shown this to be true. Recently, neuroscientists have discovered that consuming or sharing information that confirms our beliefs delivers a highly pleasurable hit of dopamine.[53] Facebook was likely aware of this when it rolled out its Like and Share features. The opposite is also true—when confronted with evidence that contradicts our beliefs, we experience cognitive dissonance, which feels crappy, especially if the contradictory information comes with a side of scorn.

There's a famous experiment involving two sets of Stanford students, one pro-death penalty and one against. The students read two fabricated studies: one that demonstrated that the death penalty has a deterrent effect and one that said it does not. After reading the *same two studies*, the students who were already pro-death penalty became more adamantly in favor of it, and the students who were already against it became even more strongly opposed.[54] Being exposed to beliefs that challenge our worldview is uncomfortable to most people and intolerable to many, and we respond by denying, ignoring, and/or forgetting the new information.

Confirmation bias can be strong when Trump supporters begin to harbor seeds of doubt. If they supported Trump initially,

only to watch him blunder spectacularly, much to the smug satisfaction of I-told-you-so liberals, they might feel humiliated. To
save face, they dismiss and deny evidence of Trump's malfeasance
as biased liberal slander. As Mark Twain said, "It's easier to fool
people than to convince them that they have been fooled." And,
more to the point, as a Trump supporter said, "You need to give
us an opportunity to admit we have been wrong without saying
we're bad people."[55]

Liberals have confirmation bias, too. Many liberals had high
hopes for Obama and remain uncritically loyal despite his record
of war, deportations, staffing the White House with corporate
elites, and protecting Wall Street executives from their misconduct. They simply don't want to hear it. Meanwhile, Obama's detractors often forget how intensely Congress obstructed him.

Just-world bias. If you strongly value freedom, hierarchy, and
competition, and, due to confirmation bias or attribution error,
don't acknowledge the advantages conferred by race, class, and
gender, then it's easy to believe that the status quo represents the
best of all possible worlds—and that any effort to introduce more
equality is a bad idea. Ninety-two percent of far-right conservatives believe that anyone who works hard can find success, no
matter what situation they were born into.[56] As ultraconservative
commentator Ben Shapiro put it, "In a free country, if you fail, it's
probably your own fault."[57]

Many low-income Americans mistakenly believe themselves
to earn more than the median income (and vice versa, with well-
off people thinking they're lower on the ladder than they really
are). For example, an incredible 19 percent of those who said
they sometimes went hungry believed themselves to be in the
top half![58] You might think that the solution then is to inform
them that they're poorer than they realized, but get this: When
asked what percent of total wealth the top 1 percent *should* own,
the average answer (of all Americans, not just conservatives) was
27 percent.[59] Apparently, a lot of folks see income inequality as
somehow desirable or beneficial. Oy.

them that you're right. We don't influence others by trying to overpower them with our facts, intellect, and morality. When you come out swinging, you may feel like you're scoring rhetorical points, but it's more likely that, in the quest to quash the other person's power, you wind up diminishing your own.

I've worked extensively with Ellison to develop an approach to engaging with conservatives nondefensively so that they have a greater opportunity to rethink their positions. The starting place, she says, is curiosity.

Curiosity is an antidote to contempt. Whereas a contemptuous stance comes from a highly defensive place of know-it-all superiority, curiosity is an innocent desire to understand where the other person is coming from. Curiosity questions are disarming.

Instead of blasting Trump, or insulting the morality or intelligence of his supporters, see if you can turn over the reins to your curious mind. You don't have to agree with what Trump supporters say; you're simply gathering information and trying to understand where they're coming from.

You can do this right now by conjuring up a right-wing belief that makes you see red. Let yourself feel how outraged and frustrated you are that any carbon-based life form could ever believe such a thing. Then, take a few breaths and let your mind quiet down. Pretend you're a recently arrived extraterrestrial with no ideology and no myths-versus-facts charts at the ready: What would your genuinely curious and humble self want to know?

For example, if you don't understand how an evangelical Trump supporter can tolerate Trump's philandering, you could ask what being a good Christian means to them. A follow-up question could ask in what ways Trump meets their standards and/or if he falls short in any way.

Sometimes people are reluctant to ask questions about offensive belief systems for fear that merely asking a question somehow implies forgiveness or acquiescence. It doesn't—you're simply gathering information and trying to understand what underlies their beliefs so that you can speak to them.

Availability bias. A father and son wreck their car and are rushed to the hospital. The emergency room surgeon looks at the boy and cries, "Oh my God, that's my son!" How can this be? If, like me, it took you more than a half-second to solve this riddle, you're afflicted with availability bias; most, if not all, of the surgeons you've been exposed to have been men, and you were slow to realize that the surgeon in the riddle was the boy's mother. I'm a feminist who has had two female surgeons, yet availability bias still got the better of me.

Availability bias leads people to fear air travel more than driving because, even though flying is far safer, grisly images of plane crashes are stuck in our heads. It makes people think crime is on the rise, even when it's not, because there's always a recent local crime event they can recall. It can also lead people to believe—or reinforce their belief—that Muslims commit more acts of terrorism or black men commit more violent crimes. So long as they have the image of the plane crashing into the World Trade Center or a mug shot of a black man flashed across their TV screen, availability bias can lead to the formation or perpetuation of stereotypes.

Loss aversion. Imagine you are given $1,000 and then asked to choose between being given an extra $500 for certain or taking a 50 percent chance to win another $1,000. Most people will go with the sure $500. Now, let's say you're given $2,000 and then asked to choose between a 50 percent chance of losing $1,000 or losing $500 for sure. Most people will take the gamble. In both scenarios, the choice is between getting $1,500 for sure or taking a risk that could make you richer but could also make you lose $500. (If you have to work this over in your mind a few times before you understand it, welcome to the club.) People will take the risk in the second scenario, but not in the first because, in the second scenario, the $500 is framed as a loss, not as a gain.[60]

Right-wing authoritarians, it turns out, are more motivated by fear of loss than are liberals.[61] This could explain why middle-class people who fear sliding into poverty are willing to take a gamble on Trump's trade wars and his vague promise of a "fantastic" health-care fix. They see the loss of white racial dominance and economic slippage as likely, have a particularly strong aversion to the prospect of such losses, and want very much to make American great again.

Intuitionism. University of Chicago political scientist Eric Oliver divides people into intuitionists and rationalists. Quick test: If you had to choose between putting a nickel from the ground in your mouth or wearing laundered pajamas that once belonged to Charles Manson, which would you choose? If you chose the latter, you're probably a rationalist.

Intuitionists go with their gut—if something seems dangerous or disgusting, they'll avoid it, no matter what the data shows. They are fearful and superstitious, and swing wildly for Trump, an extreme intuitionist who says his "gut has always been right."[62] People who score high on intuitionism are the most likely to buy into conspiracy theories involving hidden powers that control events.[63]

Gullibility. Development psychologist Stephen Greenspan is a leading expert in the study of gullibility, which he defines as a pattern of being repeatedly duped in the face of warning signs.[64] Several personality traits can predispose someone to gullibility, including agreeableness, hypnotic suggestibility, high trust, and, paradoxically, paranoia, when it comes to believing in falsehoods that align with their distorted conception of themselves as persecuted victims.[65]

Gullibility is not a function of intelligence or educational level. More educated Republicans are *more* likely to believe that Obama was a Muslim and that climate change is a hoax.[66] Rather, Greenspan says, gullibility is a function of cognitive laziness in which rationality lapses and the emotional desire to believe what one *wants* to be true takes precedence.[67]

Certain circumstances predispose people to ideological cons: We're more likely to believe falsehoods if they concern risks such as terrorism or crime. This is true even more so for conservatives.[68] People are also more likely to believe authority figures; again, this holds truer for conservatives than for liberals.[69]

Liberals are not immune to gullibility. Greenspan notes that liberals' overestimation of their intellectual abilities can make them overconfident of their ability to spot deception, and liberals' idealism can make them naïvely trusting of the intentions of nefarious actors.[70]

Liberals love to mock the gullibility of Trump supporters. I believe gullibility does play a role in some, but not all, Trump supporters' willingness to place their trust in him.

Disinformation Silos

The right-wing media empire is vast, and tribalism, authoritarianism, fear, and cognitive errors are its best friends. If you grew up watching Fox News or even mainstream "if it bleeds it leads" TV news, you can be forgiven for believing that you're in imminent danger of being murdered. Likewise, you can be forgiven for not understanding the existential threats of climate disruption and nuclear annihilation when these issues receive so little media attention.

It's frustrating when people's fear, disgust sensitivity, ignorance, cognitive errors, and gullibility combine to make them susceptible to believing spin, but they are victims of professional disinformation campaigns that infiltrate traditional and social media, political stumps, and advertising. We can wish they were savvier information consumers or had superhuman immunity to cognitive errors, but treating them with anger or condescension is not helpful. Nor should we assume that someone's media diet is 100 percent red meat. I know many conservatives who consume centrist media like *The New York Times* and *CNN* in addition to right-wing outlets.

To some extent, we're all products of cultural conditioning carried out by marketing agencies, artists, politicians, spin doctors, and media, who often distort or conceal the truth, and sometimes lie. We are all bombarded with subliminal messages expertly inserted into commercial and political advertising, like when a George W. Bush political ad attacking Al Gore's prescription drug plan allegedly flashed the word "RATS."[71]

We are all immersed in a corporate mindscape centered around personal gratification and denial of any ecological limits in the pursuit thereof. What sets the worst right-wing propaganda apart is a malicious intent to deceive, inflame, manipulate, and confuse its consumers—separating them from reality to gain their tribal allegiance to a figurehead (Trump) whose misconduct they vigorously deny and conceal.[72]

A trio of Harvard professors examined the trajectory and life span of sensational stories in both right- and left-leaning media. They found that groundless stories, such as the Clintons' pizza-parlor pedophilia ring, originated on disreputable sites like Infowars and then migrated to sites like Fox and Breitbart, which maintain a pretense of journalistic objectivity.[73] (When *The New York Times* tried to debunk Pizzagate, it succeeded only in launching Pizzagate believers—in the grips of confirmation and conformity bias—into zealous overdrive.)[74] Fake news aimed at tarnishing right-wing figures, by contrast, usually dies before it hits mainstream outlets, but it does get a fair amount of play on unreliable Facebook sites like Occupy Democrats.[75]

As if all of the above doesn't sow enough chaos, there is a concerted effort on the part of billionaires like Robert Mercer and governments like Russia to psychographically profile and target American voters, creating social media bots that bombard us with personalized bytes of disinformation designed to exploit our vulnerabilities.[76] YouTube, meanwhile, feeds its users increasingly conspiratorial and extremist content—watch a Trump rally and, up next, a Holocaust denial rant.[77] I can't be certain that I, too, haven't been fed and digested false and misleading information aimed at progressives.

How judgmental can I be of someone targeted by some of the richest and most powerful oligarchs on the planet? And how certain can I be that, if I grew up in their family and in their town, attended their school and their church, and tuned in to their TV and radio shows, I would have turned out any differently?

Is it possible to have empathy for the purveyors of right-wing disinformation? They operate in a narcissistic culture that makes a cult of celebrity and profit, a culture in which nothing is held sacred and, thus, no amount of wealth, power, or fame can ever fill the empty void. Within that system, they vie for top-shelf status, their lives devoted to the incessant grooming of their brand. I can acknowledge the ways in which they're victims of an impoverished culture at the same time that I'm infuriated by the damage they have done as perpetrators. I can also hold the possibility that they have been influenced by right-wing authoritarian social conditioning and, hence, genuinely see Trump as a benevolent strongman whose flaws and blunders must be concealed or rationalized.

The readiness of some Trump supporters to believe not only propagandistic reportage but outlandish conspiracy theories is particularly vexing to liberals. I see the rise in conspiracy media as a function of social alienation and a need to make sense of the bewildering state of future shock many Americans find themselves in. When people are unmoored from communal bonds, they can become untethered from reality, adrift in an atomistic sea of loneliness with the flotsam and jetsam of lurid conspiracy theories and racial fearmongering their only company.

What Does "Make America Great Again" Mean to Trump Supporters?

You don't know until you ask (which you'll learn how to do in the next chapter). It could be a white supremacist provocation, but it could also be a call for bringing home manufacturing jobs, a longing for greater religiosity, or an expression of patriotic pride, harkening back to an era like World War II when America was, in their minds, the unequivocal "good guy."

In *Political Tribes*, law professor Amy Chua talks about the demise of America as a "super-group" that cuts across lines of class and ethnicity. But with faith in government and the two-party duopoly collapsing, and people living in polarized red and blue zip codes, the sense of being in a supertribe has faltered. Absent a super-group, people with a strong need to belong to a tribe seek recourse in ideological, ethnic, or religious tribes.[78] You might not feel the need to belong to a tribe, but consider that some people do.

Those who pine for the good old days might be ignorant or indifferent to the quality of life for oppressed groups in the 1940s and 1950s, but that doesn't necessarily mean they want to bring back racial segregation and shutter gay bars. Perhaps what they're guilty of here is not so much bigotry as naïve and uninformed romanticization. As one MAGA defender said, "To attack the Make America Great Again concept with 'Oh, you're racist,' it doesn't make sense. It's like, I'm not racist, I'm saying, 'America did all this in this time, and now we don't.' That's what they're looking back fondly on." He went on to add, "Calling him [Trump] racist and saying, 'Hey bigots, come on over here and vote for us'; that ain't gonna work."[79]

Why Are Some Conservatives Okay with Inequality?

Conservatives have a stronger need for certainty and predictability and, hence, tend to favor the status quo.[80] And because the status quo in the United States is social inequality, many are comfortable with hierarchies of status, wealth, and power, and resist leveling efforts. This helps explain why some conservative white women might oppose equal pay and tolerate sexual harassment— male dominance is the status quo and trying to change it introduces anxiety-producing uncertainty. Subservience to men is the price women pay for social stability; if all hell breaks loose, they'll be glad to have their man to protect them. Some heterosexual white women might consciously or unconsciously rationalize patriarchy because, although it subordinates them to men, at least they still have higher status than people of color and queers.

If the system is fair and meritocratic, then mucking with it is unfair and threatens to bring down the whole system. If capitalism crashes and socialists start composing "I told you so" essays, conservatives will be sharpening their pencils, too, but with opposite explanations for what went wrong—explanations in which Big Government, personal licentiousness, and liberal social engineers figure prominently.

Conservatives also may believe that government assistance programs foster dependency and that temporary suffering can motivate someone to get their act together. They put great stock in the individual's capacity for ingenuity and grit, and are wary of policies that undermine those virtues.[81] For some, opposition to welfare programs stems from racial resentment of nonwhite beneficiaries, but opposition is not universally rooted in racial animus.

Last but not least, conservatives tend to overestimate the probability of intergenerational social mobility. When asked to predict a person's chances of rising from the bottom to the top quintile, conservative Americans (but not Europeans) are wildly optimistic relative to the *actual* empirical probability.[82] If social mobility is so attainable, the rationale goes, then the system is basically fair and there's little need for tinkering.

That said, a substantial minority of Republican voters are aware of our nation's tilt toward oligarchy. In an April 2019 ABC/ *The Washington Post* poll, one-third of them said that the economic system mainly benefits the powerful. Eighty-one percent of Democrats and 66 percent of Independents agree.[83]

Moderate conservatives support equality of *opportunity* but frown on equality of *outcome*, which they see as unfair and meddlesome. To the victor, the spoils and the losers should display stoicism instead of demanding redistribution. Even conservatives on the losing end of this proposition still endorse it—these are the working- and middle-class Americans who liberals condescendingly see as dupes for voting against their interests. But what liberals are missing is conservatives' *moral* interest in freedom and individualism. Just as high-net-worth progressives vote against their narrow *economic* interest and in favor of their *moral* interest (equality), so, too, do working-class conservatives.

Once an egalitarian shift reaches a tipping point without the sky falling, most conservatives can accept it. Take gay marriage, supported by only 18 percent of conservatives in 2001, and by 41 percent in 2017. As more and more same-sex couples wed, I predict a majority of conservatives will soon accept it.[84]

How Else Do Conservative and Liberal Values Differ?

To make a long story short and dangerously oversimplified, conservatives tend to value order, predictability, stability, obedience, sanctity, purity, tradition, family, independence, individualism, patriotism, strength, power, competition, retribution, stoicism, productivity, loyalty, tough love, freedom, and fairness.[85] Are there contradictions embedded in this set of values? Yes.

Liberals tend to value cooperation, collectivism, diversity, equality, critical thinking, questioning authority, conflict resolution, peace, harm reduction, health and safety, compassion, freedom, and fairness. Are there contradictions embedded in this set of values? None that I can see, thanks to confirmation bias, but I'm sure a conservative could spot some.[86]

As traditionalists, conservatives are cautious (liberals might say "frightened") about change. They don't want to take a fence down until they know the reason it was put up.[87]

Conservatives feel as fiercely about freedom as liberals do about equality.[88] Their notion of freedom encompasses the freedom to think and say whatever they want, free from the dictates of political correctness, and the freedom of individuals and private enterprise from regulations created by distant bureaucrats. For some conservatives, however, freedom in the bedroom takes a back seat to other conservative values relating to biblical strictures, purity, and gender roles.

Conservatives are more likely to believe in God and to look to religion as a source of guidance on right and wrong.[89] They cherish religious liberty and are leery of anything that might curtail it. Some extend this protection to other faiths, while others are preoccupied with Christianity. Some religious values (compassion, charity) align with liberal values, but the religious right has refashioned these into functional opposites such as the wealth-venerating prosperity gospel. Many Christian evangelicals subscribe quite rigidly to church-ordained beliefs concerning abortion, homosexuality, and evolution. For some evangelicals, climate disruption is the harbinger of the end times, and there's nothing that can or should be done about it; for others, environmental stewardship is ordained.

Some conservatives see government as the enemy. As Ronald Reagan said, "The nine most terrifying words in the English language are: 'I'm from the government and I'm here to help.'" Damn, he was good. When the Reagan administration devastated the government's ability to provide essential services, his clever sound bite became prophetic. Part of their antipathy toward the government stems from what I see as a healthy skepticism of one-size-fits-all solutions created by far-flung institutions that may not reflect local needs and wisdom.

Having come to understand conservative beliefs better, I can honestly say that if I were an elected official, I would count among my advisors at least one conservative who could serve as a check against liberal confirmation and conformity bias and, more generally, call attention to my blind spots.

Understanding the distinct moral foundations and deep stories of conservatives can be helpful when embarking upon a conversation across lines of difference. Rather than bending their ear with liberal talking points, it's important first to get a sense of what underpins *their* views. Listen, then speak. It all begins with asking questions.

4

Curiosity—The Antidote to Contempt[1]

Who is a wise man?
He who learns from all men.

—Talmud

Political discourse between liberals and conservatives typically goes from bad to worse in short order. Each party approaches the arena armed with selective facts and assumptions concerning their opponent's mindset. Within moments, the amygdala, the brain's fear center, activates and issues a fight-or-flight command. Both parties are now on the defensive, issuing sharp-edged retorts or retreating into silent rage and disgust. A wall goes up, and hope of productive dialogue is extinguished.

Vitriol and snide superiority rocket-launch the above chain of events into warp speed. Being made to feel inferior is perceived as a threat to our well-being, so the amygdala rings the alarm: "We're under attack: fight back, or run and hide out with your tribe—they'll protect you!" And the more routinely we telegraph snarling condescension, the more dangerously polarized the civic arena becomes.

As we saw in the first two chapters, liberals often make conservatives feel defensive (and vice versa), primarily by reducing them to a crude racist redneck stereotype. Even if someone proves themselves to be racist, how we provide feedback can mean the difference between entrenchment and receptivity.

Multicultural education scholar Robin DiAngelo, author of *White Fragility*, notes that whites get defensive because they interpret allegations of racism as denunciations of their overall character. To be called racist is to be accused of being an immoral person because the dominant understanding of racism is that that some (bad) people are racist and some (good) people aren't. On the contrary, DiAngelo points out, internalized racism is a state of mind *all* white Americans inhabit to some degree because it's baked into our history and culture.[2]

People don't take kindly to suggestions that they're immoral. They get defensive and move into fight-or-flight mode. A defensive reaction is especially likely on the part of those who see themselves (rightly or wrongly) as victims (i.e., Trump supporters). That's why, when political campaigns send canvassers out to knock on doors, they train them to ask questions and share stories rather than level moral denunciations that will likely result in getting a door slammed in their faces.

Anytime I want to weigh in on a political issue, whether I'm chatting with someone, writing a letter to the editor, or composing a Facebook post, I try to remember to ask myself at the outset who my intended audience is, who else might be listening, and what effect I want my words to have on them. Pausing to set my intention helps me check my tendency to rant. If it's just my husband, who I already know agrees with me, I'm free to blow off steam, but if it's someone whose beliefs might be different, then I try to do like the pros do.

Lessons From the Field

If taunting and shaming Republicans were effective, we'd see Democratic canvassers going door-to-door doing just that. Instead, we see the opposite.

When Working America AFL-CIO volunteers approach white working-class Trump voters, it's with an understanding that their vote was, at least in part, an unleashing of pent-up pain and frustration. Working America, like any effective canvassing operation, trains its canvassers to treat voters of all stripes with respect. "You have to care about the people you're talking with," says Josh Lewis, a Working America field manager.[3]

Karen Nussbaum, the organization's executive director, is more blunt about why their canvassers strictly avoid denouncing Trump:

> If Democrats just want to keep piling on Trump, that will be the way to get Trump reelected…I suspect that for a lot of prosperous liberals, it [Trump's reelection] wouldn't be such a bad thing. For them, there's an alternative to political victory: a utopia of scolding. Who needs to win elections when you can personally reestablish the rightful social order every day on Twitter and Facebook? When you can scold, and scold, and scold, and scold. That's their future, and it's a satisfying one: a finger wagging in some deplorable's face, forever.[4]

Working America canvassers begin by asking the person what issue is most important to them and why. From there, they share what Working America's position is on that issue and then ask if they'd like to join the organization.

The Leadership Lab of the Los Angeles LGBT Center takes canvassing to another level. They share a personal story, then invite the other person to share a story about being mistreated. As the person shares their story, the canvasser listens carefully and tries to identify common ground. Sometimes, in the course of telling a story about themselves or someone they love, the person might reveal that their real-world experience contradicts their opinion on an issue. The canvasser might ask questions or, ultimately, make a statement that brings attention to the mismatch. At no point does the canvasser say anything judgmental or dismissive, even if the other person makes a blatantly offensive statement.

The Lab's track record is impressive. During a 2014 campaign, 56 canvassers spent 10 minutes talking to 500 Miami-Dade County residents about whether they supported a local law that protected transgender residents from discrimination. According to Stanford University and University of California, Berkeley researchers who monitored the campaign, these single conversations "markedly reduced prejudice." These Floridians were substantially more supportive of the antidiscrimination law than those who had not been canvassed; their support endured when they were surveyed nine months later, even though they had been exposed to viciously transphobic attack ads in the interim. The decline in transphobic prejudice these canvassers achieved in 10 minutes was comparable to the decline in antigay prejudice over a decade.[5]

Dave Fleischer, director of The Leadership Lab, is the brain-child behind its novel "deep canvassing" technique. In his experience, people don't reconsider their opinions because someone shamed, cajoled, or browbeat them. They change their minds when they reflect on their personal experiences and connect the dots for themselves. The role of Lab canvassers is to ask questions and tell personal stories to prompt the other person to reexamine their beliefs.

I asked Fleischer if he believed someone could be shamed out of their bigotry. His response was unequivocal: "Tell me the time someone shamed you out of something and you're grateful for it."[6] Rarely, if ever, is shame a positive motivator.

In an October 2016 TED Talk, Fleischer includes video footage of a conversation between a transgender Lab canvasser named Virginia and an older man speaking in broken English. Early on, the man says that he doesn't support the transgender antidiscrimination law because, he says, where he's from in South America, "we don't like fags." Virginia asks him where his feelings come from, and then reveals that they (Virginia) are gay and don't identify as a woman. The man asks why Virginia chose to be gay; Virginia calmly explains it to him. Later, the man shares a story about caring for his ailing wife, whom he's devoted to; Virginia says his story resonates with them—Virginia is madly in love with their partner and knows they will take care of each other for the rest of their lives. At some point, Virginia casually suggests using the word "gay" rather than "fag." At the end of their conversation, the man says, "This is the first time, and I thank you, that I could ask questions like this and be responded [to] with elegance…Listen, probably I was mistaken."[7] It's clear from the video that these two made a genuine, heartfelt connection and that this connection made it possible for the man's humility to rise to the surface. If, instead, Virginia had berated him for using the word "fag," the outcome could have been very different.

Studies comparing the efficacy of various antiprejudice techniques are scant,[8] but Fleischer's intuition—and The Leadership Lab's track record—is borne out by at least one study of "non-black" Canadian college students. The students were divided into three groups and given one of two brochures or no brochure. One brochure took a controlling and threatening tone, telling students to refrain from racial prejudice because it's socially unacceptable and unlawful in Canadian society to discriminate and those who do will face serious consequences. The other brochure stressed the benefits of a diverse society and made it clear that the student had the autonomy to choose whether to be prejudiced or egalitarian. After reading one of the brochures (or not reading a brochure), the students answered questions about their motivation to be nonprejudiced. The "controlling" brochure backfired rather spectacularly, with students in that group displaying more prejudice than those who read the "autonomy" brochure. They were more prejudiced even than the students who read *no* brochure. The researchers concluded that heavy-handed attempts to shame people out of their racism might have the perverse effect of inciting hostility toward the oppressed group. Furthermore, they caution against the use of such messaging in prejudice-reduction policies and programs.[9]

Shame performs no better when directed at hard-core white supremacists than it does with everyday racists. Angela King and Christian Picciolini are co-founders of Life After Hate, a group that counsels people in the process of exiting violent hate groups. Both King and Picciolini were active in white supremacist skinhead groups in the 1990s, and both tell a similar story of disavowing hate after being shown kindness and compassion by their would-be victims. For King, it was her participation in a series of round-table talks with a Holocaust survivor who, upon hearing

King express remorse for her Holocaust denial and participation in the Aryan Nations, hugged King and told her she forgave her. For Picciolini, the path to redemption began with the Jewish and black customers who patronized his record shop and engaged him in conversation—even though they knew of his neo-Nazi affiliation.[10]

To hear King and Picciolini tell it, they joined hate groups as a way of coping with low self-esteem. It wasn't the hateful ideology that drew them in, but the feeling of belonging to a community that accepted them. The sense of meaning, purpose, and belonging came first and only later did the indoctrination into white-supremacist ideology. Both say that, without exception, people involved in hate groups have experienced some form of abuse, bullying, or other trauma and are vulnerable to the invitation to project their self-loathing onto an "other." Hate-group recruiters prey on these vulnerabilities and insecurities.

King's and Picciolini's stories are corroborated by sociologist Pete Simi, who has interviewed more than 100 former white supremacists. Eighty percent experienced childhood trauma such as abuse, neglect, or a drug-addicted parent. Some expressed fear that they had suffered brain damage, something Simi wants to explore using brain-imaging technology.[11] Researchers studying other far-right and terrorist movements have found again and again that most people join in search of meaning and belonging, and that ideology is secondary and not always strongly held.[12]

In guiding people out of hate, it's crucial to understand what drew them in and then respond to those needs with empathy. Shaming never works, King says. Never.[13]

Shame can be productive when it arises internally. When King heard the Holocaust survivor tell her story, she was so ashamed of herself she couldn't even look the woman in the eye. At that point, her belief system began to disintegrate. It wasn't necessary for someone to lecture her—the hate simply crumbled. King's experience fits with what Jeni Kubota, a psychologist at the University of Chicago's Center for the Study of Race, Politics, and

Culture, has found—that prejudice dissolves when there's an internal motivation to be a better person, not when someone tells you that your prejudice is bad.[14]

Picciolini concurs: "Treat the child, not the monster." At the end of a talk he gave in Berkeley, he challenged the audience, "Give compassion to someone you don't think deserves it, because I guarantee you, that's who needs it the most."

Such compassion was on display in the incredible story of Rabbi Michael Weisser, who befriended Larry Trapp, a lonely, elderly Klan leader who had been harassing him. Upon learning that Larry was disabled, Michael called and offered him a ride to the grocery store. A few days later, Larry called him back and said, "I want to get out of what I'm doing and I don't know how." A close friendship developed. Larry renounced the Klan, converted to Judaism, and died a year later in the home where Michael and his wife Julie were caring for him.[15]

Picciolini's call for compassion echoed through my mind when I read about Derek Black, son of Klan leader Don Black and godson of former Klan Grand Wizard David Duke. Derek was a youth leader of the white nationalist movement that sought the division of the country into separate racial enclaves. Derek and his father were credited with helping mainstream white supremacist rhetoric to make it appeal to moderates.

When Derek went to college, he was befriended by Latino and Jewish students. One of them, the descendant of Holocaust survivors, invited him to Shabbat dinners, where they engaged in respectful conversation. "What good would come from berating him if Derek simply left the table and never came back?" the Jewish host wondered. As Derek broke bread with them, the edifice of his anti-Semitic and racist beliefs began to crack. His white, nonracist girlfriend began asking him questions and sending him links to studies that contradicted his beliefs. Shortly after graduation, Derek left the movement and, to his family's shock and horror, publicly renounced white nationalism in an op-ed in *The New York Times*.[16]

At college, many students shunned and castigated him. But Derek says it was "the people who chose to invite me into their dorms and conversations rather than ostracize me" who enabled him to recognize and take accountability for the damage he had done. These friends expressed "clear and passionate outrage" regarding his beliefs, but they did so without negating his humanity.[17] Had Black attended my college in the 1980s, we would have bird-dogged him with "SHAME!" signs, patted ourselves on the back, and accomplished nothing.

If empathy is the best practice for dismantling hard-core white-supremacist beliefs, what about addressing the unconscious bias that afflicts most, if not all white Americans to some degree? Anti-racist workshop trainers under the umbrella of the Challenging White Supremacy Workshop consistently emphasize respectful dialogue.[18]

David Campt developed an approach called RACE (Reflect. Ask. Connect. Expand), which relies on active listening, empathy, and personal storytelling. Campt calls upon whites to shoulder the burden of engaging other whites in such dialogues:

> White people are in a much better position to execute [a] listening-based strategy with people who are skeptical about whether racism is real. On a daily basis, POC [People of Color] must endure the indirect expression of white skepticism that racism really matters, and they must do so as they are experiencing overt and subtle racism in many parts of their lives. Some people of color might want to choose to have conversations where white people's racial skepticism is consciously expressed. But it would not be fair to *expect* people of color to endure this. Engaging white folks…should be the primary task of white allies. *But the allies must be smart about how to do this* [emphasis in original].[19]

Campt's philosophy calls to mind Martin Luther King, Jr.'s wisdom: "We must have compassion and understanding for those who hate us. We must realize so many people are taught to hate us that they are not totally responsible for their hate."[20] King envisioned a "beloved community" bound together by goodwill across lines of difference. King believed that reconciliation—not retribution—would break the cycle of violence, and bring about enduring peace and justice.[21] Reconciliation invites racially biased whites into a beloved community; retribution pushes them out into the wilderness where white nationalist recruiters will find them.

Learning From Our Mistakes

After the 2016 election, progressive commentator Van Jones articulated this imperative:

> It takes a lot of inner work, community support, and maybe a few Jedi mind tricks to deliberately and skillfully place ourselves in conversation with people whose ideas, assumptions, and attitudes often wound us. But our present strategy of retreating further and further into self-affirming liberal echo chambers has backfired in a big way.[22]

Several bridge-building communication strategies help us be heard outside our echo chambers. The most comprehensive and effective one I've encountered is Powerful Non-Defensive Communication (PNDC). Its creator, Sharon Strand Ellison, has trained thousands of educators, government officials, and corporate and nonprofit leaders in a novel, straightforward communication style that avoids the pitfalls of a conventional adversarial approach.

PNDC is premised on recognizing every person's humanity, no matter what terrible thing they say, do, or believe. It is a method of communicating across lines of difference without soft-pedaling our own beliefs and values, or excusing hurtful behavior. It's about transcending power struggles by learning how to stand, with strength and humility, in your position of power rather than trying to knock down the other person or convince

Asking curiosity questions skillfully can prompt the other person to respond without trying to dodge and feint defensively. "If you don't get defensive no matter what the other person does," Ellison says, "you'll have more power, not less."

The right question, skillfully and nonaggressively posed, could prompt someone to gain unexpected insights; when someone realizes something for themselves, they can more easily accept it. Ellison has told me many stories of a single question resulting in an insight that changes everything. My favorite is of a young woman whose older male boss was always putting his arm around her and calling her "honey." Finally, she asked him, "Do you believe that I wanted you to touch me in that way?" He paused, then replied, "No, I don't think you did. I can see that I've humiliated you, and I'll never do it again."

For real. Long before #metoo, this man instantly took accountability in a situation in which he could have been sued or lost his job.

I was talking once with a conservative acquaintance who complained about "irresponsible" women who had more children than they could care for and then "expected the government to bail them out" with a welfare check. I asked, "Do you think it might be possible that there are some families who made decisions about their family size when they were doing well and then later fell on hard times?" It took him all of a second to process what I had said, and he replied, "Well, yes, that probably was the case a lot of the time." It seemed he had never considered the issue from that vantage point before.

Here's one more story of a nondefensive question that changed everything: Michael Bell, a diversity communications consultant, was conducting a racial equity reconciliation session for a nonprofit organization in which two people of color were experiencing disrespect from their white coworkers. Moments into the presentation, a red-headed white man raised his hand and said: "When I was a kid, I used to turn red when I got embarrassed and the other kids made fun of me. Does that make me a person of color?"

Bell could have let fly some choice words that would have made for a viral YouTube smackdown. Instead, he calmly asked, "Are you saying that you believe your experience of being a red-headed kid is the equivalent of my experience of growing up black in the segregated South?" The redhead paused, then replied, "No, I don't think it's the same." After the training, he asked Bell for a list of recommended reading. Because Bell's question didn't deny the white man's experience of being embarrassed and teased, and didn't antagonize him by labeling him a racist, the white man didn't get defensive. He was able to see the absurdity of his comparison. Imagine what would have happened if Bell had responded defensively.

A sincere question, asked with humility, can be very disarming. An adversarial or arrogant one causes the other person's defenses to go up. At this point, their brain turns off, and they'll either fight you or withdraw. Either way, the prospect of that interaction bearing fruit is dim.

One final note about curiosity questions: Though I gave some inspiring examples above of questions that prompted the other person to shift, *that is not the goal.* I can't emphasize this enough, and it's something I have to remind myself of constantly. The best questions are formed by an *open* mind, free of a persuasive agenda. I cannot enter a dialogue wearing my opinion like a suit of armor. If I'm not open to shifting my position based on what the other person says, that reflects under-confidence masquerading as overconfidence in my own beliefs. My cherished opinion will still be there, waiting for me to reclaim after I'm done listening to the other person; if I don't choose to reclaim it, it's only because I've learned something new.

There's a bit of a paradox here for people like me who are politically engaged. How can we *not* try to talk people into voting for our candidate or subscribing to our views on key issues? PNDC does require a Jedi mind trick of temporarily setting aside your agenda and engaging with humility and openness. The transgender-discrimination canvassers certainly had an agenda when they knocked on people's doors, but the Force was with them when they approached people with curiosity rather than trying to convince them to support the new law.

It's incredibly hard to abandon one's agenda, especially during these frightening times. But nondefensive communication can coexist alongside your political agenda. It's essential that you temporarily disable the part of your brain that wants to persuade.

How to Ask Curiosity Questions

Questions are part of a conversation, not a cross-examination or a Socratic inquisition. Your questions should be specific but posed in a nonjudgmental, nonleading, nonargumentative way. For me, trained as a lawyer, this is the most difficult aspect. I'm always trying to sneak an argument into the question.

Here's an argumentative question: "Given that the United States already has enough nuclear weapons to blow up the world three times over, what purpose do you believe is served by spending billions more on new nuclear weapons?" The first part of the question already gives away my position—we already have an absurdly dangerous amount of nuclear firepower—and implies that anyone who thinks we need more nukes is a fool. Instead, I could ask, "What advantages do you believe the United States would gain if we spend billions more on nuclear weapons?" Later, I could share my belief that any additional weapons would be redundant, dangerous, and a colossal waste of money.

You may be tempted (I know I am) to discharge a fusillade of Socratic questions designed to lead the person to "get it." But this will make the other person feel snookered; they will defend themselves against this unpleasant sensation accordingly.

If you ask a question to which you already know the answer just to make the other person look ignorant, that's entrapment. If someone is adamant about wanting a border wall to prevent drugs from coming in, and you already know that the Drug Enforcement Administration (DEA) says that the vast majority of drugs are smuggled in at legal entry points, then it would be entrapping to ask, "What percentage of drugs do you think are coming in through illegal border crossings?" Instead, you could begin with a question that seeks to understand *why* they feel so strongly: "What are the impacts you're seeing from the illegal drugs getting smuggled in?" Depending on their response, it may be appropriate for you to share the DEA's assessment later.

Here's the litmus test for Socratic entrapment: Are you asking the question to understand the person's experience or are you laying the foundation to prove your point? If the latter, save all that useful information and analysis for your position statement (which I'll go over in the next chapter) instead of trying to manipulate the conversation to convince them.

In my example above of asking whether the person thought it was possible that some welfare recipients fell on hard times after planning for a large family, I was bordering on entrapping. However, my tone was laid back and I was *genuinely curious* as to whether the person had considered this possibility.

Another form of entrapment is a question that leaves the person with a no-win choice: "Do you want your grandkids to die in a climate catastrophe?" leaves Grandma with the choice of either admitting that climate disruption is real or that she's willing to have her grandchildren suffer a horrible death.

There are several other crucial elements in asking questions without prompting defensive reactions, including keeping a relaxed, non-urgent tone; letting your voice come down at the end of the question instead of going up; and avoiding common (often unconscious) body language, such as shaking your head, shrugging, frowning, raising your eyebrows, squinting, or waving your arms.

You can watch a demonstration of Ellison asking the same question aggressively and curiously at this book's website. Note what words she emphasizes and whether her voice goes up or comes down at the end of the sentence. Watch her eyebrows, hands, and shoulders. Notice how you feel when she poses the very same question with a different demeanor.

At a PNDC workshop I attended, one woman practiced asking whether the other person had noticed any seasonal abnormalities in recent years. Her words were nondefensive, but she kept jerking her head back and squinting in a way that said, "You don't believe in climate change; what are you, *insane*?" After about six tries, she was finally able to keep her head still, and the intense vibe she had been transmitting noticeably downshifted.

Some questions come off as nondefensive in person but aggressive in writing; you may need to adjust your language accordingly. For example, I might ask in person, "What do you mean by 'freeloader'?" If I'm careful to not spit out the word "freeloader" contemptuously, the question is fine. But if it's a Facebook comment, the person is likely to read contempt into it. Instead, I would ask, "What does being a freeloader mean to you?" or "Would you be willing to tell me more about what you see people doing that makes them freeloaders?"

While the other person is answering your question, your job is to *listen*. Try not to half-listen while composing in your mind what you're going to say next. Listen like you want the other person to listen to you. Try to keep your facial expression neutral and your energy relaxed. Campt suggests holding your tongue on the roof of your mouth or imagining that your lips are superglued together. He also sagely warns against listening for what's wrong or offensive and, instead, listening for common experiences and underlying needs in what the person is saying.[23]

Sample Questions

On this book's website, you'll find examples of many curiosity-based questions. When you're stumped during a conversation, ask yourself, "If I were truly curious right now, what would I want to know?"

Here are some examples:

Immigration

- What do you see as some of the root causes driving immigration?

- Are there values or traditions in American culture that you feel are threatened by immigrants? What impact does it have on you? *If they reference people with different religious beliefs and say they want to maintain a Christian nation, you can ask*
  - In what way do you find immigration threatening to your own beliefs?
  - What does it mean to you that the United States is a Christian nation? What makes it a Christian nation?
  - Do you believe Christians should have a dominant role in shaping this country's culture?

Hate Violence

- What do you think is causing the uptick in white nationalist violence around the world in the past few years, like the mass shootings at mosques, synagogues, and black churches? Do you believe that the way politicians and the media talk about immigrants plays any role?
- What are the strengths and weaknesses you see in terms of each party's response to hate crimes?

Racism

- When people say "black lives matter," does it feel to you like they're saying that white lives don't matter?
- When people talk about white privilege, do you think they're saying that because you're white, your life hasn't been hard?
- What does being color-blind mean to you? *If they seem not to understand the privilege of white skin…*Have you ever been kicked out of a hotel lobby or a café when you were just sitting there, minding your own business?[24]

#Metoo

- What do you think are the most common reasons women report men as having sexually harassed or assaulted them? *If the answer focuses on vindictiveness, you might ask:* What makes you think vindictiveness is the main motivation?

- Have you ever had someone in a position of authority over you treat you badly but you were afraid to report it?

Welfare and Income Inequality

- When you say you're sick and tired of paying for welfare for people who are too lazy to work, do you feel like you're working hard so other people can get a free ride? Do you think a few, a lot, or all of the people getting welfare are not willing to work and not looking for a job?
- *If someone says they're worried about the government going broke paying for entitlements:* What do you mean by entitlements? Are you worried that there might not be enough left for you if you need it?
- Have you worked hard and felt like you didn't get to cash in on the American Dream?
- Do you believe that effort always equates to prosperity or have you seen examples where someone tries hard but doesn't succeed, sometimes because of circumstances beyond their control?

If you're talking to a wealthy conservative:

- What net worth would be enough to make you feel comfortable and secure?
- What kind of effect do you see economic inequality having on our country?

Environment

- Do you believe that if we require corporations to meet clean air and clean water standards, that people will lose jobs over it? Are you worried about losing your job if these standards are upheld?
- If an industry is polluting, like discharging chemicals into drinking water, do you think they should be responsible for cleaning it up or not? Do you see other solutions to the problem?

- Do you think it's important for the EPA to keep track of how many honey bees are dying, or not?
- How do you react to the position the military has taken that climate change is a threat to national security? Do you believe them or not?

Health Care
- What do you want most out of your health care? Are there any elements of Obamacare you'd like to keep?
- What's your impression of the quality of the health care systems in other advanced economies?

Political Canvassing
If you're canvassing for a progressive candidate ("Candidate A," below) in a swing district:
- Would you be more inclined to vote for somebody who's committed to making sure no new gun control laws are passed or somebody who will work to shift the tax burden from the middle class to the ultra-rich?
- Do you feel like, because you see abortion as immoral, that you would be immoral if you voted for Candidate A?
- Did President Trump's tax plan work out the way you expected? *If yes:* What were the things you liked best about it? Did any parts of it disappoint you? *If no:* What parts disappointed you?
- Do you see Trump's/Candidate A's policies as mainly benefiting the rich, the middle class, or the poor?
- *If the voter says they're not sure they will vote for the Republican incumbent again...*What is it that makes you question whether they deserve your vote?

General Questions
Questions about the person's state of mind, thought process, or receptivity:
- When I mentioned what the expert consensus is on this issue, does it make you feel like I'm discounting your opinion because you're not an expert?

- Do you believe that is absolutely true, or do you have any degree of doubt?
- *If they reject information from a reputable source that you've presented, you can ask:* What do you think would make them say that if it weren't true?

Better Angels' red–blue workshops begin with each "side" brainstorming the stereotypes they believe the other side has about them (e.g., "bleeding heart," "politically correct") and then discussing the ways in which the stereotypes are true and not true. A good icebreaker for any conversation could be asking the other person, "Are there perceptions or stereotypes you think liberals have of conservatives or that you've seen me having? To what degree do you believe there are any kernels of truth in the stereotypes?" Another icebreaker is to ask each person to reflect on the formative experiences and events that have shaped their political views (e.g., Iraq War, Watergate, getting bullied or sexually abused, etc.).

If you're considering engaging with a conservative family member you've been avoiding discussing politics with, you can begin by asking them if they're willing and interested in engaging, and you can share any concerns you have about damaging the relationship. If the other person is someone you love, tell them that nothing they say will change that and that you hope that nothing *you* say will cause a rupture. Establishing good intentions at the outset can serve as a homing beacon if tensions arise.

You can also ask yourself questions when you catch yourself feeling superior:
- Is it true? Have I just had more training in critical thinking and more exposure to cultural diversity? Are my critical thinking skills really so finely honed or am I just relying on my tribe's talking points?
- *If you're financially well off...* Does my affluence make it easier for me to support policies that could lead to job loss or increased consumer costs?
- Does the Trump supporter shine in areas where I don't? Does she volunteer at the senior center or take in rescue animals?

Do her contributions make her superior to me? (If not, then why do my progressive political beliefs or participation in the Trump resistance make me superior to her?)

- Does the person have dignity and worth even though they espouse beliefs I find offensive or mind-boggling? (Hint: Yes.)
- Does the other person know things I don't?
- Do I harbor implicit biases, now or in the past? Do I partake in relatively socially acceptable forms of prejudice, such as classism, ageism, sizeism, or anti-Mormonism? How much do I benefit from or actively attempt to dismantle structures of oppression?
- Does feeling or asserting my superiority serve me? What do I gain—or lose—when I indulge my sense of superiority? When was the last time I yielded during a verbal power struggle with someone who had an imploring, shaming, or know-it-all attitude?

Nondefensive questions can dissolve the walls between two people with opposing viewpoints. If they're genuinely curious, they can stimulate new insights for either or both people.

During your conversations, you'll likely hear some things that you strongly disagree with. The next two chapters will show you how to speak your truth without triggering the other person's defensiveness.

5

Speaking Your Peace

Peacemaking doesn't mean passivity.
It is about a revolution of love that is big enough
to set both the oppressed and the oppressors free.

—Common Prayer: A Liturgy for Ordinary Radicals

Once you have some understanding of another person's point of view, you can voice your opinion in the form of a nondefensive position statement. As with PNDC questions, PNDC statements are not designed to convince but, rather, to share your personal experience or perspective and to identify any contradictions in the other person's position.

A PNDC position statement is not incontrovertible truth, not dogma, not a sermon, not a guilt trip, and, above all, not a platform from which to show off your supposed superiority. It can be very passionate so long as what you're passionate about is *your* position, not the wrongfulness of the other person's position. You can be angry provided that you're not using your anger as a weapon to punish or convince.

You can't *make* someone change their mind; the harder you try, the more resistant they'll become. All you can do is *invite* the other person to consider what you're saying.

An effective position statement can serve three functions: (1) show the other person that you understand (though not necessarily agree with) their position; (2) share your story and the basis for your beliefs; and (3) hold the other person accountable for the ways in which their attitude or behavior has harmed you or others.

Playwright-activist Eve Ensler's statement below serves all three functions. Ensler's piece was a response to white women who supported Trump's mockery of Christine Blasey Ford. In an open letter, Ensler recounts the story of how her father sexually abused her and how her mother failed to protect her. Ensler says that watching women standing behind Trump, laughing and cheering while he mocked Ford, "felt like I was falling into a familiar nightmare. It compelled me to reach out to you." She continues:

> I know the risk many of you [would] take in coming out to say you believe a woman over a man…I write to you because we need you, the way I once needed my mother. We need you to stand with women who are breaking the silence in spite of their terror and shame…Here is why I believe you should take this stand with me. Violence against women destroys our souls. It annihilates our sense of self. It numbs us. It separates us from our bodies. It is the tool used to keep us second-class citizens. And if we don't address it, it can lead to depression, alcoholism, drug addiction, overeating, and suicide. It makes us believe we are not worthy of happiness. It took my mother 40 years to see what her denial has done and to apologize to me. I don't think you want to apologize to your daughters 40 years from now.[1]

Ensler could have ranted about Trump's misogyny and maligned women who support him as women who should know better, women who should be ashamed of themselves. What she did instead was far more powerful.

A woman in Wisconsin named Becca participated in a small discussion group of liberal Jews and conservative Christian Trump supporters. Before the 2018 midterm elections, she wrote a heartfelt letter to the conservatives in her group telling them that she had friends who were leaving the country out of fear, and that she, too, was considering leaving and she hoped they didn't want her to. One of them wrote back to her saying that they didn't want her to go, that they wouldn't vote for Republicans in the mid-terms, and that they wanted her to come over for dinner.[2] Wow.

A position statement is your opportunity to speak your sub-jective truth. The more you can remain subjective, the more re-ceptive the other person will be. Even if you were dealing with an absurdity such as flat-Earthism, saying "The photos of Earth from outer space make me 100 percent confident that the Earth is round," will engender less defensiveness than proclaiming, "There is no doubt whatsoever that the Earth is round, and any-one who questions that is utterly insane."

It is certainly true (or, I should say—I certainly *believe* it's true) that a society cannot function without grounding in a widely accepted understanding of reality. There is no valid or use-ful purpose served in casting doubt on, for example, the Holo-caust. However, like it or not (not!), we are in the midst of an information war, and throwing truth bombs reignites it.

Liberals revere objectivity and often throw up their hands in despair over right-wing fact-resistance and Trump's sinister un-dermining of the very notion of truth; however, I believe that some of his supporters' resistance is triggered by the judgmental and arrogant manner in which the Left communicates contradic-tory facts. When people's cherished belief systems are attacked, they double down on them. Rather than reflecting on the short-comings of their beliefs, they use them as a protective shield.[3] The shield goes up, the mind closes, and discourse short-circuits.

Imagine being a climate denier on the receiving end of this statement:

> Jesus Christ! If you believe that, you've been watching too much Fox News. Practically every scientist in the world knows that climate change is human-caused; there's simply no question about it.

Feeling a little defensive? Now react to this one:

> From everything I've read, there's strong scientific consen-
> sus that humans are causing climate change. We're close
> to a tipping point, where runaway climate change could
> become unstoppable and heat the planet to temperatures
> that humans have never encountered before. That really
> scares me. I'm afraid that, if the planet gets that hot, its life-
> support systems will start to shut down, and there will be
> more devastating droughts, fires, and floods. If I'm wrong
> and there isn't such grave danger, I'd rather be wrong than
> risk the kind of devastation scientists are predicting. If
> nine out of ten doctors told me I needed a stent to prevent
> a heart attack, I'd go with the advice of the nine.

The second statement tells the person what I believe and how I
came to believe it. It does not insist that it's the unvarnished truth
and doesn't belittle their beliefs. The person might not agree, but
they probably won't feel defensive; this leaves the door open for
them to investigate whether there's any validity to what I said.

You could also say, "When I see so many government climate-
scientist whistleblowers saying that the Trump administration is
trying to prevent the public from seeing their research, it makes
me think that the Trump administration is trying to hide something."[4] This could prompt them to do their own research.

Turning the tables for a moment, how would you react if
someone said this to you?

> You bleeding-heart liberals just want to coddle every free-
> loader. If it were up to you, everyone would be on welfare
> and the economy would collapse.

How's your amygdala doing? Are you firing up a snarky rejoinder,
or are you going to withdraw and lick your wounds? Do you see
this conversation being productive or insufferable?

Now put yourselves in the shoes of a libertarian Trump supporter impressed by Trump's wealth, who assumes he'll do for

the country what he's done for himself and his family. Someone says to you:

> Do you actually believe for a hot second that Trump gives a shit about you? He's the ultimate con man and, if you don't wise up fast, he'll turn this country into a kleptocracy.

How do you respond? Are you ready and willing to "wise up"? What if, instead, someone said this:

> I hear you saying you admire President Trump's wealth and hope he'll be able to run the country like a successful business. I agree that we've got some serious economic problems that need to be dealt with. When I look at Trump's track record, what stands out to me is that there were a lot of lawsuits against him by undocumented Polish workers, who built Trump Tower and didn't get paid, and by small business owners, who weren't paid for their services. Some of them went bankrupt.[5] I also remember reading about him settling the lawsuit brought by Trump University customers who sued him for fraud.[6] It seems to me that he has a pattern of enriching himself at the expense of ordinary Americans, and that makes me worry about whether he's abusing his position as president to increase his own family's wealth at the expense of the country. His not turning over his tax returns makes me even more worried. There are countries where there's so much corruption that it devastates the economy, and I don't want that to happen to the United States.

One more: How would a rich person respond to a populist denunciation of the venality and greed of rich people? I would bet you $1 million: Defensively. Even nonrich people might rush to their defense. Now, lo and behold, the wealthy are victims! Instead, what if you said, "From what I've seen, people with a lot of money don't usually represent the interests of the majority of working- and middle-class people very well. I think it might be hard for them to relate to the day-to-day struggles of making ends meet or saving for a down payment on a house or a car. I think they may tend to see the system as fairer than it is because it works for them."

When you compare each of the above statements, do you see any loss of meaning or power in the nondefensive version? I don't. What I see is a straightforward articulation—without self-righteousness or bitter sarcasm. Nothing lost, much gained.

For socialists and progressive populists, there's a temptation to bash the well-to-do with populist blame-the-rich rhetoric. But like Reverend McBride counsels, it's wise to go soft on people, hard on structures. Be as hard as you want on capitalism, globalization, and corporate cronyism, but keep in mind that even the richest among us are complicated human beings with fine points and flaws and, just like all of us, are deserving of basic kindness and respect.

Sometimes, liberals act like it's a burden to have to explain the obvious to conservatives. All too often, we don't even bother trying. Fleischer, director of The Leadership Lab, criticizes liberals who hide in their silos: "We don't talk to people who don't already agree with us, and we don't explain the way we see things. We don't make the case for our ideals. It's almost as if we think our ideas are so good we shouldn't have to defend them."[7] Though more subtle than a snarky meme, avoidance can reflect contempt toward people who don't automatically subscribe to our views.

Verbal Crossfire

On November 5, 2017, a man slaughtered 26 people at a church in rural Texas. Many Republican politicians responded with thoughts and prayers—and nothing else. One woman tweeted, "Why not just ban guns, and when people are upset about it, just send them thoughts and prayers?"

The tweet captured the mounting frustration and rage many progressives felt about decades of Republican obstruction of gun-safety laws. Spot-on, clever, and a little bit snarky, it instantly became the tweet heard 'round the world.[8]

The woman, Erica Buist, received thousands of responses, most of them love notes from gun-control supporters grateful for the insight into Republicans' shirking of responsibility. But pro-gun Americans fired back. Although roughly one in five of them attempted to engage Buist in a respectful exchange of opinions, the vast majority responded with heavy sarcasm or hateful abuse.

I spent an enjoyable hour chatting with Buist about her tweet. She's a talented British writer who feels something akin to survivor's guilt over the tragedy of American gun violence. Buist believes that Second Amendment absolutists are motivated by fear—as citizens of a country that does not guarantee health care or basic income security, guns serve as a substitute security blanket.

I asked Buist if, in light of the vitriolic responses, she would have composed her tweet differently. She said she wouldn't have, because so many people found her framing of the issue valuable. She went on to say that the people who attacked her were missing the point—she wasn't advocating a gun ban but calling out do-nothing politicians who "pilfer the language of the faithful." She never imagined her tweet would even be seen outside her small liberal following.

The trouble is, gun rights conservatives *did* see the tweet, interpreted it as a call for a gun ban, and instantly became defensive. If Buist is right that their attachment to their guns is a function of fear and insecurity, then their reaction is even more understandable and predictable—they see their guns as a form of protection, and now someone is threatening to take them away.

If I wrote a pithy, clever tweet with viral appeal, I probably wouldn't want to go back in time and alter it, either. I suspect, however, that appreciation for her tweet was confined to the choir and that it put gun-control opponents into a defensive stance. Given that, I would consider something with broader appeal. If, as she noted, her foes were "missing the point," is there a way to rephrase it to avoid misunderstanding? And could the tweet leave room for the possibility that religious Americans, even politicians (some of whom are born-again Christians) may be sincere in praying for victims and their families?

> I know many people are praying for the victims. At the same time, when politicians offer thoughts and prayers while defending laws that allow people to commit mass murder, the thoughts and prayers ring hollow to me.

Granted, my tweet doesn't have viral appeal, but it's also not polarizing because it represents my subjective stance. It's also less threatening because it doesn't imply that I'm coming for their guns. There's a time and place for sharing cogent insights like Buist's with people already on your side of an issue, but in an open forum like Twitter, the downsides are worth weighing.

I know from speaking with Buist that her intent was not to insult gun owners or religious folk, but many interpreted it that way. Following the tweet's social-media trail led me to an encounter with a man I'll call Frank, an ex-Marine whose Facebook profile image is a machine gun. I began my exchange with Frank in mid-February 2018, just after the Parkland, Florida, school shooting. I asked Frank what it was about Buist's tweet that, as he put it, "got under [his] skin."

Frank sent me a long, thoughtful reply, explaining that sometimes people of faith offer thoughts and prayers when they can't find other words to express how they feel about a horrific event. He said he understood that it might not resonate for nonreligious people, but that it's meant in earnest and that he considers the mockery of thoughts and prayers to be mean-spirited and provocative.

I'd never paused to consider that the invocation of thoughts and prayers might be genuine, and his response enlightened me. I wrote him back:

> When I first read her tweet, I loved it because I had been feeling so frustrated with politicians who offered thoughts and prayers and, at the same time, didn't take action to prevent gun violence. Given that they were defending

laws that, in my view, were enabling mass murder, their thoughts and prayers rang hollow to me.

Reading what you've written, I now understand that thoughts and prayers can be sincere and heartfelt. I do wonder if all of the politicians who talk about "thoughts and prayers" were touched by the shooting and mean it genuinely, or are mouthing it just to have something to say or to avoid having to talk about gun control.

Frank and I had a lengthy exchange, during which I learned a lot about firearms and why gun enthusiasts want to keep their guns, and Frank learned that the weight of evidence shows that guns in the home endanger more than protect household members.

Frank read the articles I sent him and appreciated the balanced information they provided. In the end, he agreed with me that AK-15-style rifles make mass shootings more likely (though as of this writing, he still opposes an assault rifle ban).

We gave each other a fair hearing. Months later, Frank asked out of the blue what I thought about the Kavanaugh hearings. I sent him an article detailing Kavanaugh's lies; he responded that the article was "very compelling" and added that Trump was behaving like an "insufferable ass." I believe that the respectful tenor of our prior communication was what made him genuinely curious about my position on Kavanaugh.

Liberal rhetoric about gun violence is often highly contemptuous. In the comments section of a Fox News article about the Florida massacre, someone wrote, "Keep it up deplorables...kids who aren't shot become adults who vote."[9] Presumably, the commenter was a liberal seeking to win over Fox News consumers by insulting and taunting them. A Facebook friend of a friend posted a meme that pilloried gun-toting, pink-eyed, toothless "hillbillies" who let their kids play in empty refrigerators. Hilarious.

After the Florida massacre, David Brooks wrote an op-ed in *The New York Times* suggesting that gun-control advocates make overtures of respect toward gun-rights advocates rather than issuing blanket condemnations of guns and gun culture.[10] He was swiftly ridiculed.[11] For his detractors, doing anything other than shaming and denouncing gun-rights proponents as heartless monsters was an absolute non-starter. They would sooner toss grenades at stereotyped cardboard cutouts of trigger-happy hill-billies than come to the table and find out what gun-rights advo-cates think about gun violence.

In *The Washington Post*, columnist E.J. Dionne, Jr., chimed in, lambasting the notion of giving gun-rights advocates the time of day:

> And as the mass killings continue, we are urged to be pa-tient and to spend our time listening earnestly to the views of those who see even a smidgen of action to limit access to guns as the first step toward confiscation…What is odd is that those with extreme pro-gun views—those pushing for new laws to allow people to carry just about anytime, any-where—are never called upon to model similar empathy toward children killed, the mourning parents left behind, people in urban neighborhoods suffering from violence, or the majority of Americans who don't own guns.[12]

Dionne implies that empathy is a tit-for-tat commodity. When I extend empathy to someone, I hope they'll reciprocate, but I can't demand it. If I withhold it until the other person meets my behav-ioral standards, then I'm using it manipulatively; it's no longer genuine empathy.

Empathy is the act of taking the other person's perspective, stepping into their shoes, and trying to understand what they're feeling. Empathy is not agreement or compromise. You can em-pathize with the feelings and experiences underlying someone's opinions without liking or agreeing with those opinions. Many gun owners are scared of violent crime and convinced their guns will protect them. I can empathize with their fear without agreeing that having guns makes us safe. Sometimes, empathy is unavailable: If you're talking with someone who is very argu-mentative, reveals nothing about themselves, and/or says hateful things, then you're not likely to be able to feel empathy unless, perhaps, you happen to be the Dalai Lama. But if I'm talking to someone who's telling me why guns are important to them and I have no knowledge of them ever perpetrating or condoning violence, then I can empathize with whatever underlies their attachment to their guns.

The NRA's success is a function of its ability to mobilize its members to vote, turn up at town halls, and put their legislators on speed dial.[13] Every time we demean a gun owner, we're doing free outreach for the NRA. Furthermore, when we refuse to acknowledge people's opposition to gun control respectfully, we widen the cultural divide and inflame simmering resentment against liberals who, they believe, don't understand or care about them.

Framing Your Position Statement

Position statements can be used to share your values and worldview. What's crucial here is to share your values without denigrating others' values. Express your position as your opinion, not gospel, and use factual citations sparingly. Meet the other person where they're at, not where you *wish* they were at.

Your position statement is your chance to share information or experiences that contradict any false assumptions the other person has. For example, you might have had positive experiences with people the other person has expressed stereotypes or animosity toward. Or you may have researched an issue and learned some things that contradict the other person's assertions. Or you may notice a contradiction between what you understand the person's values to be and the ideological position they espouse— for example, if they enjoy the National Parks but are in favor of opening them up to mining. Naming a contradiction should never be a "gotcha" but, rather, simply an observation.

Make it into a story—a description of what you've read, heard, think, or believe, and why—as opposed to a statement of fact that refutes their position. Sometimes, the story is a personal experience, but often it's simply your thought process—what did you read, hear, or watch; why did you trust it; and what was your takeaway?

In her book, *So You Want to Talk About Race*, writer Ijeoma Oluo tells a compelling story about going to a scholarship conference for students of color and how liberating it was to be free from microaggressions for the first time in her life:

> Not once in the two days I was at the conference did anybody make fun of my name. Not once in the two-day conference did anybody even glance at my hair. Not once in the two-day conference was I aware of the loudness of my voice or the size of my ass. Not once in the two-day conference did anybody question the academic achievements that had brought me there—we were all there because we were smart kids who had worked very hard...I don't know how to describe what those two days were like for me except to say that I hadn't known before then that there was so much air to breathe.[14]

A person who isn't black might have a different kind of story to tell concerning race:

> I grew up watching the local news on TV with my parents, and I had the impression that black people committed the vast majority of crime because that's whose mug shots I was always seeing. And then I found out that the media is more likely to show images of black people getting arrested than whites.[15] I realized how that early experience had distorted my perspective. Even though I have this new information, those images of black faces associated with crimes made a deep impression; I have to keep reminding myself that the vast majority of black people are law-abiding.

Ellison recommends trying to fashion your statement according to the following formula:

1. **Active listening.** "I hear you saying that..." (If "I hear you say-

ing" gets old, you can use alternatives like "it sounds like" or "I think what you're saying is…") Summarize what you think the other person is saying without parroting it.

2. **Name any contradictions** you identify based on what the person said, their tone or body language, your experience, or outside data: "At the same time, I'm aware that…" (Personal stories are better than data because they're stickier and less contestable, but sometimes all you've got is data.) The purpose here is *not* to prove the other person wrong but to hold up a mirror. Exploring contradictions can lead to greater insights.

3. **Interpret and draw a tentative conclusion** regarding the meaning of the contradictions and/or the other person's motivations or intentions: "And so it seems to me that…"

4. **Share your reaction**—your thoughts, feelings, beliefs, conclusions, and/or what you're going to do in response to what the other person said ("I believe that…").

The first three steps are feedback for the other person, which is best delivered in a firm but neutral tone to avoid triggering defensiveness. In the fourth step, you can express emotions, including anger, ideally in a non-punitive, authentic manner. If you're in a place of uncontrollable, raw pain or white-hot rage, it might be best to forget about the four parts and simply tell your story. Expressing a lot of outrage will alienate many but, so long as it's not vicious, others may be able to take it in.[16]

Here's an example that conforms to the four-part formula:

1. I hear you saying that you're okay with separating families at the border because, even though you know it's hard on them, they're breaking the law and that you hope that the threat of being separated will deter migrants from coming, which is important to your sense of safety.

2. At the same time, what I'm seeing is that almost a third of immigrants present themselves legally at the border and apply for asylum under federal law, but they're still detained and separated—without even having an attorney or a hearing. I've

heard some of their stories of why they've fled their home countries; the three biggest reasons I've heard are gang violence, political violence, and hunger due to crop failures from drought. One woman said she was willing to walk thousands of miles knowing she might not get in; she said she's praying that Trump will change his mind because she's afraid she'll die if she has to go back.[17]

3. So it seems to me that there are families seeking safety and keeping within the law, but they are being labeled and treated like criminals; they're being punished by having their families torn apart. And I think that you're focusing so much on your safety that you're not considering theirs.

4. When I think about a young child being taken away from their mother or father, and how terrifying and traumatic that would be for them, I think about how I would feel if that happened to me and my child, or you and your child. It makes me feel sick to my stomach. I worry about the long-term effects on the children, especially the very young ones, who end up not even recognizing their parents after being separated for weeks or months. Even if people are trying to get in illegally, I think it's cruel to take their children away from them. I don't feel that these people are doing anything that justifies that treatment.

Position statements can be used in conversation, oral or written, with friends, family members, and colleagues. They can also be used to great effect with elected officials during town halls or in-person meetings. If you're a concerned constituent, you'll already know your elector's position on the issue, so step one of the position statement writes itself. The rest of the position statement can be a powerful presentation of what you think the elected is overlooking and what you believe, followed by a prediction of what you think will happen if the elected persists in enacting bad policy. The prediction can include the negative impacts on the public and on the elected official—e.g., losing the next election and/or having advocates escalate their tactics.

Abbreviated Position Statements

If someone asks your opinion about a topic before you know anything about their views, you can make a brief position statement rather than a four-part statement. A position statement can be followed by a prediction of what you foresee will occur if one policy or another is implemented.

Health care. Given that universal health care in Canada and Europe costs much less than health care here and the people in those countries are healthier, I predict that, if we have a similar system here, we'll have the same outcome. If we don't have Medicare for All, what I think will happen is that health care will become more and more expensive, and countless people will have to go without and die prematurely.

Estate tax. I thought that cutting the estate tax would put more money in my pocket. Then I found out that no one pays it unless their estate when they die is worth at least $11 million. That leaves me out! (This simple statement is enough for the other person to realize, if they didn't already, that estate taxes apply only to the ultra-rich.)

Trump's fitness for office. Imagine that a Trump supporter asks you, "What's your problem with Trump anyway? I mean, he won. Why can't you just get over it?"

(Note: I know you've got a list of 100 reasons why you can't get over it—just pick one. Below, I've chosen violent divisiveness as the focus.)

> I believe that a crucial quality a president needs to have is to be able to bring the country together. I remember that after 9/11, President Bush said that we need to stop terrorism, but he also said that Islam is a peaceful religion, that Muslims are our brothers and sisters and our fellow Americans, and that we should treat them with respect because

that's our highest calling as Americans—to accept each other.

I'm extremely upset about Trump being president because, instead of bringing people together, I see him being divisive and inciting group violence, like when the guy at one of his rallies shouted out that migrants at the border should be shot and Trump's response was to laugh.[18] I've watched him leading people in chants that fuel anger and hatred, telling people to beat up protesters and even to kill them, and telling members of Congress like AOC and Ilhan Omar that they should go back where they came from.[19]

He also lumps groups of people together as "bad people" to be feared and hated. I saw a video of a woman telling a Latino man to go back to Mexico because Latinos are rapists. When he asked why she thought he was a rapist, she said President Trump says so.[20] The shooters at the Pittsburgh synagogue and the New Zealand mosque said Trump inspired them, and I've seen neo-Nazis calling him their leader and giving him the Nazi salute.[21]

When a leader, the commander-in-chief, targets entire groups of people as threats, I believe it encourages people to bully, attack, and even murder them. I see it tearing our country apart and violating the essence of what it means to be a democracy. I believe that President Trump has used his position to encourage hatefulness, and it makes him unfit to be president.

You'll find additional position statements on other topics at this book's website.

The Self-Righteous Moralizing Pitfall

I got into trouble when I allowed self-righteousness to creep into my position statement during a heated discussion on my online neighborhood forum about how to respond to a homeless encampment. Several people had been making hateful comments that vilified homeless residents, at times even wishing them ill.

Others were less overt but, from my perspective, had begun to see *themselves* as the primary victims of the homelessness crisis.

Early in the discussion, I acknowledged that, while I was someone who supported the encampment's right to exist, I understood that people have varying degrees of tolerance for disorder. While I felt safe walking by the encampment, I also realized that others, especially if they're disabled or elderly, might feel vulnerable. People responded favorably to that. However, after someone made a comment asserting that most of the encampment residents were "service-resistant" spoiled kids choosing to do drugs and live in squalor, I got triggered. I responded thusly, my superiority leaking out:

> As the numbers of homeless people swell, I see more of a tendency among housed people to make assumptions and judgments about homeless people—where they're from, why they're homeless, whether they deserve assistance, their criminal backgrounds, etc. Often, these assumptions don't seem to be based on facts or might be generalized based on the behavior of a small number of homeless individuals.
>
> [*So far, so good…I've stated my observations and the contradictions I saw.*]
>
> Given the reality of Berkeley's finite resources, I acknowledge the necessity of prioritizing who gets services, just like a hospital has to triage patients during a natural disaster.
>
> At the same time, I think it's important to avoid dichotomies of "good" and "bad" homeless people.
>
> [*Boom, there it is…"it's important to avoid" was a passive-aggressive way of saying, "You people who label homeless as good or bad are committing a moral error."*]
>
> Even those we cannot assist are human beings who are suffering. I believe that denying them their humanity contributes to the erosion of social trust and breaching of interconnectedness that is, perhaps, the root cause of this

and all other contemporary crises. We can't help everyone,
but still have a choice of how to treat people who don't get
served: with contempt or with dignity.

Because I framed my little sermon as "my belief," I thought it was
nondefensive, but it smacked of superiority (especially so because
I was writing in a formal, non-conversational style that helped me
come across as a pompous ass). A woman I'll call Linda promptly
called me out for "compassion-shaming."

I ran the whole affair by Ellison, who observed that I had given
short shrift to housed residents' fears and concerns. I paid lip service to their concerns—I knew I was supposed to, and I wanted
to check that box and quickly return to my "superior" position. In
so doing, I was covertly judging them for not being graced with
the saintly virtue I possessed. Superiority leads to judgment, and
judgment leads to alienation and resentment.

Ellison suggested I apologize, which I resisted doing, rational-
izing that other people's behavior on the forum had been so much
worse than mine. But she was right: I needed to be accountable
for my behavior regardless of whether other people were taking
accountability for theirs.

I apologized for my self-righteousness, and Linda responded
graciously. My apology helped reduce the level of divisiveness
in the forum. In the days following my apology, several people
thanked me, and I noticed people on both sides toning down
their rhetoric, brainstorming more creatively about solutions
to the homelessness crisis, and applauding each other's civility.
The love fest lasted for a few weeks, at which point newcomers
to the forum began trolling each other and repolarizing the issue,
a dynamic I, too, slipped into more than once (much to Linda's
dismay).

An interesting side note is that, early on, I was on the cusp
of ceasing to participate because it was eating up a lot of time.
However, I was lured into a power struggle with a participant
who was trolling me hard. I not only continued participating in
that forum but started keeping tabs on related forums to rebut

other assertions of his that I deemed to be erroneous or biased. It was a case study of how we dig in our heels when under attack. If I ever want to inspire a Trump supporter to dedicate their life to reelecting Trump, I'll be sure to troll them.

A few months after my exchange with Linda, I was driving on the freeway and saw two men hitchhiking. They looked bedraggled as they trudged along the shoulder with heavy backpacks in the ninety-degree heat. As I whizzed by in my air-conditioned VW, I didn't even consider stopping for them. The rational part of my mind knew that there was only a very small chance that these men would have harmed me, but my fear center was in the driver's seat. A few days later, it dawned on me that just as I was casting judgment on people for allowing their fear to override their compassion toward unhoused residents, so, too, might someone who picks up hitchhikers cast judgment on me. And if they judged me for my choice, I'd be pretty damn defensive about it.

We all have our judgments toward people whose moral equations pencil out differently or who have character traits we deem negative. I'm judgmental of people I regard as selfish, incompetent, prejudiced, arrogant, and, ironically, judgmental. Someone else might be judgmental of people who are closed-minded, weak-willed, unintelligent, hedonistic, or blasphemous. There's no ultimate arbiter of who's worthy of praise or condemnation. If you attempt to play the role of arbiter, all you're likely to achieve is alienating the object of your judgment.

Instead of judging, you can observe when a person's beliefs contradict your own or when their behavior harms themselves or others. You can call their attention to this without blaming or shaming and, in so doing, you are far likelier to enable them to reconsider the mark they're leaving on this little world of ours.

Dealing with Bigotry

Having a president who is openly hostile to people of color lends a new urgency to an issue that has plagued and shaped our country since its inception. But calling out racism unskillfully can backfire. Skillful navigation begins with listening empathetically to the fears and resentments—legitimate or not—of white people experiencing or fearing downward mobility and casting about for an "Other" to blame. This can then be followed up with stories about the lived experiences of people of color, and the obstacles and violence they face; belief statements about who benefits and who is hurt by racial discrimination; and expressions of concern about the ways in which Trump has emboldened racists. One of the most important things whites can do is to be transparent about their own implicit bias and learn to recognize and counteract it. We're all somewhere along the journey, none of us perfect beings.

When racists are attacked and ridiculed, they don't get woke, they get resentful, and the last thing we need is more white resentment. At one of Ellison's workshops, an older black woman said she'd spent a lifetime watching well-meaning white people "call out" racists and then watching those racists unleash their rage on people of color. She implored us to resist the urge to label others as racists and, instead, to engage them in respectful dialogue.

Putting people on the defensive makes them double down on their offensive beliefs. Recall ambivalent Trump voter Cindy Kiser who talked about how she recoils at labels like racist even though she acknowledges the reality and harm of white privilege. The problem with labels is that there's a subtle implication that the person doing the labeling is superior: "I'm not a racist, but you are." From there, the accused will defend their character by denying that they're a racist, and the conversation is derailed without the person understanding why what they said was racist. If the person you're talking to is someone who sees racism as shameful and strives to be nonracist, they will feel humiliated and preoccupied with their self-image instead of their impact on people of color.

Lastly, when someone is branded a racist, they don't learn anything. They may associate racism with wearing a white hood or saluting Hitler. They may not be familiar with concepts like structural racism and implicit bias. Sometimes, we slap a racism label on offensive speech as a shortcut rather than taking the time to explain how what the person said is rooted in and perpetuates white supremacist history and culture.

"Telling people they're racist, sexist, and xenophobic is going to get you exactly nowhere," says Alana Conner, executive director of the Social Psychological Answers to Real-World Questions Center at Stanford University. "It's such a threatening message. One of the things we know from social psychology is when people feel threatened, they can't change, they can't listen." Instead, Conner says, "we should strive to reassure these groups that they are being respected, that they are being listened to."

You can challenge racist *beliefs* without labeling the person a racist and without scolding them for being unaware of their white privilege. How? By asking curiosity questions and then sharing stories, like The Leadership Lab canvassers do, or by making a PNDC position statement. As *White Ally Toolkit* creator Campt puts it, "Effective White Allies must fight against the natural tendencies to resist finding common cause with racism skeptics. Try to understand the various influences impacting the beliefs and actions of each side."[22] Just as people of color "code switch" when speaking in different settings, Campt notes, so too must white allies when speaking with whites of varying degrees of "wokeness."[23]

Robin DiAngelo, author of *White Fragility*, offers similar advice to white people providing feedback to other whites. To avoid triggering defensiveness, DiAngelo recommends starting a conversation by owning one's white privilege or prejudice and telling the story of how one began to gain insights and hold oneself accountable. "Ultimately, I let go of changing the other person," DiAngelo writes. "[M]y actions are driven by my own need for integrity, not a need to correct or change someone else."[24] (Ironically, the concept of "white fragility" is now sometimes misused as an epithet to taunt and shame ignorant whites in ways that would make any *Homo sapien* react defensively.)

Again, it comes back to the challenging practice of meeting people where they're at. Racial justice organizers Tarso Luis Ramos and Scot Nakagawa put it beautifully:

> White antiracist activists are critical to successfully competing with the right for the attention of those vulnerable to their appeals. We should also remember that white nationalist movements are identity movements. We must take seriously the sense among a growing number of whites that white identity is under attack. That older white voters seem to feel this threat most acutely could be a reflection of generationally bound values, but it is also very likely an indication of the vulnerability that many feel as they age.
>
> Good organizing *meets people where they are, and not where we wish they were.* Moreover, good organizing focuses on the egos of those being organized, and not on the egos of the organizers. This isn't a pissing contest over who gets it. It's a fight for economic and social justice for everyone.[25]

I think I understand why some people of color bristle when white people like me engage in "tone policing," regarding how they call out racism. This burdens them with the responsibility of catering to white fragility, on top of everything else they have to deal with. My intent is to offer an alternative, which people of color may or may not choose to try. I can't know what it's like to live as a person of color in a white supremacist society and so am not offering a prescription so much as food for thought. I also respect the need for people of color to outsource this difficult work to white people.

If you're someone who feels personally threatened by the overt bigotry Trump's ascent has unleashed, please don't feel that you're required to engage in any conversation with people who scare or offend you. Though some people of color and LGBTQ people choose to participate, others feel, quite legitimately, that such an exercise is not for them. For those who want to engage, there are some tips in the next chapter concerning how to hold boundaries that protect your physical and emotional safety.

R-E-S-P-E-C-T

Do people who say and do hurtful things deserve our respect? Not necessarily, but that doesn't mean we should treat them with cruelty. Ellison says, "I don't believe we have to respect a person in order to honor their humanity. Honoring it can come from the simple act of being honest and straightforward without any attempt to demean the person." We can have more of an impact by expressing compassion for people who are oppressed rather than trying to punish the oppressors and their sympathizers.

At the same time, anger is a valid reaction to oppression. If you're angry, try to communicate from a place of authentic hurt. If your goal is to punish the other person or make them change, and your feelings are conveyed with vitriol or steely coldness, it will trigger defensiveness. If you show them your wound—or the pain you feel for other people's wounds—there is more chance that they will shift their attitude. If you try to wound them back, the only response they will be capable of is defensiveness.

When *The Washington Post* asked Speaker of the House Nancy Pelosi if she respects Trump, she dodged and feinted: "I respect the office that he holds and the agencies of government that he appoints to—I think I respect them more than he does, looking at who he has appointed to those offices." She went on to note his "lack of shared values about our country" and "disrespect for the dignity and worth of a person." She finished on a note of superiority, asserting that the Democrats would not "stoop to his level."[26]

Pelosi didn't directly answer whether she respects Trump, though it's clear she doesn't. If there was any doubt, her contemptuous clapback during the 2019 State of the Union address put it to rest.[27] Instead, she criticized him for appointing bad apples and held herself up as superior in her values, her demeanor toward, and her respect for the presidency. Pelosi could have spoken more straightforwardly as follows: "My values are very different from those I've seen expressed by President Trump. I see much of his attitude and behavior as being disrespectful of the dignity and worth of other people and of democracy. For these reasons, I do not respect him."

At the end of the day, whether or not you seek to find something worthy of respect in people whose values you find abhorrent is a deeply personal call. But even if you decide to withhold respect, that doesn't necessitate inflicting punishment in the form of contempt.

Ten More Tips

Avoid strong hand gestures and facial expressions when giving feedback. Use a neutral, relaxed tone while sharing information or observations. When sharing a personal story, revealing your authentic feelings is appropriate. (You can watch a recording of Ellison making position statements at the book's website.)

Controlling your body language may seem trivial compared to the words coming out of your mouth, but it can make all the difference. I was canvassing in a swing district and encountered a Trump supporter who started telling me how much he valued honor and integrity. I tried to keep from grimacing as my mind began inventorying Trump's lapses in integrity. The man stopped midsentence and said in a tone of resignation, "You don't agree with me. I can see it in your eyes." At that moment, I became aware that, while my face was neutral, my gaze was boring a hole into his head. I had conveyed unmistakable contempt. Whoops.

Transcend partisanship. If you're a Democratic Party loyalist, it can be hard to admit that icons like Obama and Clinton have made mistakes, acted unethically, or failed to fulfill their campaign promises. Acknowledging their imperfections allows the other person to see you as trustworthy and open-minded. Defending them against *all* criticism, on the other hand, can deepen anti-establishment swing voters' suspicion that the Democratic Party doesn't give a hoot about people like them.

Unless someone brings up Trump, it may be best to steer clear.

For me, just hearing his name is so triggering I'm apt to blow my stack. The one time someone did ask me what I thought of him, I said, "I don't think he cares about people like me. I think all Trump cares about is Trump." She nodded approvingly, then said she had considered voting for him in 2016 but was glad she hadn't.

Mock not. The most counterproductive thing you can do is mock someone's beliefs, foibles, or lifestyle. Whatever you do, don't make fun of their diet, occupation, faith, pride of place, hobbies (including guns, NASCAR, and ATVs), mental health, gullibility, physical appearance, or loyalty to the president. (I don't remember too many liberals criticizing Obama when he deported more immigrants than Bush and killed thousands of civilians in drone strikes, though I wish they had.) Conservatism is not a mental illness. Trailer trash is not a thing. Flyover states are people's beloved homes.

And don't mock Trump, no matter how tempting a target he is. We live in an appearance-obsessed culture in which many people do whatever they can to conceal signs of aging and body fat. Calling him an obese Cheeto is an unkind cheap shot and is entirely beside the point.

Take it easy. Bring to mind for a moment a recent political argument you've had. What was the *energy* like between you two? Was it relaxed and comfortable, or charged and tense? Were you able to empathize with anything the other person said or did you withhold empathy for fear of somehow validating their viewpoint? How we deliver our statements creates a vibe that can either amp up the discord or harmonize it. Slow down, pause, and think before you speak, and release the need to control the outcome—it's just one conversation out of a lifetime and is unlikely to change the course of history. Chill.

Avoid the royal "we." Sometimes, it's unavoidable, but often people say "we" when they mean "I" or "the government" or "the public."

Saying "we" subtly implicates the other person in ways they might not consent to, thereby triggering their defensiveness. "We" can also be passive-aggressive. If I say, "We really need to work harder to avoid buying into racist stereotypes," but by "we," I mean "you" (because I'm an enlightened, antiracist higher being), I'm being passive-aggressive.

No personal or group-based attacks. Try to keep the focus on the issue, not the person—no one enjoys being the target of an *ad hominem* attack. Don't accuse the other person of being irrational, illogical, emotional, fact-resistant, stubborn, or gullible. Look for opportunities to empathize—remember, empathy does not imply agreement or approval, and it doesn't cost you anything.

Own up to uncertainty and ignorance. If you don't know a lot about the topic of discussion, feel free to say, "I haven't heard much about that; it sounds like something I should read up on." Sometimes, someone makes a statement that you disagree with, but you're not sure exactly why; it just feels "off." If you're stumped, it's fine to say that you'd like to think about it more before responding.

You don't have to win. Often, I feel like I must win or, at least, wear down my opponent enough to get the last word in. Once you've stated your position, there's nothing to gain by belaboring the conversation. Let it sink in and come back to it another time if you believe doing so could potentially be productive. If you're conversing with someone you won't see again, you can just let it lie. Though you may never know, it's possible you'll have planted a seed that, with some future fertilization, sprouts into a new way of looking at things. Speak your piece, then hold your peace; otherwise, prepare for war.

If you screw up, apologize. It's inevitable that, at some point, you'll choose the wrong words or say it in a tone or with a facial expression that triggers a defensive reaction. Don't hesitate to say, "I'm sorry, I just said that in a judgmental way," or "I'm sorry, did what I just say rub you wrong?" Humility can go a long way toward bridging the divide.

Keep an open mind. If your only purpose in conversing with someone is to convince them of your rightness, they will notice. When you think about it, closed-mindedness is an absurdity—if someone presents sound information and analysis about how one policy would better serve your values than another, why *wouldn't* you change your mind? As Mark Twain said, "An open mind leaves a chance for someone to drop a worthwhile thought in it."

6

Putting It All Together

Speak the truth but not to punish.[1]

—Thich Nhat Hanh

This chapter shows how a dialogue concerning immigration could unfold, PNDC-style, with a series of curiosity questions, statements, and a prediction. Observe how, in this sample dialogue, the person practicing PNDC avoids directly countering the other person's statements, which can lead to a defensive back-and-forth rally. Instead, the person gathers information to make sure they understand what the other person is saying and then states their own position. Also, note that not every statement is a formulaic four-part position statement—that would be pretty weird and annoying! A four-part position statement is appropriate when you feel you've gathered enough information to understand the person's experience and reasoning, and have identified key differences between their perspective and yours.

If I were to boil down the entire process into one sentence, it's this: *Find out how the other person came to believe, think, and feel a certain way, and tell them how you came to believe, think, and feel a certain way, without trying to convince them that you're right.*

In crafting this dialogue, Ellison and I found again and again how crucial, yet difficult, it is to avoid arguing about facts. Though there are some facts woven in, our use of data is judicious and proffered in ways that we hope will reduce the potential for an infowar.

Immigration Dialogue

Immigration is an incredibly complex issue that, to be fully and justly reckoned with, requires discussion of numerous economic, social, and foreign policy issues, and profound questions of morality. However, trying to cover everything in a single conversation will undermine your ability to share your perspective on whatever the other person is basing *their* anti-immigrant beliefs on, whether that's crime, terrorism, nativism, or labor-market impacts (an issue that some left-wing economists have concerns about, too).

Barbara Jordan, a civil rights icon who was one of the first black women in Congress, decried the scapegoating of immigrants. At the same time, she warned back in the 1990s that, if immigration were not sufficiently restricted, nativists would rise and demand that the border be sealed. We are now living out the nativist backlash Jordan predicted, one that presents painfully complicated legal, political, and moral issues, including the issue of how to respond to nativist resentment without either inflaming or surrendering to it. Jordan believed compromise was a moral necessity to protect both immigrants and native-born workers from a worst-case scenario, a conclusion I wrestle with as someone who sees the entire concept of borders as morally fraught. Jordan died before her Commission on Immigration Reform's agenda was enacted, and the framework she had worked so hard to create fell apart.[2]

The dialogue presumes you and your discussion partner (we'll call him "Alan") are white, native-born citizens, neither of whom is an expert. The statements made are for demonstration purposes only and do not necessarily reflect either my own or Ellison's views.

> **You:** Immigration is such a divisive issue. If you're willing, I'd like to try to understand where each of us is coming from without us getting into an argument about it.

Alan: Yeah, sure. I think immigration is complicated. Some amount is okay, but we have to secure our borders. I don't care if we do that with a wall or some other way, but it's got to be done. The problem I have is with liberals who want open borders because that's more votes for Democrats. They turn a blind eye to all the crime illegals bring in and all the jobs they're taking.

You: Which of those things you just mentioned is the biggest issue for you?

Alan: The job issue for starters—illegals are taking millions of jobs that unemployed citizens could have and when they work under the table, that drives down wages.

Now that Alan has identified worker displacement and wage suppression as his key issue, stick to it and leave behind the other issues he mentioned. If you try to address everything, the conversation will become disjointed and argumentative.

You: Where are you getting the information about immigration's impact on native-born workers?

Alan: It's on the news, and I can see the influx of foreign workers in Houston. Here's the thing—when illegals accept lower wages, it drives down wages and working conditions for all workers in that occupation. So then those jobs are crappy and, of course, American workers don't want them. The only solution is to stop the flow of illegals—then, employers will be forced to raise wages to attract American workers. You can't have it both ways, so which do you want—open borders or decent-paying jobs?

You: If there weren't any immigrants working here illegally, how much do you think wages would increase?

Alan: I don't know; someone could run the numbers on that, I guess. And it's not just illegals—I mean, you could give them all amnesty and then, poof, they'd be legal residents, but they'd still be willing to work for peanuts.

You: Besides immigration, do you think there are other factors causing wage stagnation?

Alan: Oh yeah, probably. I mean, all the regulations businesses have to deal with and all the taxes—that probably cuts down on how much they can afford to pay workers.
You: Do you think raising the minimum wage would help solve the problem of wage stagnation?
Alan: What is it now, $7.25? I feel bad for anyone trying to live on that, but if you raise it, that will put some companies out of business. Sorry to say, but a lousy job is better than no job.

For now, wait to address the issue of whether raising the minimum wage will increase unemployment.

You: I can't even imagine trying to live on $7.25 an hour—for an adult with a kid, working full time, that's below the federal poverty line. I don't see how a parent could even afford to buy their kid new shoes. And it's not just minimum-wage workers who are in poverty, there are also teachers who are moonlighting and sleeping in their cars, so it's impacting the middle class, too.
Alan: Yeah, we've got issues—that's why it's so important to get a handle on immigration. It's making a bad situation even worse.
You: I think what you're saying is true about immigrants doing, for example, most of the farm labor in the country—and a lot of it for substandard pay because they're desperate for work and also afraid they'll get deported if they complain. That upsets me, too. I don't want immigration policy to be driven by employers wanting cheap labor.

You may now be tempted to say a whole lot more about farm-worker abuse, climate chaos, and colonialism. However, if you do that, you'll be overriding the issue that Alan identified, which could make him defensive. What you can do instead is to springboard off Alan's identified concern of labor-market impacts and then explain how you view that problem.

Alan: Me, neither, so what I'm trying to spell out for you is that if you open the border to every Latin American who wants to come here, believe me, they'll take every low-skilled job in sight because they're willing to work for less. Even if you raise the minimum wage, they'll still undercut citizens. How would you prevent that from happening?

You: I don't have a perfect understanding of it all, but I can think of a few ways that might prevent that. One would be for them to get working papers and be here legally so that employers couldn't take advantage of them so easily. Another thing I think would help is to have laws like we used to have that protect labor unions' ability to organize for better wages and working conditions. Another piece that seems really important is the offshoring and automation of jobs, which is putting so many people out of work so fast, it's terrifying. There's something like 14 million people in other countries working for offshore US factories, and they can get away with paying them next to nothing and giving them no benefits. Fourteen million—that's more than all the immigrants living here illegally! My guess is that the low-paid offshore factory workers might be having a far greater impact on the blue-collar job market than immigrants are.[3]

I've heard economists say that keeping workers hungry and keeping at least 5 percent unemployment is the best way to have a stable economy, but stable for who? We're such a rich country, but we have so much poverty. Where's all the money going?

Alan: Hmm, good question. But you know what, I'll tell you where the money's going: it's going to support all the illegals sending their kids to our schools, getting free school lunches, free medical care. We just keep opening our wallets. I understand wanting to be charitable, but there's a limit. That probably makes me sound like the bad guy, but I think we have to protect the home team first.

Leave the topic of how much in government benefits undocumented immigrants receive for another day. (Not-so-fun fact: Undocumented immigrants pay billions into Social Security even though, under current law, they won't receive any of these benefits.[4])

> **You:** I don't see you as a bad guy, Alan. I think you have lots of legitimate concerns about the financial problems so many Americans are facing. And I do, too. Where I think we differ is in what we see as causing the problem and how to solve it.

Now you can make a four-part statement:

Step 1: Active Listening
What I hear you saying is that the problem is immigrants working for such low pay, sometimes even below minimum wage, and that if they weren't here, employers would pay more and citizens would take those jobs. For you, the solution is to keep as many immigrants as possible out of the labor market so they won't compete with American workers or drive down wages. I also heard you suggesting that even though the minimum wage isn't a livable wage, raising it could put companies out of business and employees out of work.

Step 2: Naming Contradictions
At the same time, I've been hearing a lot about American farmers being short of the help they need. In some parts of California, farmers are paying more than minimum wage, and local people still aren't willing to take the jobs. There are farmers in Florida and North Carolina who say they'll go under if they can't hire immigrants because citizens aren't willing to do the backbreaking work. And the dairy industry was quoted saying if immigrant labor were cut in half, thousands of dairies would close, and milk prices would shoot up.[5]

Step 3: Drawing a Conclusion

It seems to me that keeping out immigrants will likely leave US farmers without crews, which could have a devastating impact on our food supply.

Back to Step 2: Naming Contradictions

On the issue of raising the minimum wage, what I'm looking at is that corporate profits are at record highs and wages haven't gone up in proportion.

Back to Step 3: Drawing a Conclusion

Given the high profits, it doesn't seem likely to me that corporations would go out of business if they increased wages. So long as the minimum wage isn't raised, those workers are in a no-win situation, with low pay and potentially higher food prices.

All this is happening at the same time that CEOs are getting astronomical salaries and shareholders are getting huge profits; I see that money as coming out of the pockets of the employees, whose hard work creates those profits.

Step 4: Discuss Your Reaction

When immigrants are blamed for all of these economic problems, I get upset. I want them to be treated fairly for all the work they do, like putting food on our tables. I see blaming them as a distraction from what I believe is the real problem: the 1 percent are getting richer, and the poor and middle-class are getting poorer. I think the way politicians and the media talk about immigration makes everyone more polarized and angry instead of bringing us together to find solutions.

For me, the solutions are policies that give everyone better wages and working conditions and changes to the tax code that ding companies offshoring jobs. It enrages me to think that as one of the richest countries in the world, we still have families working full time and living in poverty, and worrying that the factory they work for is going to move to China or that they're going to lose their job to a robot.

As far as stopping immigrant workers from under-cutting wages, I like the idea that President George W. Bush proposed: give them visas so they're documented, which makes it more likely they'll earn minimum wage and pay taxes.

Step 5: Prediction
If we continue to blame immigrants and ignore the root causes of our economic problems, I believe that we may face a severe economic breakdown. If we make the changes in labor and tax policies I mentioned, I think we could give people better wages and job security and be able to take in a lot of immigrants.
Alan: If the farms need field hands, so be it, but that doesn't mean just opening up everything and turning America into Mexico. It sounds like you just want open borders. The Democrats all want open borders so these foreigners can come in, become citizens, and vote for Democrats.

Alan introduces two new topics (open borders and Latinx voters):

You: For me, having open borders is a difficult moral and political issue. I have conflicting thoughts about it, and my own family's immigration story is wrapped up in it. The more I think about immigration, the more complicated it seems. I think you said that earlier, too, about it being complicated.
Alan: Yeah, we agree on that much. But what's your response to what I said about Democratic politicians just wanting more Democratic voters?

You: Do you believe that's what's motivating all Democrats or some?

Alan: Maybe not all, but certainly the ones in power—Nancy Pelosi, AOC; they'd stop at nothing.

You: I believe there are people with and without integrity in any group, including Democrats and Republicans, and there's no way for me to know what's motivating any particular politician. If I were a cynical Democratic politician who didn't truly care about immigrants but just wanted their votes, I don't think open borders would be a winning strategy. If they let in a lot more immigrants now, those immigrants won't get to vote until they become citizens, which takes at least five years. In the meantime, there would likely be a backlash that costs Democrats votes in 2020, so they would lose more than they would gain—and could lose the 2020 election. My opinion about immigration is based on wanting to create an immigration program that's workable; it's not about trying to predict who immigrants will vote for, if and when they become citizens.

Alan: Fair enough. But at the end of the day, are you for open borders or not?

You: I'd like to think about that some more. Would you be willing to talk about it another time?

Alan: Sure.

You: It means a lot to me to be able to talk about these issues and at least hear each other.

To see a sample dialogue and position statements concerning other facets of immigration, including open borders, nativism, crime, and terrorism, visit the book's website.

Troubleshooting

When you're talking politics with someone you don't know well, it's helpful to break the ice before diving in. Canvassers often begin by inquiring what's top of mind for the person they're interviewing, drawing out their story as much as possible. Listening to and validating someone's concerns can create a rapport that helps both of you ease into areas of disagreement.

When you hit an impasse, asking curiosity questions can help you find common ground. Let's say you're talking to someone who adamantly believes that immigrants are responsible for the economic problems afflicting his town. You can ask, "Other than cracking down on illegal immigration, are there other things you'd like to see done that would help your town get back on its feet?"

At times, you may find yourself on what Ellison calls "shifting sands," which are a series of questions that, intentionally or unintentionally, hijacks the conversation by shifting focus or context, like when Alan suddenly accused Democrats of wanting open borders to increase their base. A gay-marriage opponent once asked me, "You're okay with gay marriage—well then, what if I'm okay with incest? What if I'm okay with pedophilia? How about bestiality?" He was trying to suggest that gay marriage would put society on a slippery slope to harmful, taboo sex acts, so I asked him what made him think one would lead to the other.

But attempting to answer an onslaught of such questions can derail your focus on your position, and leave you confused as you slip and slide on the shifting sands. It can also make you so frustrated and irritated that your curiosity shatters into shards of anger, and you become too furious, confounded, or helpless to continue talking.

If you feel the sands shifting, you can set a boundary that makes clear what you are and are not willing to discuss. I could have said, "I don't want to switch from the topic of gay marriage to incest because I don't see any connection between the two. If you're interested in talking about gay marriage without bringing in issues like incest, then I'd like to do it. If you aren't willing to do that, then I don't want to continue the conversation." If he tried to convince me, I could hold my boundary: "I've made my decision and won't discuss it further."

Another rhetorical hazard is "whataboutism"—deflecting attention from the issue at hand or accusing the other person of hypocrisy. Whataboutism was at play when Trump downplayed white-nationalist violence by pointing at Antifa; when climate deniers attacked Al Gore's carbon-intensive lifestyle to discredit climate science; and when Fox News hosts asked Bernie Sanders why he wasn't voluntarily paying more in taxes if he was so eager to tax millionaires.[6] I frequently encountered whataboutism on my online neighborhood forum, where people suggested that if I wasn't willing to invite homeless people to sleep on my couch, then I had no right to advocate for the city's humane treatment of them.

Sometimes, the additional topic *is* relevant. If you think it might be but you're not sure, you can ask the person how the new topic relates to the original one. Then, you can evaluate the person's answers and proceed accordingly. If someone points out a possible contradiction in your position, consider whether the contradiction actually might call your position into question or whether it's a manipulative tactic. If it's the latter, you can call that out. Sanders, for example, could have said, "Are you saying that, because I don't pay more taxes than I'm required to under the current law, my proposal for a higher top tax rate lacks merit?"

Avoid using "whatabouts" to discount the other person's concerns. For example, if someone is outraged about effigies of a decapitated Trump, don't rush in and say, "Yeah, but what about the effigies of Obama being lynched—that's even worse!" Instead, you could say something like, "Even though I have huge issues with Trump, I don't believe in dehumanizing or encouraging violence against anyone, and I agree with you that it's a problem. I remember when people were hanging effigies of Obama; I was horrified and scared for him, especially with the history of lynching in this country." By framing the issue of hypocrisy in relation to your thought process, you allow them to compare and contrast their reactions without accusing them of a double standard.

Another common problem is when someone says a whole bunch of things without coming up for air—how do you keep track of everything they said and respond to it all? In short, you don't. Instead, you can pick one point and respond.

In general, if someone is talking to you in a way that makes you feel defensive (telltale signs: steam comes out of your ears or your brain freezes up), name it. You can say, "You know, I'm realizing that the way you're talking (very quickly/shouting/sounding annoyed) is making it hard for me to stay in the conversation. If you can talk to me more slowly/calmly/respectfully, I think we could have a good conversation. If you can't, then I don't think I'm going to be able to stay with it." If you find yourself getting defensive, you can always own it by saying, "I'm sorry, I can feel myself reacting defensively. Can I have a do-over?"

Logical missteps such as the ones discussed above often arise innocently, just like any cognitive error. We can tease them out and get past them without accusing the other person of nefarious intentions.

As your conversation wraps up, it's likely to end on a note of ambiguity. Don't expect them to say, "OMG, I see now that Trump is a dangerous, fraudulent superpredator whose clownish shenanigans create a smokescreen behind which white supremacists and oligarchs are consolidating their control of government even as they demolish it, and no way in hell will I vote for him again." You've given them something to think about, and that's sufficient. Don't ruin it by laying a "gotcha" statement on them. Instead, thank them for talking with you, even if you didn't like what they had to say.

If the other person reiterates their position without adding anything new, rather than repeating yourself and getting caught in a back-and-forth argument, you can say, "I've said everything I have to say, and I don't want to try to convince you to agree with me. It's a hard topic to talk about, and it means a lot to me that we were able to listen to each other's perspectives."

If it feels like the conversation is ending on a sour note, you could say something lighthearted such as, "Wow, we sure figured that one out, eh?" Or you could acknowledge the tension and say, "I don't want to have this conversation end with bad feelings between us." Many people "agree to disagree," but this phrase can convey passive-aggressive bitterness.

Boundaries Against Bigotry

What if you're interacting with an overt bigot? If the person is a stranger and is acting aggressively, your safety is paramount and you should disengage. If you're witnessing someone harassing or threatening someone else, there are organizations, like Holla-back!, that offer bystander intervention training.

If it's someone you know and feel safe with, you can ask questions about the basis for their animosity and then make a position statement. Tell them what it feels like to hear people express hatred or bias toward you (or people you know/love); how it affects your life; and why it's difficult/impossible for you to be around people who demean others. You can leave it there. There's no debate: You've spoken your truth, and the other person will either be impacted by it or they won't. If they persist in making offensive comments, you can tell them it's too hurtful to continue talking or simply walk away.

Responding to Classism

If you're a blue-state liberal, you'll inevitably come across people who use classist slurs like "redneck" and "white trash." You can ask them, "What does it mean to you when you say someone is a redneck?" They may say something like, "Oh, you know, all those ignorant racists with their guns and pickups who voted for Trump." Then you can say, "I thought that was what you meant, but I wasn't sure. You know, I used to call people rednecks. I lumped them all together and had a lot of negative assumptions. And then I started realizing that the word "redneck" refers to farmers or other people who work outdoors and get sunburned. So now I'm trying to catch myself making assumptions about what people are like or what they believe based on their education or where they live or what kind of work they do. I don't want to blame Trump's presidency on working-class voters, especially since it was mostly middle-class and wealthy people who voted for him."

If someone gives voice to "culture of poverty" classist (and often racist) stereotypes, you can ask them what they're basing their impressions on and then make reference to studies or stories that debunk these myths.[7]

Does PNDC Work?

As you've seen throughout this book, there have been many instances of non-adversarial communication leading to profound shifts—hate-group activists who left the movement; the Miami man who gratefully acknowledged the teachings of the transgender canvasser who knocked on his door; the Wisconsin Trump voter who decided not to vote Republican after hearing the fears of a Jewish woman.

But often, what "works" isn't such an obvious, instant transformation. PNDC's objective is defusion, *not* persuasion. It can bring people out of their defensive crouch in the corner, the place where they have been digging in their heels and getting more deeply entrenched in their mindset. Inviting the other person to converse freely, without fear of verbal retribution, makes a shift *possible*. It might not be immediate (and it might not happen at all), but it creates an opening that adversarial-style communication typically forecloses.

If someone can take in the information or perspective you've shared with them, they may file it away for future reference. You may never know how your words have affected them and, if you're participating in an online discussion, you may never know how many silent observers are impacted by your refreshingly nondefensive communication.

I've had the experience of someone seeking out my opinion after previously engaging with them respectfully on an unrelated topic. A rural Californian who attended one of Ellison's workshops told me that she, too, has cultivated ongoing relationships with conservatives who actively seek out her views and, in some instances, seem to have softened their stance or learned that they were relying on disreputable sources of information. It's a start, a softening, an opening.

As an activist, what do I want? Results! When do I want them? Now! Talking across the divide is a kind of "slow politics" with an unfamiliar, amorphous quality. It's an exercise in humility and uncertainty as to whether that seed will take root, and an act of faith that it just might.

Developing skill in PNDC takes practice, but you can reap huge benefits right away simply by shedding your sense of superiority and by cultivating humility. You might not become a PNDC Jedi master who can pose a question that prompts someone to profoundly shift their perspective (then again, you just might). But the act of engaging authentically, openly, and nonjudgmentally, with the goal of learning from a fellow human rather than schooling a deplorable, can dramatically change the quality of the interaction.

More Help

You may find it helpful to start practicing PNDC by shifting just one of your habitual patterns for a week or two and then moving on to another. For example, for the first week, you could focus on keeping a relaxed, receptive facial expression instead of shaking your head and frowning. During week two, you could practice making your voice come down at the end of a question. At some point, you could try abstaining from sarcasm, condescension, and convincing.

Some people find writing easier than face-to-face conversations. Believe it or not, social media is a good training ground for PNDC: You can take your time to craft thoughtful responses. Remember what the latent liberal *Cracked* magazine writer from chapter one said about all of the quiet social media lurkers influenced by what others post. Give it a try, but be careful not to let yourself get baited by trolls, some of whom might even be bots.

The Bridge Alliance is a network of groups like Better Angels and Living Room Conversations that can connect you with conservatives interested in engaging in civil discourse. A SMART Politics Facebook community provides a place for people who are trying to practice "radical civility" (which has some elements in common with PNDC) in their social media interactions. If you live in a liberal bubble and want to know what conservatives are thinking without having to watch Fox News, subscribe to the "Red for the Blue" newsletter (redfortheblue.com) or *The Flip Side* (theflipside.io/).

It's also fun to listen to Dylan Marron's podcast, *Conversations with People Who Hate Me* (dylanmarron.com/podcast/), in which he has phone conversations with people who post racist, homophobic comments in response to his educational social justice videos. "Most people soften when they feel listened to," says Marron. "And they'll even listen to you in return."[8]

Marron's ability to extend the olive branch of empathy and gentle humor to verbally abusive individuals is remarkably brave and wonderful. In a TED Talk, Marron says,

> Before I started this project, I thought that the real way to bring about change was to shut down opposing viewpoints through epically worded video essays and comments and posts, but I soon learned those were only cheered on by the people who already agreed with me...Sometimes, the most subversive thing you could do was to actually speak with the people you disagreed with, and not simply at them.[9]

To hone your skills, I highly recommend participating in a PNDC webinar or workshop, which will give you many additional tools and insights for fostering better communication. And get your hands on Ellison's CDs or her book, *Taking the War Out of Our Words*, which provides a comprehensive overview of PNDC and numerous real-life stories of PNDC miracles. Lastly, check out this book's website, where you'll find video demonstrations and sample questions, position statements, and dialogues concerning many hot-button topics, and can sign up to get notifications for PNDC trainings.

Conclusion:
To Bridge or to Break

Building a movement is ultimately about just that—
restoring humanity to all of us,
even those of us who have been inhumane.

—Alicia Garza, cofounder of the Black Lives Matter movement[1]

It is surely a reflection of how tattered the fabric of civic virtue has become that I'm compelled to end this book with an answer to a question that I've asked myself repeatedly during the past few years: Why bother talking to the other side?

Democracy cannot function well without public deliberation across lines of difference. Public deliberation requires an informed public and a public who has trust in institutions and one another. Absent either of these elements, people are ruled by whoever is best at invoking tribal loyalty, and manipulating their predispositions, fears, and cognitive errors.

Right-wing media disinformation and the corporate-friendly nature of mainstream media leave the public oversaturated yet ill-informed, a state of affairs unlikely to change anytime soon. We can't control people's news sources, but we *can* talk to them. Yet fewer than one in four of us can name a single person with oppositional views in our social network.[2]

Most Americans are conflict-avoidant, and they steer clear of politics for fear of getting embroiled in something that's likely to turn ugly.[3] They are the "Exhausted Majority" who believe it's important to listen to the other side but are so disgusted by partisan rancor that they've disengaged from politics. And they represent 67 percent of the country.[4]

The Exhausted Majority's apathy is frustrating, but their open-mindedness is laudable. Open-mindedness is underrated. In an atmosphere of extreme tribalism, we tend to criticize open-minded people as cavorting with the enemy.

There are a handful of issues, such as white supremacy, which we're necessarily and utterly closed-minded about—if someone starts telling me that Africans enjoyed being enslaved, I'm not about to mull that over. But what can quickly happen is that the concept of white supremacy expands and becomes so all-encompassing that we feel we cannot be open-minded about affirmative action or reparations—that even considering a more-conservative position is to perpetuate white supremacy and, therefore, forbidden.

It's up to every individual to circumscribe the boundaries of what they will and will not openly consider—the point is to draw your boundary consciously, based on *your* needs, not your tribe's. It's not an easy call. As a climate activist, I can't be open-minded to the notion that climate change is a hoax. But can I be open-minded about whether fracked natural gas should be used as a bridge fuel? Even though I'm adamantly against it, I'm capable of having that conversation. Opening up your belief system to reconsideration can be uncomfortable and vulnerable. Brené Brown calls it "braving the wilderness" in her book by that name, the wilderness being the place where you strike out on your own with humility.

If a person or group disagrees with you and their opposition is an obstacle to the kind of change you want to see in the world, it's vital that you understand their objections and address them, or decide that they're right and you're wrong. If you don't consider other's concerns but just reiterate your talking points, you're talking right past them. Political theorist Hannah Arendt wrote about the importance of cultivating an "enlarged mentality": "The more people's standpoints I have present in my mind while I am pondering a given issue, and the better I can imagine how I would feel and think if I were in their place, the stronger will be my capacity for representative thinking and the more valid my final conclusions, my opinion."[5]

At a cross-partisan workshop, I learned something important about conservative antipathy toward welfare programs. *They* viewed welfare as an *antipoverty* program. By that measure, it had failed: Most people on welfare are poor before, during, and after receiving aid. *I* saw welfare as a *survival* program designed, tragically, to do little more than keep people alive. I voiced to the group the different expectations we had for welfare programs and then articulated our common ground: None of us wanted people to be poor and rely on welfare in the first place. I also noted that we probably had different ideas about what causes poverty and how to tackle it. A lot of heads nodded. This is not something I would ever have thought to say had I been in an adversarial dialogue with them.

The dialogue made me reflect further on how framing government assistance programs as "lifting people out of poverty" not only sets these programs up to fail in the eyes of fiscal conservatives but also undermines real economic justice. I will defend the right of any person to keep their benefits, but if I act like welfare is the solution, rather than a wholly inadequate stopgap, then I won't advocate for better income equality and redistribution measures. By stress-testing my opinions, I refined my position, as Arendt suggested, and, possibly, laid the groundwork for a less polarized discussion of how to keep people from needing welfare.

The potential for productive dialogue is evident in a process developed by James Fishkin, director of the Center for Deliberative Democracy at Stanford University. Deliberative Polling is a highly structured process in which a representative sample of individuals comes together for a weekend to deliberate on a policy issue. Participants on both sides of the issue present competing analyses; the participants review materials and talk to the "experts" and each other at length.

Minds change during these weekends. During a Deliberative Poll gathering in Texas, the participants went from 52 percent to

84 percent in favor of paying a little more for renewable electricity, leading Texas to become a wind-power leader. During a national Deliberative Poll gathering of voters, support for increased federal education spending went up 14 points, while support for the flat-rate tax cratered.[6]

At the 2019 Better Angels Convention, New York Black Lives Matter leader Hawk Newsome shared the stage with Cincinnati Tea Party leader Ray Warrick. Newsome delivered a civil and cogent message to Warrick and the mostly white audience: *Black people are dying, and most whites are acting as though they don't care.* Newsome was passionate and angry but also gracious and respectful, and he was heard. Following the dialogue, a white woman from Arkansas stood up and apologized for her prior use of "All Lives Matter" which, after hearing from Newsome, she understood was wrong.[7]

In my own experience at cross-partisan workshops, I haven't observed any apparent shifts in opinion, but I have shifted out of my tendency to caricature Republicans. Most are more nuanced, thoughtful, open-minded, well-informed, and kind than I had presumed. If by some miracle, they feel the same way about me, then our tribal animosity is neutralized. I have some reason to believe that such miracles can and do happen. At one workshop, several of the conservatives said that they recognized in the liberal participants' defense of social welfare programs a degree of authentic caring that they weren't previously aware of. We aren't, as one said he'd suspected, partisans ginning up votes from the downtrodden; we genuinely care about people's well being. They *saw* us, and that felt validating.

Outside the occasional cross-partisan workshop, most Americans live in either liberal or conservative bubbles. Increasingly, these partisan bubbles have become intensely tribal and defensive, with both sides perceiving the other to be significantly more extreme in their views than they are. (The more news one consumes, the more inaccurate one's perceptions.)[8]

Political scientist Lilliana Mason, an expert in partisan polarization, believes that extreme polarization was the ideal landscape for someone with Trump's talent for divisiveness.[9] He riles white Christians experiencing low self-esteem by telling them how unfair it is that their tribe's numerical and cultural dominance is slipping. The only solution is to empower him, as leader of the tribe, to lash back at the other tribe. Trump's frequent references to "winners" and "losers" cue anyone who feels like a "loser" to join the "winning" team. Remember the experiment in which people chose a smaller payout for themselves—so long as it meant an even smaller payout for the "others?" Vengeance against the "other" *trumps* rational self-interest.

Trump's victory is what political scientists call "negative polarization" at its most extreme.[10] Think of all the Republicans who admitted they didn't like Trump, but boy did they *hate* Clinton. This wasn't solely misogyny—they saw her as the emblem of everything that was wrong with the Democratic Party, their sworn enemy, who under no circumstances could be allowed to win.

Negative tribal polarization helped Trump and, if that's not bad enough, has also mired us in gridlock, weakening people's faith in democracy, inspiring apathy, and lending credence to the Republican insistence that government doesn't work. Very bad.

An Israel–Palestine experiment demonstrates what happens when tribal loyalty overrides open-minded consideration. Social psychologists presented a group of Israelis with an Israeli-authored peace plan. Half of the test group was told that Iraelis had developed the plan; the other half was told Palestinians had developed it. Guess which half liked the plan and which half hated it?[11]

Here at home, Republicans have relentlessly pilloried Obamacare, a program actually modeled after a proposal by the conservative Heritage Foundation.[12] Had Bush, not Obama, championed the program, conservatives would likely have supported it. In another example of partisanship taking precedence over beliefs, only a slim majority of Republicans supported a background-check law in 2013, when Democrats controlled Congress and the White House, even though 81 percent of

Republicans favored background checks.[13] Again and again, political scientists have found that people increasingly take knee-jerk political stances based not on their substantive beliefs but on their perception of whether it's a Republican or Democratic proposal.[14] The result of incessant partisanship is stalemate across a range of critically important issues.

How liberals and conservatives define and seek to resolve problems appear to be worlds apart, but I believe that, just like with the Israelis, there is overlap that gets missed because of partisan polarization. In 2018, 65 percent of Florida voters supported a measure that restored the voting rights of 1.4 million Floridians with felony convictions. The measure garnered the support of unlikely allies, including the Christian Coalition of America and far-right business barons David and Charles Koch. Voting-rights activist Desmond Meade, who led the effort, credits the campaign's ability to eschew divisive labels of "left" and "right," and appeal to people's capacity for love and redemption. They didn't write anyone off, including people at Trump rallies who signed the petition to put the measure on the ballot.[15] Bridging, not breaking, won the day. Meade urges progressives to get out of their silos and talk to the other side, likening it to the necessity of talking to our kids about sex—if we don't, someone else will.

Political activist Ralph Nader identified 25 issues that could potentially unite liberals and (some) conservatives, including corporate crime, civil liberties, trade, and military spending.[16] I would add to Nader's list monopoly-busting, artificial intelligence, and infrastructure repairs, and social issues like mass incarceration, pornography, opioid over-prescription, and teen screen-addiction. Conservatives might not admit that human activities destabilize the climate, but they may agree on the need for flood-resilient infrastructure and drought-resistant agriculture— heck, even Trump is building seawalls to protect his golf courses. Republican Senator Ted Cruz and Democratic Representative Alexandria Ocasio-Cortez have flirted with joint legislation to make oral contraceptives available over-the-counter and to ban former members of Congress from lobbying.[17]

There are also glimmers of philosophical commonalities like shared skepticism of impersonal bureaucracies and one-size-fits-all solutions; heartsickness concerning cynicism, greed, and depravity; and yearning for the restoration of sacred purpose, community bonds and the social contract, the deterioration of which gives rise to conditions none of us like—substance abuse, loneliness, crime, corruption, greed, and the profusion of red tape and criminal penalties that play whack-a-mole with bad behavior.

In a political arena riven by wedge issues, Nader's suggestion that we turn our attention to potential bridge issues is apropos. At the same time, let's be real: Common ground is elusive and may not surface during even the most exemplary dialogue. But where there's no common ground, there's still common life. We're all on the same life raft and the better we get along and the more we recognize the core humanity of every person, the less inclined we'll be to try to elbow each other off.

Rehumanizing each other is no small thing. It may feel soft and inconsequential, but reducing the level of alienation and hostility is of unique and urgent importance. Thirteen percent of Americans ended a relationship with a family member or close friend over the 2016 election. Twenty percent of both Republicans and Democrats say that members of the other party are subhuman. Almost as many believe the country would be better off if large numbers of their adversaries died.[18] It's not, by and large, the most socially or economically vulnerable who feel this way, but the most educated, urban, white, and politically segregated.[19] This scary state of affairs cannot be blamed on Republicans alone; it's our bad, too. When we join the Right in reducing political discourse to a spectacle of self-righteous performative outrage, we contribute to the dangerous demise of civic literacy and engagement. And we stoke the kind of negative polarization that Trump thrives on.

Psychologists Kirk Schneider and Sayyed Mohsen Fatemi believe that polarized thinking "has caused more human torment and misery than virtually any other factor" and now constitutes "a major threat to humanity." Polarized thinking arises when people feel afraid and helpless, states of mind that have become rampant. The antidote they prescribe is "mindful, widespread dialogue," and they call for a massive—and urgent—public investment in civility infrastructure.[20]

Paula Green, an acclaimed intercommunal dialogue facilitator who has worked in conflict zones all over the world, believes that the United States is in grave danger of a civil war. She notes that, for many nonwhite and immigrant communities, the war has already begun.[21] With militias patrolling the border, gunmen shooting up mosques and black churches, "alt-right" hate-group activists and Antifas (or agent provocateurs) attacking each other, self-identified black nationalists shooting Dallas police, and a machete-wielding political foe hacking at Democratic college students in Kentucky, Green's concern appears to be spot-on.[22]

A lifelong activist, Green is well aware that dialogue alone won't change the world but is a key ingredient.

> Dialogue is a social change process...We know you can bring all these people into a room and have these wonderful Kumbaya moments and we can all be very tender with each other and very hopeful. So what? If you work only at the structural-change level and you don't bring the people along with you, the change won't hold. And if you work only with the people and not at the structural level, then the unjust structures continue. So there's always this balance.[23]

Dialogue isn't a panacea, but I believe that we're not going to get out of this mess and create enduring positive change unless we start talking to each other and depolarizing our tribes. Our elected officials aren't about to do it, so we must lead the way. There's no quick fix, just painstaking transformation over a time horizon of unknowable length. Best get started.

As we go about our social and environmental justice and anti-war advocacy; as we try to shore up democratic institutions and labor unions, restore voting rights, and get money out of politics;

as we campaign for progressive candidates at every level of government or build a progressive third party, we will obviously be more successful if we have strong public support. To garner such support, we must not only energize but also *enlarge* the choir, and we can't invite newcomers to the choir if we're refusing to talk to them or if we approach them with contempt. No one has ever been browbeaten into changing their stupid little minds. Never. If it's an issue we're fired up about, we can express that anger and passion, but if we're amped up to level ten outrage every time we open our mouths, we'll be tuned out.

In addition to wanting strong support, we want tepid opposition. We will always face opponents, but if our contempt riles up their hostility, we will face steeper odds of achieving our goals and defending them against a backlash. If we show people respect and empathy, and we meet them where they're at (not where we wish they were at), they might still disagree, but perhaps not as fervently. Likewise, when moderates observe us sneering condescendingly at Trump and his supporters, this may trigger feelings of protection toward the objects of our scorn and feelings of disgust toward us. When our counter-attacks turn the bully (Trump) into a victim, we pay dearly at the ballot box. Trump, well aware of this dynamic, trolls the Left every chance he gets.

I don't want to get too Machiavellian—respect and empathy are virtues in and of themselves, pillars of democracy and morality, not weapons of manipulation. To the extent that they disarm the opposition, that's a side effect. Parker Palmer, founder of the Center for Courage & Renewal, writes, "It is in the common good to hold our political differences and the conflicts they create in a way that does not unravel the civic community on which democracy depends."[24] To give up on the possibility of productive discourse, to abandon or pollute civic culture, is to surrender to the riptide of fascism and nihilism that tug at the body politic. When the people drop out, the tyrants take over.

The polarization that afflicts our politics is, according to political scientists Jacob Hacker and Paul Pierson, "asymmetric." Politics are skewed strongly toward the right with policies far

removed from majority public opinion.[25] Take it from David
Frum, George W. Bush's speechwriter, who says the right has
embraced "a reactionary radicalism unlike anything seen in
American party politics in modern times."[26] Needless to say, the
rightward tilt has gathered momentum under Trump. We can't
immediately eradicate many of the causes of asymmetric polarization Hacker and Pierson identify, but we can avoid behaving
in a manner that drives swing voters into disgusted apathy or a
reactionary embrace of Trump. We can stop rigidifying the "us
versus them" mindset and start acting like we understand we're
all in this together.

Even within the Left, the internecine squabbling sometimes
feels like a *Mean Girls* sequel. A friend of mine's 17-year-old
daughter was canvassing for a Democratic candidate for state
assembly and was repeatedly berated—*and spat upon*—by volunteers for the opposing Democratic candidate. With all the contempt we heap on conservatives, it's a wonder we have any left to
spare for one another.

Frances Lee, a Chinese-American trans activist who was
named one of the most influential intersectional activists on the
2017 Bitch 50 list, braved the wilderness with an essay challenging
the Left's increasingly unkind and intellectually elitist "call-out
culture." In Lee's view, the "quest for purity" has been taken to
a counterproductive extreme in which self-righteous comrades
abuse and humiliate each other: "[A]fter witnessing countless
people be[ing] ruthlessly torn apart in community for their mistakes and missteps, I started to fear my own comrades."[27]

Lee's article prompted a torrent of reader comments affirming Lee's observations and sharing painful feelings of humiliation, betrayal, and anger toward those who seem more invested
in thought-policing than in movement-building. A queer student
activist published a very similar piece in *The McGill Daily*, cred-
iting the dedication and good intentions of her fellow activists,
but denouncing their dogmatism, self-righteousness, and cul-
tish certainty that they're right about everything, and "others"
are deluded.[28]

What's become of us? Is someone who volunteers for the "wrong" candidate or isn't versed in the latest lexicon of oppression wicked? Does having empathy for Trump voters make us evil? Have we come to define our self-worth as a function of the intensity of our disdain?

Our communication style is contagious. When we tear each other down, people notice. Our friends and family notice. Our resistance movement comrades notice. Silent lurkers on social media notice. The effects spread out across the world. This contagiousness is one way, maybe the principal way, in which culture changes, for better or worse. We have the power to make our culture more or less kind and humane.

Getting past the Trump era and rebuilding requires modeling the opposite of everything this regime stands for, beginning with dehumanization. We will never out-hate the haters or out-divide the dividers any more than we can outgun them. We will not win by becoming what we are resisting.

Author-activist Sally Kohn says, "I want everyone to hate less. And I think progressives should lead the way because somebody has to go first."[29] Me too. I want people to act less like the woman who heckled the autistic Patriot Prayer man who couldn't rip the sign and more like Virginia, the trans activist who let compassion be their guide; more like the voting rights activists who drummed up support at Trump rallies in Florida; more like the graduate student who taught me about red-baiting and homophobia without shaming me. I want less talk of "stupid white men" and more talk of unaccountable corporations; less about how stupid and ignorant Fox News viewers are and more about creating new media models; less about how reactionary they are and more about what working people of all races and nationalities have in common. I want progressives to be able to tell voters why they're voting for whomever they're voting for in 2020 without telling them that they'd be fools to vote for Trump.

Our national emergency is far from over, and moving beyond contempt can liberate our better angels to speak from the heart, repair what's broken, and rekindle the spirit of democracy.

Notes

Introduction

1. *The Daily Show with Jon Stewart*, "Modern Romance: An Investigation," 2-655, directed by Chuck O'Neil, written by Elliott Kalan, Comedy Central, June 16, 2015, cc.com/video-clips/gyhfub/the-daily -show-with-jon-stewart-democalypse-2016---white-house-don.

2. Tim Parks, "The Limits of Satire," *The New York Review of Books*, January 16, 2015, nybooks.com/daily/2015/01/16/charlie-hebdo-limits -satire/.

3. Jodie Shokraifard, "The Conversation," *The Atlantic*, March 2019, theatlantic.com/magazine/archive/2019/03/the-conversation/580423/.

4. Edward Wasserman, "Why News Media Must Embrace Online Rules," Markkula Center for Applied Ethics at Santa Clara University, September 22, 2015, scu.edu/ethics/focus-areas/journalism-ethics /resources/why-news-media-must-embrace-online-rules/.

5. For a discussion of the lucrative business model of media "outrage outlets," see Jeffrey M. Berry and Sarah Sobieraj, *The Outrage Industry: Political Opinion Media and the New Incivility* (Oxford: Oxford University Press, 2016).

6. Evan Halper, Matt Pearce, and Michael A. Memoli, "Sanders' Supporters Are Lashing Out, But Here's How They Might Be Hurting His Campaign," *Los Angeles Times*, April 15, 2016, latimes.com/nation /politics/la-na-bernie-sanders-supporters-20160415-story.html; Rick Hampson, "Hillary Clinton, No Fan of 'Bernie Bros,' Could Use Their Energy vs. Trump," *USA Today*, May 13, 2016, usatoday.com /story/news/politics/elections/2016/05/12/hillary-clinton-bernie -sanders-social-media-supporters/84284322/.

7. Andy Borowitz, "Many in Nation Tired of Explaining Things to Idiots," *The New Yorker*, October 3, 2017, newyorker.com/humor /borowitz-report/many-in-nation-tired-of-explaining-things-to -idiots.

8. Evelin Lindner, *Making Enemies: Humiliation and International Conflict* (Westport, CT: Praeger Security International, 2006), xiii–xvi.

9. Lindner, *Making Enemies*, xvi.

10. Allyson Chiu, "'Queen of Condescending Applause': Nancy Pelosi Clapped at Trump, and the Internet Lost It," *The Washington Post*, February 6, 2019, washingtonpost.com/nation/2019/02/06/queen -condescending-applause-nancy-pelosi-clapped-trump-internet-lost -it/?utm_term=.a06eea9013b1&wpisrc=nl_most&wpmm=1.

11. Manu Raju and Caroline Kelly, "Pelosi Questions Trump's Manhood," CNN, December 12, 2018, cnn.com/2018/12/11/politics/pelosi -aide-trump-meeting-own-shutdown-wall-manhood/index.html.

12. "#LoveArmy Guiding Principles," Dream Corps Unlimited, accessed March 20, 2019, lovearmy.org/principles.

13. Martin Luther King, Jr., "Address at the Thirty-Sixth Annual Dinner of the War Resisters League," February 02, 1959, The Martin Luther King, Jr. Research and Education Institute, Stanford University, kinginstitute.stanford.edu/king-papers/documents/address-thirty -sixth-annual-dinner-war-resisters-league.

14. Ben McBride, "The Urgency of Bridging," Lecture, at the *Othering & Belonging Conference*, from the Haas Institute for a Fair and Inclusive Society at UC–Berkeley, Oakland, CA, April 10, 2019.

15. Alicia Garza, Opening ceremony keynote address, at the *19th Annual Allied Media Conference*, Detroit, MI, June 16, 2017, alliedmedia .org/news/2017/09/05/alicia-garza-speaks-building-power-amc2017 -opening-ceremony.

16. Dream Corps Unlimited, "Is Unity What We Need?" #LoveArmy, lovearmy.org/is_unity_what_we_need.

17. Mark Kingwell, *A Civil Tongue* (University Park, Pennsylvania: The Pennsylvania State University Press, 1995), 247–48.

18. Charles Duhigg, "The Real Roots of American Rage," *The Atlantic*, December 18, 2018, theatlantic.com/magazine/archive/2019/01 /charles-duhigg-american-anger/576424/.

19. "The King Philosophy," The King Center, accessed March 10, 2019, thekingcenter.org/king-philosophy#sub4.

20. Philip Rucker, "Bush Funeral: Trump Sits with Fellow Presidents but Still Stands Alone," *The Washington Post*, December 5, 2018, washingtonpost.com/politics/bush-funeral-trump-sits-with-fellow -presidents-but-still-stands-alone/2018/12/05/fdc6663a-f8a3-11e8 -8d64-4e79db33382f_story.html?utm_term=.e67fe136c7f1&wpisrc =nl_most&wpmm=1.

21. Stephen Hawkins, Daniel Yudkin, Miriam Juan-Torres, and Tim Dixon, *Hidden Tribes: A Study of America's Polarized Landscape*,

(New York, NY: More in Common, October 2018), 113–16, hidden tribes.us/pdf/hidden_tribes_report.pdf.

22. Leo Gerard, "The Rich Want to Take Away Your Right to Vote," *Our Future* (blog), September 26, 2018, ourfuture.org/20180926/stealth -coup-by-the-rich; Annalyn Censky, "Why the Rich Vote More," *CNN Business*, September 24, 2012, money.cnn.com/2012/09/24/news /economy/rich-vote-more/index.html.

23. Art Cullen, "Hope From The Heartland: Interview with Art Cullen," by Ralph Nader, *Ralph Nader Radio Hour*, podcast, 59:27, December 1, 2018, ralphnaderradiohour.com/hope-from-the-heartland -robot-lawyer/.

24. David Eggers, "None of the Old Rules Apply," in *What We Do Now: Standing Up for Your Values in Trump's America*, eds. Valerie Merians and Dennis Johnson (New York: Melville House, 2016), 202.

25. Lee Drutman, "Political Divisions in 2016 and Beyond," Democracy Fund Voter Study Group, June 2017, voterstudygroup.org /publications/2016-elections/political-divisions-in-2016-and-beyond.

26. Yair Ghitza, "Revisiting What Happened in the 2018 Election," *Medium*, May 21, 2019, medium.com/@yghitza_48326/revisiting -what-happened-in-the-2018-election-c532feb51c0.

27. Michael Scherer, "White Identity Politics Drives Trump, and the Republican Party Under Him," *The Washington Post*, July 16, 2019, washingtonpost.com/politics/white-identity-politics-drives-trump -and-the-republican-party-under-him/2019/07/16/a5ff5710-a733-11e9 -a3a6-ab670962db05_story.html?utm_term=.1fa21933250d.

28. Working America, "100 Days into the Trump Era, Working-Class 'Searchers' Who Voted for Him Are Having Doubts, Open to Appeals," *Working America, AFL-CIO*, April 2017, workingamerica.org/100days; Working America, "Disaffected and Down on Their Economic Prospects, Swing Voters Are Up for Grabs in Eastern Iowa," *Working America, AFL-CIO*, May 2018, workingamerica.org/IowaSwingVoters.

29. Kaitlyn Harrold, interview by author, May 1, 2018.

30. Satyen Bordoloi, "Surviving Trump: Tips from the World's Largest Democracy to the Oldest," in *Rules for Resistance: Advice from Around the Globe for the Age of Trump*, eds. Melanie Wachtell Stinnett and David Cole (New York: The New Press, 2017).

31. Rod Dreher, "'Rednecks' And The Two Randys," *The American Conservative*, July 16, 2019, theamericanconservative.com/dreher/red necks-randy-rainbow-randy-newman-donald-trump-ilhan-omar/. Dreher is riffing off a line in the 1974 Randy Newman song, "Rednecks," about a white Southern racist who calls out Northern white liberal condescension and hypocrisy.

32. Margaret Sullivan, "Journalism in the Age of Trump," in *Rules for Resistance: Advice from Around the Globe for the Age of Trump*, eds. Melanie Wachtell Stinnett and David Cole (New York: The New Press, 2017), 159.

Chapter 1: Contempt and Its Discontents

1. "Research FAQ," *The Gottman Institute*, accessed January 15, 2018, gottman.com/about/research/faq/.
2. Nate Gowdy, "Man Gets Schooled By Anti-Fascism Sign," YouTube video, 1:41, May 1, 2018, youtu.be/Ylfto5YnOww.
3. David Neiwert, "Seattle 'Patriot Prayer' Rally Takes a Twist As Leader Gibson Denounces Supremacists," *Hatewatch*, Southern Poverty Law Center, August 15, 2017, splcenter.org/hatewatch/2017/08/15 /seattle-patriot-prayer-rally-takes-twist-leader-gibson-denounces -supremacists.
4. Refuse Fascism is an offshoot of the sectarian Revolutionary Communist Party (RCP) which, as late as the 1980s, denounced homosexuality as a symptom of "capitalist degeneracy." Now that it sports rainbow pride signage, the RCP attacks the alt-right's homophobia with self-righteous amnesia. Reddebrek, "The RCP's Current Solution to the Gay Question," *Libcom.org* blog, August 21, 2016, libcom .org/blog/rcps-current-solution-gay-question-21082016.
5. Clarence Page, "Page: Incels, the New Hate Movement," *Evansville Courier & Press*, May 6, 2018, courierpress.com/story/opinion /2018/05/06/page-incels-new-hate-movement/584555002/.
6. Christian Picciolini, "Uniting Against Hate: A Conversation with Christian Picciolini," Lecture, Berkeley City College, Berkeley, CA, June 15, 2018.
7. Agneta Fischer and Roger Giner-Sorolla, "Contempt: Derogating Others While Keeping Calm," *Emotion Review* 8, no. 4 (2016): 346–57, doi:10.1177/1754073915610439; Joe Navarro, "Body Language vs. Micro-Expressions," *Psychology Today* blog, December 24, 2011, psychologytoday.com/us/blog/spycatcher/201112/body-language-vs -micro-expressions.
8. David Matsumoto, "Contempt," in *International Encyclopedia of the Social Sciences, 2nd ed.*, ed. Williams A.Darity, Jr. (New York: Macmillan Reference USA, 2008), 113.
9. Fischer and Giner-Sorolla, "Contempt," 346–57.
10. Fischer and Giner-Sorolla, "Contempt," 348.
11. Katie Reilly, "Hillary Clinton Transcript: 'Basket of Deplorables' Comment," *Time*, September 10, 2016, time.com/4486502/hillary -clinton-basket-of-deplorables-transcript/.

12. Paul Street, "Deplorables II: The Dismal Dems in Stormy Times," *CounterPunch*, March 23, 2018, counterpunch.org/2018/03/23 /deplorables-ii-the-dismal-dems-in-stormy-times/.

13. Dan Balz, "Midwestern Voters Gave Trump a Chance. Now, They Hold the Key to His Political Future," *The Washington Post*, May 10, 2018, washingtonpost.com/graphics/2018/national/trump-voters /?utm_term=.0e213541ca5e&wpisrc=nl_most&wpmm=1.

14. Susan T. Fiske, *Envy Up, Scorn Down: How Status Divides Us* (New York: Russell Sage Foundation, 2011), 35.

15. Salena Zito, "Why Liberal Elites Are So Resentful of Middle America," *New York Post*, January 23, 2017, nypost.com/2017/01/11 /why-liberal-elites-are-so-resentful-of-middle-america/.

16. Alyson Shontell, "Bill Maher: 'What the F— Does It Take' for GOP Die-Hards to Be 'Human Beings' and Not Vote for Trump?" *Business Insider*, October 19, 2016, businessinsider.com/bill-maher-video -trump-support-2016-10.

17. Sarah Smarsh, "Dangerous Idiots: How the Liberal Media Elite Failed Working-Class Americans," *The Guardian*, October 13, 2016, theguardian.com/media/2016/oct/13/liberal-media-bias-working -class-americans.

18. Laura Ingraham, *Shut Up and Sing* (Washington, DC: Regnery Publishing, 2003), 79.

19. Cindy Boren, "Meryl Streep's Trump Speech Hit Right Notes for Many—Until She Dinged Football, MMA," *The Washington Post*, January 10, 2017, washingtonpost.com/news/early-lead/wp/2017/01/10 /meryl-streeps-trump-speech-hit-right-notes-for-many-until-she -dinged-football-mma/?utm_term=.dac9420036d8; Guardian News, "Robert De Niro's 'Fuck Trump' Speech at Tony Awards," YouTube video, 0:44, June 11, 2018, youtube.com/watch?v=1zNr8Pf1QkY.

20. Jason Newman, "Michael Moore to Trump Voters: 'You're Legal Terrorists,'" *Rolling Stone*, October 21, 2016, rollingstone.com/movies /features/michael-moore-to-trump-voters-youre-legal-terrorists -w446067.

21. Michael Moore, *Stupid White Men* (New York: Harper Collins, 2001), 148, 173.

22. Jon Snow, "Anderson Cooper's Magnificent Response To Trump Proving Why He Is 'Rac!st,'" YouTube video, 17:13, January 16, 2018, youtube.com/watch?v=VN6R268lvCo.

23. Luke O'Neil, "Mika Brzezinski Apologizes for Calling Mike Pompeo a 'Butt Boy,'" *The Guardian*, December 12, 2018, theguardian.com /media/2018/dec/12/mika-brzezinski-apology-mike-pompeo-butt -boy; Pete Kasperowicz, "Joe Scarborough: Americans Are 'Stupid'

for Believing There's a Border Crisis," *Washington Examiner*, January 8, 2019, washingtonexaminer.com/news/joe-scarborough -americans-are-stupid-for-believing-theres-a-border-crisis.

24. Jeffrey M. Berry and Sarah Sobieraj, *The Outrage Industry: Political Opinion Media and the New Incivility* (Oxford: Oxford University Press, 2016), 31, 61; Rich Lieberman, "'Lib Radio Host Mike Malloy Hopes Glenn Beck Commits Suicide on TV; Dumb and Dumber," City Brights: Rich Lieberman, *SFGate* blog, August 6, 2009, blog .sfgate.com/lieberman/2009/08/06/lib-radio-host-mike-malloy -hopes-glenn-beck-commits-suicide-on-tv-dumb-and-dumber/.

25. David Matsumoto, interview by author, May 20, 2018.

26. Berry and Sobieraj, *Outrage Industry*, 7.

27. Berry and Sobieraj, *Outrage Industry*, 37–40.

28. Rod Dreher, "Least Tolerant: Educated White Liberals," *The American Conservative*, March 4, 2019, theamericanconservative.com /dreher/educated-white-liberals-intolerance/.

29. Caitlin Flanagan, "How Late-Night Comedy Fueled the Rise of Trump," *The Atlantic*, May 2017, theatlantic.com/magazine /archive/2017/05/how-late-night-comedy-alienated-conservatives -made-liberals-smug-and-fueled-the-rise-of-trump/521472/.

30. Hoopologic, "John Oliver Once Begged Donald Trump to Run for President," YouTube video, 0:28, November 6, 2016, youtu.be/HlHo -F1z_aw.

31. Charles Duhigg, "The Real Roots of American Rage," *The Atlantic*, January/February 2019, theatlantic.com/magazine/archive/2019/01 /charles-duhigg-american-anger/576424/.

32. Ipsos Public Affairs, "Ipsos Poll Conducted for Reuters: Media Poll 2.28.2019," Ipsos, February 28, 2019, ipsos.com/sites/default/files/ct /news/documents/2019-02/2019_reuters_tracking_-_media_poll_2 _28_2019.pdf.

33. Bryce Covert, "In Defense of the Much-Maligned IRS," *The Nation*, April 8, 2019, thenation.com/article/internal-revenue-service-irs -budget-cuts/.

34. Charles M. Blow, "About the 'Basket of Deplorables'," *The New York Times*, September 12, 2016, nytimes.com/2016/09/12/opinion/about -the-basket-of-deplorables.html.

35. Paul Krugman, "How Many People Just Voted Themselves Out of Health Care? (Updated) (Updated Again) (And Again)," *The New York Times*, November 29, 2016, krugman.blogs.nytimes.com /2016/11/29/how-many-people-just-voted-themselves-out-of-health -care/?_r=0.

36. Daily Kos Staff, "Be Happy for Coal Miners Losing Their Health

Insurance. They're Getting Exactly What They Voted for," *Daily Kos*, December 12, 2016, dailykos.com/stories/2016/12/12/1610198/-Be-happy-for-coal-miners-losing-their-health-insurance-They-re-getting-exactly-what-they-voted-for.

37. "The Furor Over a Forum for Trump Fans," *The New York Times*, January 18, 2018, nytimes.com/2018/01/18/opinion/trump-voters.html.

38. Hamilton Nolan, "Can Donald Trump Ever Be Too Stupid For His Stupid Supporters?" *Gawker*, October 22, 2015, gawker.com/can-donald-trump-ever-be-too-stupid-for-his-stupid-supp-1738005727; Hamilton Nolan, "Dumb Hicks Are America's Greatest Threat," *Gawker*, November 19, 2015, gawker.com/dumb-hicks-are-americas-greatest-threat-1743373893.

39. David Masciotra, "Who Are These Idiot Donald Trump Supporters? Trump Loves the Poorly Educated—And They Love Him Right Back," *Salon*, March 21, 2016, salon.com/2016/03/20/who_are_these_idiot_donald_trump_supporters_trump_loves_the_poorly_educated_and_they_love_him_right_back/; David Masciotra, "We Must Shame Dumb Trump Fans: The White Working Class Are Not Victims," *Salon*, May 2, 2016, salon.com/2016/04/30/we_must_shame_dumb_trump_fans_the_white_working_class_are_not_victims/.

40. Timothy Egan, "We're With Stupid," *The New York Times*, November 17, 2017, nytimes.com/2017/11/17/opinion/were-with-stupid.html.

41. Jonathan Chait, "Why Republicans Love Dumb Presidents," *Intelligencer*, January 10, 2018, nymag.com/daily/intelligencer/2018/01/why-conservatives-love-dumb-presidents.html.

42. Steve Chapman, "Donald Trump's Biggest Flaw: He's Not That Bright," *Chicago Tribune*, November 7, 2017, chicagotribune.com/news/opinion/chapman/ct-perspec-chapman-donald-trump-dumb-20171103-story.html.

43. Paul Waldman, "Trump Wants a Big Parade (For Himself). It's a Surpassingly Dumb Idea," *The Washington Post*, February 7, 2018, washingtonpost.com/blogs/plum-line/wp/2018/02/07/trump-wants-a-big-parade-for-himself-its-a-surpassingly-dumb-idea/?utm_term=.6ef1233e563b.

44. Robert Reich, "Seriously, How Dumb Is Trump?" *HuffPost*, January 7, 2018, huffingtonpost.com/entry/seriously-how-dumb-is-trump_us_5a525a1ee4b003133ec8cb66.

45. Harry Caines, "Too Stupid to Know They're Stupid," *Cache Valley Daily*, September 21, 2017, cachevalleydaily.com/news/archive/2017/09/21/89c8abae-9e80-11e7-a0be-b3f2b107c235/#.XJQemShKjIU.

46. Chauncy DeVega, "Are American Voters Actually Just Stupid? A New Poll Suggests the Answer May Be 'Yes,'" *Salon*, April 26, 2017, salon .com/2017/04/26/are-american-voters-actually-this-stupid-a-new -poll-suggests-the-answer-may-be-yes/.

47. Eugene Robinson, "Trump Is Hoping You're Too Stupid to Notice," *The Washington Post*, April 2, 2018, washingtonpost.com/opinions /trump-is-hoping-youre-too-stupid-to-notice/2018/04/02/b20a6e9a -36a6-11e8-8fd2-49fe3c675a89_story.html?utm_term=.fdcc843ba500.

48. Jennifer Rubin, "How Republicans Got So Mean and Clueless," *The Washington Post*, August 13, 2018, washingtonpost.com/blogs /right-turn/wp/2018/08/13/how-republicans-got-so-mean-and-clue less/?noredirect=on&utm_term=.ea55a3021fb9.

49. John McWhorter, "Linguistic Expert: Trump Sounds Like Your Beer-Swilling Uncle," interview by Brian Williams, *The 11th Hour with Brian Williams*, MSNBC, September 7, 2017, video, 06:44, msnbc.com/brian-williams/watch/linguist-expert-trump-sounds -like-your-beer-swilling-uncle-1315606083641?v=railb&.

50. Joshua Corell, Steven J. Spencer, and Mark P. Zanna, "An Affirmed Self and an Open Mind: Self-Affirmation and Sensitivity to Argument Strength," *Journal of Experimental Social Psychology*, 40 (July 10, 2003): 350–56, pdfs.semanticscholar.org/cccc/85d618c07 d70a38aeab5ec700a1a6da07110.pdf; Corinne Bendersky, "Resolving Ideological Conflicts by Affirming Opponents' Status: The Tea Party, Obamacare and the 2013 Government Shutdown," *Journal of Experimental Social Psychology* 53, 163–168, dx.doi.org/10.1016/j.jesp .2014.03.011.

51. Brian Resnick, "A New Brain Study Sheds Light on Why It Can Be So Hard to Change Someone's Political Beliefs," *Vox*, January 23, 2017, vox.com/science-and-health/2016/12/28/14088992/brain -study-change-minds; Jonas Kaplan, Sarah Gimbel, and Sam Harris, "Neural correlates of maintaining one's political beliefs in the face of counterevidence," *Scientific Reports* 6, 39589 (2016), nature.com /articles/srep39589.

52. Karin Tamerius, "How to Have a Conversation With Your Angry Uncle Over the Holidays," *The New York Times*, November 19, 2018, nytimes.com/interactive/2018/11/18/opinion/thanksgiving-family -argue-chat-bot.html.

53. Fiske, *Envy Up*, 30–31.

54. Fiske, *Envy Up*, 143–50.

55. Shimul Melwani and Sigal Barsade, "Held in Contempt: The Psycho-

logical, Interpersonal, and Performance Consequences of Contempt in a Work Context," *Journal of Personality and Social Psychology,* 101 (3) (September 2011): 503–520. doi:10.1037/a0023492.

56. June Price Tangney, Jeff Stuewig, and Debra J. Mashek, "Moral Emotions and Moral Behavior," *Annual Review of Psychology* 58 (January 2007): 345–372, doi:10.1146/annurev.psych.56.091103.070145.

57. Diana C. Mutz, "Status Threat, Not Economic Hardship, Explains the 2016 Presidential Vote," *PNAS* 115 (19), May 8, 2018, pnas.org /content/115/19/E4330.full.

58. Nicholas Kristof, "In Trump Country, Shock at Trump Budget Cuts, but Still Loyalty," *The New York Times,* April 1, 2017, nytimes .com/2017/04/01/opinion/sunday/in-trump-country-shock-at-trump -budget-cuts-but-still-loyalty.html.

59. Nicholas Kristof, "My Most Unpopular Idea: Be Nice to Trump Voters," *The New York Times,* April 6, 2017, nytimes.com/2017/04/06 /opinion/my-most-unpopular-idea-be-nice-to-trump-voters.html.

60. Colby Itkowitz, "He Dramatically Changed His Views on Gay Marriage. Here's How He Says the Nation Can Come Together," *The Washington Post,* February 28, 2017, washingtonpost.com/news /inspired-life/wp/2017/02/28/he-dramatically-changed-his-views-on -gay-marriage-heres-how-he-says-the-nation-can-come-together /?utm_term=.64292ed29b8b.

61. Thomas Frank, *Rendezvous with Oblivion: Reports from a Sinking Society* (New York: Metropolitan Books, 2018), 200.

62. Rod Dreher, "He Doesn't Care If You Call Him Racist," *The American Conservative,* November 17, 2016, theamericanconservative.com /dreher/he-doesnt-care-if-you-call-him-racist/.

63. Rod Dreher, "Creating The White Tribe," *The American Conservative,* January 25, 2017, theamericanconservative.com/dreher/creating -the-white-tribe/comment-page-1/.

64. Sam Altman, "What I Heard From Trump Supporters," *Sam Altman* blog, February 21, 2017, blog.samaltman.com/what-i-heard-from -trump-supporters.

65. Berry and Sobieraj, *Outrage Industry,* 144–49.

66. Hawkins et al., *Hidden Tribes,* 12.

67. As I listened to the podcast of a facilitated conversation between Cindy and her liberal sister Diana, I was struck by Cindy's earnest desire to learn about white privilege, voter disenfranchisement, police brutality, and other topics she admitted being ignorant about because her news sources skewed right. Samia Mounts, "Cindy

& Diana—The Sister Show," in *Make America Relate Again*, produced by Better Angels Media, podcast, season 2, episode 6, 1:13:07,
makeamericarelatepodcast.com/s2ep6-transcript.

68. Arlie Russell Hochschild, *Strangers in Their Own Land: Anger and
Mourning on the American Right* (New York: New Press, 2016), 22–23.

69. Nancy Jo Sales, "'They Say We're White Supremacists': Inside the
Strange World of Conservative College Women," *Vanity Fair*, Holiday
2018, vanityfair.com/news/2018/11/conservative-college-women
-university-of-north-carolina-republicans.

70. Christina H., "I Was a Hardcore Conservative: What Changed My
Mind," Cracked.com, March 18, 2017, cracked.com/blog/what-helped
-convince-me-to-stop-being-hardcore-republican/.

71. Ingraham, *Shut Up*; Todd Starnes, *The Deplorables Guide to Making
America Great Again* (Lake Mary, FL: Frontline, 2017); Michelle
Malkin, *Unhinged: Exposing Liberals Gone Wild* (Washington, DC:
Regnery Publishing, 2005).

72. Wayne LaPierre, "Conservative Political Action Conference, Wayne
LaPierre Remarks," February 22, 2018, in C-SPAN video, 38:06,
c-span.org/video/?441475-3/conservative-political-action-conference
-rifle-lapierre-remarks.

73. "President Trump Ranted for 77 Minutes in Phoenix. Here's What
He Said," *Time*, August 23, 2017, time.com/4912055/donald-trump
-phoenix-arizona-transcript/.

74. Phillip Hagerman, "Confessions of a Trump Voter," *Los Angeles Review of Books*, March 1, 2017. lareviewofbooks.org/article/confessions
-of-a-trump-voter#!.

75. Fiske, *Envy Up*, 39, 148.

76. Macalester Bell, *Hard Feelings: The Moral Psychology of Contempt*
(New York: Oxford University Press, 2018), 46–48.

77. Amanda Marcotte, "Festival of Phony Outrage: No, Conservatives
Don't Actually Care about Late-Term Abortion," *Salon*, February 4,
2019, salon.com/2019/02/04/festival-of-phony-outrage-no-conserv
atives-dont-actually-care-about-late-term-abortion/.

78. Manyika Review, "Democrat Kathy Tran Presents Virginia Third
Trimester Abortion Bill in Virginia Legislature," YouTube video, 6:41,
January 29, 2019, youtu.be/OMFzZ5I3odg.

79. Fiske, *Envy Up*, 114–116.

80. Jenna Johnson and Robert Costa, "'It's the Culture War on Steroids.'
Kavanaugh Fight Takes on Symbolism in Divided Era," *The Washington Post*, September 24, 2018, washingtonpost.com/politics/its-the

-culture-war-on-steroids-kavanaugh-fight-takes-on-symbolism-in
-divided-era/2018/09/24/15ccc792-c028-11e8-be77-516336a26305
_story.html?utm_term=.b32c7d71f64a&wpisrc=nl_most&wpmm=1.

81. Jonathan Haidt, "The Moral Emotions," in *Handbook of Affective Sciences*, eds. R. J. Davidson, K. R. Scherer, and H. H. Goldsmith (Oxford: Oxford University Press, 2003), 852–70, faculty.virginia .edu/haidtlab/articles/alternate_versions/haidt.2003.the-moral -emotions.pub025-as-html.html.

82. Matsumoto, interview; see also Pamela B. Paresky, "The Psychology of Political Violence," *Psychology Today* blog, August 30, 2017, psychologytoday.com/us/blog/happiness-and-the-pursuit-leadership /201708/the-psychology-political-violence.

83. See Ira Roseman's treatment of the upsides and downsides of contempt in "Rejecting the Unworthy: The Causes, Components and Consequences of Contempt," in *The Moral Psychology of Contempt*, ed. Michelle Mason, (Lanham, MD: Rowman & Littlefield International, 2018), 116.

84. Ira Roseman, interview with author, May 8, 2018.

85. Kyle Mattes, David. P. Redlawsk, Ira. J. Roseman, and Steven Katz, "Contempt and Anger in the 2016 US Presidential Election," *Conventional Wisdom, Parties, and Broken Barriers in the 2016 Election*, eds. Jennifer Lucas, Christopher J. Galdieri, and Tauna S. Sisco (Lanham: Lexington Books, 2018), 101–12.

86. Katie Reilly, "Read Hillary Clinton's Speech on Donald Trump and National Security," *Time*, June 2, 2016, time.com/4355797/hillary -clinton-donald-trump-foreign-policy-speech-transcript/. WikiLeaks emails later revealed the Clinton campaign's efforts to make Trump the GOP nominee, a strategy that says as much about Clinton's "common sense" as Trump voters'; Gabriel Debenedetti, "They Always Wanted Trump," *Politico*, November 7, 2016, politico.com/magazine/ story/2016/11/hillary-clinton-2016-donald-trump-214428.

87. Lyz Lenz, "The Mystery of Tucker Carlson," *Columbia Journalism Review*, September 5, 2018, cjr.org/the_profile/tucker-carlson.php.

88. Lilliana Mason, *Uncivil Agreement* (Chicago: University of Chicago Press, 2018), 84.

89. Erik Wemple, "In On-Air Apology, Samantha Bee Presents False Choice," *The Washington Post*, June 7, 2018, washingtonpost.com/ blogs/erik-wemple/wp/2018/06/07/in-on-air-apology-samantha-bee -presents-false-choice/?utm_term=.0774ba980f4a&wpisrc=nl_most &wpmm=1.

90. David P. Redlawsk, Ira J. Roseman, Kyle Mattes, and Steven Katz, "Donald Trump, Contempt, and the 2016 GOP Iowa Caucuses," *Journal of Elections, Public Opinion and Parties*, 28:2 (2018), 173–89, tandfonline.com/doi/full/10.1080/17457289.2018.1441848.

Chapter 2: Class-Based Contempt—Red with Shame

1. Chris Sommerfeldt, "President Trump Doesn't Mention Paul Manafort or Michael Cohen During Chaotic West Virginia Rally," *New York Daily News*, August 21, 2018, nydailynews.com/news /politics/ny-news-trump-manafort-cohen-mueller-virginia-rally -20180821-story.html.

2. James Boyd, "Nixon's Southern Strategy 'It's all in the charts'," *The New York Times*, May 17, 1970, nytimes.com/packages/html/books /phillips-southern.pdf; Thomas Frank, *What's the Matter with Kansas?* (New York: Metropolitan Books, 2004). Interestingly, Frank argues (in Chapter 9) that the backlash in Kansas was achieved without racist appeals but with ample homophobia and anti-Semitism.

3. "President Trump Ranted for 77 Minutes in Phoenix. Here's What He Said," *Time*, August 23, 2017, time.com/4912055/donald-trump -phoenix-arizona-transcript/.

4. Jenna Johnson and Anne Li, "What the Sounds of a Trump Rally Tell Us about His Fans," *The Washington Post*, June 22, 2018, washington post.com/graphics/2018/politics/trump-crowd-sound/?utm_term =.6596dd81a2ee.

5. Timothy J. Lombardo, "Why White Blue-Collar Voters Love President Trump," *The Washington Post*, September 16, 2018, washington post.com/outlook/2018/09/17/why-white-blue-collar-voters-love -president-trump/?utm_term=.f7baf189fbf3; Arlie Hochschild, "I Spent 5 Years With Some of Trump's Biggest Fans. Here's What They Won't Tell You," *Mother Jones*, September/October 2016, motherjones .com/politics/2016/08/trump-white-blue-collar-supporters/.

6. Donald Trump, "Donald Trump Holds a Political Rally in Lebanon, Ohio—October 12, 2018." *Factbase* video, 01:06:13, October 12, 2018, factba.se/transcript/donald-trump-speech-maga-rally-lebanon -oh-october-12-2018.

7. Alexandra Pelosi, "Outside the Bubble: On the Road with Alexandra Pelosi," directed by Alexandra Pelosi, *HBO* video, 57:00, 2018.

8. Most Trump voters are either wealthy or middle-class with incomes above the US median. Among white voters, Trump won handily in every income category—57 to 34 for whites making less than $30,000; 56 to 37 for whites in the $30,000–$50,000 range; 61 to 33 for those

making between $50,000 and $100,000; 56 to 39 for those making between $100,000 and $200,000; and so on, with diminishing margins in higher income brackets. Smarsh, "Dangerous Idiots."

9. Nicholas Carnes and Noam Lupus, "It's Time to Bust the Myth: Most Trump Voters Were Not Working Class," *The Washington Post*, June 5, 2017, washingtonpost.com/news/monkey-cage/wp/2017/06/05/its -time-to-bust-the-myth-most-trump-voters-were-not-working-class /?utm_term=.d4facd3fd936; Nate Silver, "Education, Not Income, Predicted Who Would Vote for Trump," *FiveThirtyEight*, November 22, 2016, fivethirtyeight.com/features/education-not-income-predict ed-who-would-vote-for-trump/.

10. Rod Dreher, "Least Tolerant: Educated White Liberals," *The American Conservative*, March 4, 2019, theamericanconservative.com /dreher/educated-white-liberals-intolerance/.

11. Candace Smith and John Santucci, "Trump Calls on Working Class to 'Strike Back' in Final Day of Campaigning," ABC News, November 8, 2016, abcnews.go.com/Politics/trump-calls-working-class-strike -back-final-day/story?id=43378378.

12. Altman, "What I Heard."

13. Nathan J. Robinson, "All About Pete." *Current Affairs*, March 29, 2019, currentaffairs.org/2019/03/all-about-pete.

14. John Nichols, "A Progressive Populist From the Heartland," *The Nation*, March 25, 2019.

15. Stanley G. Greenberg, "Trump Is Beginning to Lose His Grip," *The New York Times*, November 17, 2018, nytimes.com/2018/11/17 /opinion/sunday/trump-is-beginning-to-lose-his-grip.html; Re: progressive politics of 2018 midterm winners, see D. D. Guttenplan, "9 Lessons from the 2018 Midterms," *The Nation*, November 21, 2019, thenation.com/article/democrats-2018-midterms-lessons/; and Jim Naureckas, "'Moderation' and the Midterms," Fairness & Accuracy in Reporting, November 9, 2018, fair.org/home/moderation-and-the -midterms/.

16. Joan Williams, *White Working Class: Overcoming Class Cluelessness in America* (Boston: Harvard Business Review Press, 2017), 10–11.

17. Kathryn Vasel, "Most Americans Can't Cover a $1,000 Emergency," CNN Money, January 18, 2018, money.cnn.com/2018/01/18/pf/lack-of -savings-cover-unexpected-expense/index.html.

18. Shankar Vedantam, "Voting with a Middle Finger: Two Views on the White Working Class," *Hidden Brain*, NPR, October 15, 2018, audio, 49:14, npr.org/templates/transcript/transcript.php?storyId =657547685.

19. Chris Hayes, "Why Is This Happening? Debating the Concept of Political Tribalism with Amy Chua," *Think: Opinion, Analysis, Essays,* NBC News, June 22, 2018, audio, 43:07, nbcnews.com/think/opinion /debating-concept-political-tribalism-amy-chua-podcast-transcript -ncna882186.

20. Jon Huang, Samuel Jacoby, Michael Strickland, and K. K. Rebecca. "Election 2016: Exit Polls," *The New York Times,* November 9, 2016, nytimes.com/interactive/2016/11/08/us/politics/election-exit-polls .html?_r=0; isreview.org/issue/104/we-got-trumped; Daniel Cox, Rachel Lienesch, and Robert P. Jones, "Beyond Economics: Fears of Cultural Displacement Pushed the White Working Class to Trump," PRRI/*The Atlantic,* May 9, 2017, prri.org/research/white-working -class-attitudes-economy-trade-immigration-election-donald-trump/.

21. Michael Moore, *Fahrenheit 11/9* (USA: Dog Eat Dog Films, 2018), 128 min.

22. Sarah Smarsh, *Heartland* (New York: Scribner, 2018), 132–33.

23. Caines, "Too Stupid," *Cache Valley Daily.*

24. Renee Schiavone, "LIST: The 100 Most 'Redneck' Cities in California," *Patch,* November 3, 2015, patch.com/california/lake elsinore-wildomar/list-100-most-redneck-cities-california.

25. Alexandra Petri, "Every Story I Have Read about Trump Supporters in the Past Week," *The Washington Post,* April 4, 2017, washingtonpost.com/blogs/compost/wp/2017/04/04/every-story-i -have-read-about-trump-supporters-in-the-past-week/?utm_term =.0eab3ef0c22c.

26. Mark Hensch, "Olbermann: Trump Hosted 'Trailer Park Trash," *The Hill,* video, 0:30, April 20, 2017, thehill.com/homenews/administra tion/329762-olbermann-trump-hosted-trailer-park-trash.

27. James Fallows, "Welcome to American Futures 3.0," *The Atlantic,* March 9, 2015, theatlantic.com/national/archive/2015/03/welcome-to -american-futures-30/387265/

28. Hochschild, *I Spent 5 Years*

29. Balz, "Midwestern."

30. Hagerman, "Confessions."

31. David Roberts, "Hillary Clinton's 'Coal Gaffe' is a Microcosm of Her Twisted Treatment by the Media," *Vox,* September 20, 2017, vox.com /energy-and-environment/2017/9/15/16306158/hillary-clinton-hall-of -mirrors.

32. Ibid.

33. Gwen Johnson, interview with author, February 21, 2019.

34. Alex Gibson, interview with author, February 27, 2019.

35. Greg Jaffe, "For a Groundbreaking Candidate in West Virginia, Big

Money and Attention Come with Downsides," *The Washington Post*, November 1, 2018, washingtonpost.com/politics/for-a-groundbreak ing-candidate-in-west-virginia-big-money-and-attention-come-with -downsides/2018/10/31/84e0f4f8-d6d2-11e8-aeb7-ddcad4a0a54e_story .html?utm_term=.7eb21cb2fbb6&wpisrc=nl_most&wpmm=1]; Ryan Grim, "Richard Ojeda, West Virginia Lawmaker Who Backed Teachers Strikes, Will Run for President," *The Intercept*, November 11, 2018, theintercept.com/2018/11/11/richard-ojeda-2020-president/.

36. Laura Ingraham, *Shut Up*, 15.

37. German Lopez, "The Past Year of Research Has Made It Very Clear: Trump Won Because of Racial Resentment," *Vox*, December 15, 2017, vox.com/identities/2017/12/15/16781222/trump-racism-economic -anxiety-study.

38. Isaac Chotiner, "A New Theory for Why All Those Obama Voters Went for Trump," *Slate*, April 24, 2018, slate.com/news-and-politics /2018/04/a-new-theory-for-why-obama-voters-went-trump.html.

39. Isaac Chotiner, "The Disturbing, Surprisingly Complex Relation- ship Between White Identity Politics and Racism," *The New Yorker*, January 19, 2019, newyorker.com/news/q-and-a/the-disturbing -surprisingly-complex-relationship-between-white-identity-politics -and-racism.

40. Some whites find satisfaction in what W.E.B. DuBois called the "psy- chological wage" of whiteness, the delusion originally cultivated by the Southern planter class and Northern industrialists that it's better to be poor than black. To this day, white American aspirations toward upward mobility lead many to spurn the notion that their interests align more with working- and middle-class blacks than with billion- aire Donald Trump. See David R. Roediger, *The Wages of Whiteness: Race and the Making of the American Working Class* (London: Verso, 2007).

41. Kenan Malik, "White Identity Is Meaningless. Real Dignity Is Found in Shared Hopes," *The Guardian*, October 21, 2018, theguardian.com /commentisfree/2018/oct/21/white-identity-is-meaningless-dignity -is-found-in-shared-hopes.

42. CNN Politics, "Exit Polls," CNN, November 23, 2016, cnn.com /election/2016/results/exit-polls/national/president.

43. Joan Williams, "The Democrats' White-People Problem," *The Atlan- tic*, December 2018, theatlantic.com/magazine/archive/2018/12/the -democrats-white-people-problem/573901/.

44. David Atkins, "It Was Prejudice. It Was Economics. It Was Both," *The American Prospect*, July 7, 2017, prospect.org/article/it-was-prejudice -it-was-economics-it-was-both.

45. E.J. Dionne, Jr., *Why the Right Went Wrong* (New York: Simon and Schuster, 2016), 320.

46. Brian Thiede et al., "The Divide Between Urban and Rural America, in 6 Charts," *U.S. News & World Report*, March 20, 2017, usnews.com /news/national-news/articles/2017-03-20/6-charts-that-illustrate-the -divide-between-rural-and-urban-america.

47. Chris Arnade, "What I Learned after 100,000 Miles on the Road Talking to Trump Supporters," *The Guardian*, November 3, 2016, theguardian.com/society/2016/nov/03/trump-supporters-us -elections.

48. Gary Younge, "How Trump Took Middle America," *The Guardian*, November 16, 2016, theguardian.com/membership/2016/nov/16/how -trump-took-middletown-muncie-election.

49. Erin Cooley, Jazmin L. Brown-Iannuzzi, Ryan F. Lei, and William Cipolli III, "Complex Intersections of Race and Class: Among Social Liberals, Learning about White Privilege Reduces Sympathy, Increases Blame, and Decreases External Attributions for White People Struggling with Poverty," *Journal of Experimental Psychology: General*, 2019, psycnet.apa.org/record/2019-22926-001.

50. Pacific Standard staff, "Meeting Trump Voters Where They Live: An Interview with Alexander Zaitchik," *Pacific Standard*, September 9, 2016, psmag.com/news/meeting-trump-voters-where-they-live-an -interview-with-alexander-zaitchik.

51. Alexander Zaitchik, *The Gilded Rage: A Wild Ride through Donald Trump's America* (New York: Hot Books, 2016), 5; *Salon* staff, "Donald Trump's Minions: 'The Gilded Rage' Delves Deep inside the Lives of Trump Supporters," *Salon*, November 6, 2016, salon.com /2016/10/31/donald-trumps-minions-the-gilded-rage-delves-deep -inside-the-lives-of-trump-supporters.

52. Robert B. Reich, "The Common Good," Lecture, from KFPA Radio 94.1 FM, First Congregational Church of Berkeley, Berkeley, CA, February 6, 2019.

53. Balz, "Midwestern."

54. Stephen L. Morgan and Jiwon Lee, "Trump Voters and the White Working Class," *Sociological Science* 4 (2018): 234–245; Pew Research Center, "The Partisan Divide on Political Values Grows Even Wider," Pew Research Center U.S. Politics & Policy, October 5, 2017, people -press.org/2017/10/05/4-race-immigration-and-discrimination/.

55. Marianne Bertrand and Mullainathan Sendhil, "Are Emily and Greg More Employable than Lakisha and Jamal? A Field Experiment on Labor Market Discrimination," *American Economic Review* 94, no. 4

(September 2004): 991–1013, nber.org/papers/w9873; Sarah Smarsh, "Liberal Blind Spots Are Hiding the Truth About 'Trump Country'," *The New York Times*, July 19, 2018, nytimes.com/2018/07/19/opinion /trump-corporations-white-working-class.html.

56. Joe Heim, "Hate Groups Make Unprecedented Push to Recruit on College Campuses," *The Washington Post*, January 12, 2018, washing tonpost.com/local/education/hate-groups-make-unprecedented -push-to-recruit-on-college-campuses/2018/01/12/c66cf628-e4f8-11e7 -833f-155031558ff4_story.html?utm_term=.b1dc457c5d1d.

57. Michael Scherer, "White Identity Politics Drives Trump, and the Republican Party Under Him" *The Washington Post*, July 16, 2019, washingtonpost.com/politics/white-identity-politics-drives-trump -and-the-republican-party-under-him/2019/07/16/a5ff5710-a733-11e9 -a3a6-ab670962db05_story.html?utm_term=.1d8799be78ab.

58. Matthew Stewart, "The 9.9 Percent Is the New American Aristoc- racy," *The Atlantic*, June, 2018, theatlantic.com/magazine/archive /2018/06/the-birth-of-a-new-american-aristocracy/559130/.

59. Salena Zito and Brad Todd, *The Great Revolt: Inside the Populist Co- alition Reshaping American Politics* (New York: Crown Forum, 2018), 32–34.

60. Ibid., 55–58.

61. Working America, "100 Days."

62. Matt Morrison, e-mail message to author, November 4, 2018.

63. Eduardo Porter, "The Hard Truths of Trying to 'Save' the Rural Economy," *The New York Times*, December 14, 2018, nytimes.com /interactive/2018/12/14/opinion/rural-america-trump-decline.html.

64. Jim Geraghty, "Chuck Schumer: Democrats Will Lose Blue-Collar Whites But Gain in the Suburbs," *National Review*, October 10, 2017, nationalreview.com/corner/chuck-schumer-democrats-will-lose-blue -collar-whites-gain-suburbs/.

65. Briahna Joy Gray, "The Politics of Shame," *Current Affairs*, March 11, 2018, currentaffairs.org/2018/02/the-politics-of-shame.

66. Joshua Holland, "New Study: You Don't Have to Choose Between 'Populism' and 'Identity'," *The Nation*, June 11, 2018, thenation.com /article/new-study-dont-choose-populism-identity/.

67. Ibid.

68. Jonathan Metzl, "It's Time to Talk about Being White in America," *The Washington Post*, April 29, 2019, washingtonpost.com/opinions /its-time-to-talk-about-being-white-in-america/2019/04/29/20aed8 3a-6a9b-11e9-be3a-33217240a539_story.html?utm_term=.2a0d8b851 c51&wpisrc=nl_most&wpmm=1.

69. Claudia Rankine, "I Wanted To Know What White Men Thought About Their Privilege. So I Asked," *The New York Times*, July 17, 2019, nytimes.com/2019/07/17/magazine/white-men-privilege.html?search ResultPosition=1.

70. YES! Magazine, "Being Fearless: Van Jones Part 1," YouTube video, 9:36, December 07, 2017, youtube.com/watch?time_continue=2&v =9ROwRnsxD48.

71. Van Jones, *Beyond the Messy Truth: How We Came Apart, How We Come Together* (New York: Ballantine, 2017), 92–114.

72. Sarah Jaffe, "The Democrats' Deadly Error," *The New York Times*, November 9, 2016, nytimes.com/interactive/projects/cp/opinion /election-night-2016/the-democrats-deadly-error.

73. Eric Alterman, "What Can Democrats Learn from Robert F. Kennedy's Presidential Campaign?" *The Nation*, March 28, 2018, thenation.com/article/what-can-democrats-learn-from-robert-f-kennedys-presidential-campaign/.

74. Nate Cohn and Alicia Parlapiano, "How Broad, and How Happy, Is the Trump Coalition?" *The New York Times*, August 9, 2018, nytimes.com/interactive/2018/08/09/upshot/trump-voters-how -theyve-changed.html?rref=collection/issuecollection/todays-new -york-times&action=click&contentCollection=todayspaper°ion =rank&module=package&version=highlights&contentPlacement =1&pgtype=collection.

75. Deepak Bhargava, "Wrong About the Right," *The Nation*, June 29, 2015, thenation.com/article/wrong-about-right/.

76. Scott Nakagawa and Tarso Luis Ramos, "What Time Is It? Why We Can't Ignore the Momentum of the Right," Political Research Associates, July 14, 2016, politicalresearch.org/2016/07/14/what-time-is-it -why-we-cant-ignore-the-momentum-of-the-right/.

77. Highlander Research & Education Center. "Update: Devastating Fire at Highlander Research & Education Center Destroys Main Office." April 2, 2019.

78. Theo E.J. Wilson, "A Black Man Goes Undercover in the Alt-Right," filmed July 2017 in Denver, CO, TED video, 18:21, ted.com/talks/theo _e_j_wilson_a_black_man_goes_undercover_in_the_alt_right.

79. Altman, "What I Heard."

80. George Packer, "Hillary Clinton and the Populist Revolt," *The New Yorker*, June 19, 2017, newyorker.com/magazine/2016/10/31/hillary -clinton-and-the-populist-revolt.

81. Zaitchik, *The Gilded Rage*, 84.

82. David Leonhardt, "The American Dream, Quantified at Last," *The*

New York Times, December 8, 2016, nytimes.com/2016/12/08/opinion
/the-american-dream-quantified-at-last.html.

83. Eleanor Krause and Isabel V. Sawhill, "Seven Reasons to Worry about
the American Middle Class," The Brookings Institution, October 15,
2018, brookings.edu/blog/social-mobility-memos/2018/06/05/seven
-reasons-to-worry-about-the-american-middle-class/.

84. Rakesh Kochhar, "The American Middle Class Is Stable in Size,
but Losing Ground Financially to Upper-Income Families," Pew
Research Center, September 6, 2018, pewresearch.org/fact-tank
/2018/09/06/the-american-middle-class-is-stable-in-size-but-losing
-ground-financially-to-upper-income-families/.

85. Steve Fraser, *The Limousine Liberal: How an Incendiary Image
United the Right and Fractured America* (New York: Basic Books,
2016), 168–75.

86. "The Troubled American: A Special Report on the White Majority,"
Newsweek, October 6, 1969.

87. Anne P. Haas, Phillip L. Rogers, and Jody L. Herman, *Suicide Attempts Between Transgender and Gender Non-Conforming Adults*,
The Williams Institute, UCLA School of Law, January 2014, williams
institute.law.ucla.edu/research/suicide-attempts-among-transgender
-and-gender-non-conforming-adults/.

88. Frank Hobbs and Nicole Stoops, "Demographic Trends in the 20th
Century," US Census Bureau, US Department of Commerce, November 2002, census.gov/prod/2002pubs/censr-4.pdf.; Lindsay Hixon,
Bradford Hepler, and Myoung Ouk Kim, "The White Population:
2010," US Census Bureau, US Department of Commerce, September
2011, census.gov/prod/cen2010/briefs/c2010br-05.pdf.

89. Amy Chua, *Political Tribes: Group Instinct and the Fate of Nations*
(New York: Penguin Books, 2019), 171–72.

90. Ibid, 171; Daniel George, "Monumental Hypocrisy," *Current Affairs*,
November 6, 2018, currentaffairs.org/2018/11/monumental-hypocrisy.

91. Briahna Joy Gray, "The Problem with Calling Trump a Racist,"
Rolling Stone, June 25, 2018, rollingstone.com/politics/politics-news
/the-problem-with-calling-trump-a-racist-117010/.

92. See Ibram Kendi, *Stamped from the Beginning* (New York: Nation
Books, 2017).

93. David Neiwart, *Alt-America* (New York: Verso, 2017), 325.

94. Michael Massing, "Journalism in the Age of Trump," *The Nation*, July
19, 2018, thenation.com/article/journalism-age-trump-whats-missing
-matters/; Hannah Fingerhut, "Campaign Exposes Divisions Over
Issues, Values and How Life Has Changed in the U.S.," Pew Research

Center, March 31, 2016, people-press.org/2016/03/31/campaign
-exposes-fissures-over-issues-values-and-how-life-has-changed-in
-the-u-s/; Monica Ortiz Uribe, "Workers in Mexico's Border Factories Say They Can Barely Survive, so They're Turning to Unions,"
Public Radio International's *The World*, February 29, 2016, pri.org
/stories/2016-02-29/workers-mexicos-border-factories-say-they-can
-barely-survive-so-theyre-turning.

95. Susan B. Garland, Douglas Harbrecht, and Richard Dunham, "Sweet
Victory: The NAFTA War is Won," *Bloomberg*, November 29, 1993,
bloomberg.com/news/articles/1993-11-28/sweet-victory.

96. Warner Todd Huston, "Electrical Union Workers Display Big Pro-
Trump Banner in Philadelphia," *Breitbart News*, January 26, 2017,
breitbart.com/politics/2017/01/26/union-electrical-workers-show
-trump-banner/.

97. Shawn Donnan, "Rhetoric and Reaction: The Trade War in Northern
Minnesota," December 12, 2018, in *1A*, produced by James Morrison
and Amanda Williams, podcast, 29:50, the1a.org/shows/2018-12-12/a
-miner-discussion-on-trade.

98. Charlie Post, "We Got Trumped," *International Socialist Review*,
April 2017, isreview.org/issue/104/we-got-trumped.

99. Fox Business, "Michael Moore Supports Clinton, But Predicts a
Trump Win," YouTube video, 4:10, October 27, 2016, youtube.com
/watch?v=3Tfts5YOUHs.

100. David Wasserman, "The One County In America That Voted In
A Landslide For Both Trump And Obama," *FiveThirtyEight*, ABC
News, November 9, 2017, fivethirtyeight.com/features/the-one
-county-in-america-that-voted-in-a-landslide-for-both-trump-and
-obama/.

101. Michelle Alexander, "Why Hillary Clinton Doesn't Deserve the
Black Vote," *The Nation*, February 10, 2016, thenation.com/article
/hillary-clinton-does-not-deserve-black-peoples-votes/; Philip
Bump, "4.4 Million 2012 Obama Voters Stayed Home in 2016—More
than a Third of Them Black," *The Washington Post*, March 12, 2018,
washingtonpost.com/news/politics/wp/2018/03/12/4-4-million-2012
-obama-voters-stayed-home-in-2016-more-than-a-third-of-them
-black/?utm_term=.89a3cf284513.

102. Sabrina Tavernise, "Many in Milwaukee Neighborhood Didn't
Vote—and Don't Regret It," *The New York Times*, December 22, 2017,
nytimes.com/2016/11/21/us/many-in-milwaukee-neighborhood-didnt
-vote-and-dont-regret-it.html.

103. Stanley Greenberg, "The Democrats' 'Working-Class Problem,'" *The American Prospect*, June 1, 2017, prospect.org/article/democrats'-'working-class-problem'.

104. Thomas Frank, *Listen, Liberal—or—What Ever Happened to the Party of the People?* (New York: Metropolitan Books, 2016).

105. Matt Stoller, "After the Fumble," *The Nation*, March 1, 2017, thenation.com/article/after-the-fumble/.

106. Nai Issa and Louis Jacobson, "Viral Meme Says 1956 Republican Platform Was Pretty Liberal," *Politifact*, October 28, 2014, politifact.com/truth-o-meter/statements/2014/oct/28/facebook-posts/viral-meme-says-1956-republican-platform-was-prett/.

107. Frank, *What's the Matter*, 245.

108. Thomas Frank, *Rendezvous with Oblivion* (New York: Metropolitan Books, 2018), 218–19.

109. George Saunders, "Who Are All These Trump Supporters?" *The New Yorker*, June 19, 2017, newyorker.com/magazine/2016/07/11/george-saunders-goes-to-trump-rallies.

110. Charles Eisenstein, "Please Stop Thinking You're Better Than Trump Supporters," *YES! Magazine*, November 18, 2016, yesmagazine.org/people-power/please-stop-thinking-youre-better-than-trump-supporters-20161118.

Chapter 3: Why Not Everyone Is a Liberal

1. Hawkins et al., *Hidden Tribes*, 137.

2. Eric Levitz, "Ammon Bundy Quits Militia Movement in Solidarity with Migrant Caravan," *Intelligencer*, December 7, 2018, nymag.com/intelligencer/2018/12/ammon-bundy-quits-militia-movement-defends-migrant-caravan.html.

3. Shankar Vadantam, "Nature, Nurture and Your Politics," October 8, 2018, in *Hidden Brain* podcast, 26:15, October 8, 2018, npr.org/templates/transcript/transcript.php?storyId=654127241.

4. Vicki Haddock, "Republicans' Fertile Future," SFGate, January 12, 2012, sfgate.com/opinion/article/Republicans-fertile-future-Through-the-past-2488626.php; Erica Etelson, *For Our Own Good: The Politics of Parenting* (Berkeley: Left Coast Press, 2010), pp; George Lakoff, *Moral Politics: What Conservatives Know That Liberals Don't* (Chicago: University of Chicago Press, 1996).

5. John Hibbing, Kevin Smith, and John Alford, *Predisposed: Liberals, Conservatives, and the Biology of Political Differences* (New York: Routledge, 2013), 23.

6. Ibid, 252.

7. John Bargh, "At Yale, We Conducted an Experiment to Turn Conservatives into Liberals. The Results Say a Lot about Our Political Divisions," *The Washington Post*, November 22, 2017, washingtonpost .com/news/inspired-life/wp/2017/11/22/at-yale-we-conducted-an -experiment-to-turn-conservatives-into-liberals-the-results-say-a-lot -about-our-political-divisions/?utm_term=.6708d0111f01.

8. Sasha Abramsky, *Jumping at Shadows: The Triumph of Fear and the End of the American Dream* (New York: Nation Books, 2017), 12–13.

9. Jennifer S. Lerner, Roxana M. Gonzalez, Deborah A. Small, and Baruch Fischhoff, "Effects of Fear and Anger on Perceived Risks of Terrorism: A National Field Experiment," *Psychological Science* 14 (2), March 2003, doi.org/10.1111/1467-9280.01433.

10. Bargh, "At Yale"; Emily Deans, "How Stress Makes You Sick and Sad," *Psychology Today*, March 27, 2011, psychologytoday.com/us/blog /evolutionary-psychiatry/201103/how-stress-makes-you-sick-and -sad; Abramsky, *Jumping*, 117.

11. Hawkins et al., *Hidden Tribes*, 82.

12. Kathleen McAuliffe, "The Yuck Factor," *The Atlantic*, March 2019, theatlantic.com/magazine/archive/2019/03/the-yuck-factor/580465/.

13. Hibbing et al., *Predisposed*, 163–63.

14. Ralph DiClimente, Chris Martin, and Nihari Patel, "Ebola-Related Attitudes in the U.S. Vary by Party Affiliation and Education," *SSRN Electronic Journal*, January 2016, researchgate.net/publication /318000701_Ebola-Related_Attitudes_in_the_US_Vary_by_Party _Affiliation_and_Education.

15. McAuliffe, "Yuck Factor."

16. Thomas G. Adams, Patrick A. Stewart, and John Blanchar, "Disgust and the Politics of Sex: Exposure to a Disgusting Odorant Increases Politically Conservative Views on Sex and Decreases Support for Gay Marriage," *PLOS One* 9(5): May 5, 2014, journals.plos.org/plosone /article?id=10.1371/journal.pone.0095572.

17. Samia Mounts, "Ellen, Sarah & Anne—Catching Up with the Women of Season 1," in *Make America Relate Again*, produced by Better Angels Media, podcast, season 2, episode 12, 1:07:00, makeamerica relatepodcast.com/s2ep12-transcript.

18. Samia Mounts, "Cindy & Diana."

19. Abramsky, *Jumping*, 111–12.

20. Greg Sargent, "Trump Takes an Old Republican Lie and Makes It Even Worse," *The Washington Post*, October 23, 2018, washingtonpost

.com/blogs/plum-line/wp/2018/10/23/trump-takes-an-old-republican
-lie-and-makes-it-even-worse/?utm_term=.faa7a9a43daa&wpisrc=nl
_most&wpmm=1.

21. Thomas B. Edsall, "The Contract with Authoritarianism," *The
New York Times*, April 5, 2018, nytimes.com/2018/04/05/opinion
/trump-authoritarianism-republicans-contract.html; Matthew
MacWilliams, Benjamin Ginsberg, Jane Mayer, Jack Shafer, David
Greenberg, John F. Harris, and Joanna Weiss, "The One Weird Trait
That Predicts Whether You're a Trump Supporter," *Politico*, January
17, 2016, politico.com/magazine/story/2016/01/donald-trump-2016
-authoritarian-213533.

22. Daniel Cox and Robert P. Jones, "Two-Thirds of Trump Supporters
Say Nation Needs...," PRRI, July 4, 2016, prri.org/research/prri
-atlantic-poll-republican-democratic-primary-trump-supporters/.

23. Amy Chua and Jed Rubenfeld, "The Threat of Tribalism," *The Atlantic*, September 14, 2018, theatlantic.com/magazine/archive/2018/10
/the-threat-of-tribalism/568342/.

24. David McRaney, "Uncivil Agreement," in *You Are Not So Smart*,
produced by David McRaney, podcast, episode 133, 1:20:07, August 4, 2018, youarenotsosmart.com/2018/08/04/transcript-uncivil
-agreement/.

25. Bobby Duffy, *The Perils of Perception* (London: Atlantic Books,
2015), 12

26. Drew Westen, *The Political Brain* (New York: Perseus Books, 2007),
52.

27. Pew Research Center, "For Most Trump Voters, 'Very Warm' Feelings
for Him Endured," August 9, 2018, people-press.org/2018/08/09/an
-examination-of-the-2016-electorate-based-on-validated-voters/.

28. Tom Jacobs, "For Americans, Partisanship Trump Values," *Pacific
Standard*, April 10, 2019, psmag.com/news/partisanship-trumps
-morality-for-todays-americans.

29. Kristen Russell, "Are We Born Racist? The Talk You Must Have with
Your Children," *ParentMap*, August 14, 2017, parentmap.com/article
/are-we-born-racist-the-talk-you-must-have-with-your-children;
see also Amy Chua, *Political Tribes: Group Instinct and the Fate of
Nations* (New York: Penguin Books, 2018), 38–39.

30. Carrie L. Masten, Cari Gillen-O'Neel, and Christia Spears Brown,
"Children's Intergroup Empathic Processing: The Roles of Novel
Ingroup Identification, Situational Distress, and Social Anxiety," *Journal of Experimental Child Psychology* 106, no. 2-3 (June/July 2010):
115–28, ncbi.nlm.nih.gov/pubmed/20202649.

31. Lillliana Mason, *Uncivil Agreement* (Chicago: University of Chicago Press, 2018), 10–11.

32. Hilary Brueck, "These Key Psychological Differences Can Determine Whether You're Liberal or Conservative," *Business Insider*, April 19, 2018, businessinsider.com/psychological-differences-between-conservatives-and-liberals-2018-2#liberals-and-conservatives-extend-feelings-of-compassion-to-different-people-11.

33. Hawkins et al., *Hidden Tribes*, 87.

34. David Roberts, "Donald Trump and the Rise of Tribal Epistemology," *Vox*, May 19, 2017, vox.com/policy-and-politics/2017/3/22/14762030/donald-trump-tribal-epistemology.

35. Asymmetric polarization is documented in Jacob Hacker and Paul Pierson, *Off Center* (New Haven: Yale University Press, 2005); and Thomas Mann and Norman Ornstein, *It's Even Worse Than It Looks* (New York: Basic Books, 2016).

36. Aaron Blake, "Republicans' Views of Blacks' Intelligence, Work Ethic Lag Behind Democrats," *The Washington Post*, March 31, 2017, washingtonpost.com/news/the-fix/wp/2017/03/31/the-gap-between-republicans-and-democrats-views-of-african-americans-just-hit-a-new-high/?utm_term=.e12b0ef379fc.

37. Edsall, "Contract with Authoritarianism."

38. Jennifer Agiesta, "CNN Poll: Majority Oppose Kavanaugh, But His Popularity Grows with GOP," CNN, October 11, 2018, cnn.com/2018/10/08/politics/cnn-poll-kavanaugh-confirmation.

39. Jeremy W. Peters, "As Critics Assail Trump, His Supporters Dig in Deeper," *The New York Times*, June 23, 2018, nytimes.com/2018/06/23/us/politics/republican-voters-trump.html.

40. Hawkins et al., *Hidden Tribes*, 87; see also Jonathan Haidt, *The Righteous Mind: Why Good People Are Divided by Politics and Religion* (New York: Vintage Books, 2013).

41. Hochschild, *Strangers*, 135–51.

42. Ibid, 208–9, 303–4; Gray, "The Problem."

43. Krista Tippett, "Daniel Kahneman: Why We Contradict Ourselves & Confound Each Other," by Krista Tippett, *The On Being Project*, podcast audio, 52:32, October 5, 2017, onbeing.org/programs/daniel-kahneman-why-we-contradict-ourselves-and-confound-each-other-oct2017/.

44. Daniel Kahneman, *Thinking, Fast and Slow* (New York: Farrar, Straus and Giroux, 2015), 12–13.

45. Stephen J. Dubner and Christopher Werth, "Why Is My Life So Hard? (Ep. 280)," *Freakonomics*, podcast audio, 30:32, March 15, 2017, freakonomics.com/podcast/why-is-my-life-so-hard/.

46. Sandro Spano, "Present Bias and the Consequences of Instant Gratification?" *ING*, March 19, 2017, think.ing.com/articles/what-is -present-bias-the-consequences-of-instant-gratification/.

47. Gregory S. Berns, Jonathan Chappelow, Caroline F. Zink, Guiseppe Pagnoni, Megan E. Martin-Skurski, and Jim Richards, "Neurobio- logical Correlates of Social Conformity and Independence During Mental Rotation," *Biological Psychiatry* 58, no. 3 (August 1, 2005): 245–53, doi.org/10.1016/j.biopsych.2005.04.012.

48. Chris Crandall, Amy Eshleman, Laurie O'Brien, "Social Norms and the Expression and Suppression of Prejudice: The Struggle for Inter- nalization," *Journal of Personality and Social Psychology*, 82: 359–78.

49. Pew Research, "The Politics of Climate Change in the United States," Pew Research Center: Internet, Science & Tech, October 4, 2016, pewinternet.org/2016/10/04/the-politics-of-climate/.

50. Hawkins et al., *Hidden Tribes*, 74.

51. Jane Coaston, "Tucker Carlson Has Sparked the Most Interesting Debate in Conservative Politics," *Vox*, January 10, 2019, vox.com/2019 /1/10/18171912/tucker-carlson-fox-news-populism-conservatism -trump-gop.

52. David W. Campt, *The White Ally Toolkit Workbook: Using Active Lis- tening, Empathy, and Personal Storytelling to Promote Racial Equity* (Newton Center, MA: I AM Publications, 2018), 194.

53. Tim Adams, "Changing Your Mind Has Never Been Easy. But We Must Start Listening Again," *The Guardian*, February 25, 2018, theguardian.com/commentisfree/2018/feb/25/on-the-other-hand -behavioural-psychology-sunday-essay?CMP=share_btn_link.

54. Elizabeth Kolbert, "Why Facts Don't Change Our Minds," *The New Yorker*, June 19, 2017, newyorker.com/magazine/2017/02/27/why-facts -dont-change-our-minds.

55. Altman, "What I Heard."

56. Hawkins, et al., *Hidden Tribes*, 90.

57. Nathan J. Robinson, "Text of University of Connecticut Speech," *Current Affairs*, January 26, 2018, currentaffairs.org/2018/01/text-of -university-of-connecticut-speech.

58. Daniel Treisman, "Why the Poor Don't Vote to Soak the Rich," *The Washington Post*, February 27, 2018, washingtonpost.com/news/ monkey-cage/wp/2018/02/27/why-the-poor-dont-vote-to-soak-the -rich/?utm_term=.0f14f79767c0.

59. Bobby Duffy, "What We Just Don't Understand About the 1%," *BBC Worklife*, November 7, 2018, bbc.com/worklife/article/20181107-what -we-just-dont-understand-about-the-1.

60. Kahneman, *Thinking*, 279.

61. John T. Jost, Jack Glaser, Frank J. Sulloway, and Arie W. Kruglanski, "Political Conservatism as Motivated Social Cognition," *Psychological Bulletin* 129, no. 3 (2003): 339–75.

62. Dana Milbank, "Does Trump's Great Gut Mean a Tiny Brain?" *The Washington Post*, November 28, 2018, washingtonpost.com /opinions/why-would-trump-need-brains-when-he-has-a-gut/2018 /11/28/75bc6c38-f341-11e8-80d0-f7e1948d55f4_story.html?utm_term =.1fc421822cbf&wpisrc=nl_most&wpmm=1.

63. Jesse Singal, "Can a New Book on 'Intuitionism' Explain America's Political Crisis?" *Intelligencer*, October 16, 2018. nymag.com /intelligencer/2018/10/enchanted-america-tries-to-explain-conspiracy-thinking.html.

64. Stephen Greenspan, *Annals of Gullibility: Why We Get Duped and How to Avoid It* (Westport, CT: Praeger, 2009), 2.

65. Greenspan, *Annals of Gullibility*, 68, 158–62.

66. Singal, "Can a New Book…"

67. Greenspan, *Annals of Gullibility*, 150–55.

68. Olga Khazan, "Why Conservatives Are More Susceptible to Fake Threats," *The Atlantic*, February 3, 2017, theatlantic.com/science/ archive/2017/02/why-fake-news-targeted-trump-supporters/515433/.

69. John Ehrenreich, "Why Are Conservatives More Susceptible to Believing Lies?" *Slate*, November 9, 2017, slate.com/articles/health _and_science/science/2017/11/why_conservatives_are_more _susceptible_to_believing_in_lies.html.

70. Greenspan, *Annals of Gullibility*, 63–66.

71. Studies conducted after the ad aired confirmed that the subliminal message of "RATS" led voters to view Gore more negatively: Westen, *The Political Brain*, 58–59; Dylan Love, "The Shocking Drink and Incredible Coke History of Subliminal Advertising," *Business Insider*, May 26, 2011, businessinsider.com/subliminal-ads-2011-5.

72. *Breitbart*, for example, cannot be cited on Wikipedia because of its track record of intentionally misleading stories. "Breitbart News," Wikipedia, accessed January 31, 2019. en.wikipedia.org/wiki /Breitbart_News#cite_note-contextual-nightmare-17; see also Jane Mayer, "The Making of the Fox News White House," *The New Yorker*, March 11, 2019, newyorker.com/magazine/2019/03/11/the-making-of -the-fox-news-white-house; Yochai Benkler, Robert Faris, and Hal Roberts, *Network Propaganda: Manipulation, Disinformation, and Radicalization in American Politics* (Oxford: Oxford University Press, 2018); David Brock, *The Republican Noise Machine: Right-Wing Media and How It Corrupts Democracy* (New York: Crown, 2004).

73. Jeffrey Toobin, "A New Book Details the Damage Done by the Right-Wing Media in 2016," *The New Yorker*, August 28, 2018, newyorker.com/news/daily-comment/a-new-book-details-the-damage-done-by-the-right-wing-media-in-2016.

74. Amanda Robb, "Pizzagate: Anatomy of a Fake News Scandal," *Rolling Stone*, June 25, 2018, rollingstone.com/politics/politics-news/anatomy-of-a-fake-news-scandal-125877/.

75. Craig Silverman, Lauren Strapagiel, Hamza Shaban, Ellie Hall, and Jeremy Singer-Vine, "Hyperpartisan Facebook Pages are Publishing False and Misleading Information at an Alarming Rate," *BuzzFeed News*, October 20, 2016, buzzfeednews.com/article/craigsilverman/partisan-fb-pages-analysis#.wo2EG4oed.

76. Carole Cadwalladr, "Robert Mercer: The Big Data Billionaire Waging War on Mainstream Media," *The Guardian*, February 26, 2017, theguardian.com/politics/2017/feb/26/robert-mercer-breitbart-war-on-media-steve-bannon-donald-trump-nigel-farage.

77. James Hoggan, *I'm Right and You're an Idiot* (Gabriola Island, BC: New Society Publishers, 2019), 87.

78. Chua, *Political Tribes*, 204.

79. Samia Mounts, "Ricky & Bradley—Liberal Messaging," in *Make America Relate Again*, produced by Better Angels Media, podcast, season 2, episode 9, 51:18, makeamericarelatepodcast.com/s2ep9.

80. Jost et al., "Political Conservatism," 345, 349, 369.

81. Philip E. Tetlock and Gregory Mitchell, "Liberal and Conservative Approaches to Justice: Conflicting Psychological Portraits (1993)," *Psychological Perspectives on Justice: Theory and Applications (2008)*: 234–56, 241, ssrn.com/abstract=2479864.

82. Yves Smith, "Americans Tolerate Inequality Because They Overestimate Their Odds of Coming Out on Top," *Naked Capitalism* blog, *Aurora Advisors Inc.*, June 22, 2017, nakedcapitalism.com/2017/06/americans-tolerate-inequality-estimate-odds-coming-top.html.

83. Seung Min Kim and Scott Clement, "Populist Economic Frustration Threatens Trump's Strongest Reelection Issue, Post-ABC Poll Finds," *The Washington Post*, April 29, 2019, washingtonpost.com/politics/populist-economic-frustration-threatens-trumps-strongest-reelection-issue-post-abc-poll-finds/2019/04/28/44f64cbc-6a02-11e9-9d56-1c0cf2c7ac04_story.html?utm_term=.8ee22d12fa7c.

84. Pew Research Center, "Attitudes on Same-Sex Marriage," *Pew Research Center Religion & Public Life*, May 14, 2019, pewforum.org/fact-sheet/changing-attitudes-on-gay-marriage/.

85. Thomas Byrne Edsall, "Studies: Conservatives Are from Mars, Liberals Are from Venus," *The Atlantic*, February 7, 2012, theatlantic

.com/politics/archive/2012/02/studies-conservatives-are-from-mars
-liberals-are-from-venus/252416/; Jost et al., "Political Conservatism."

86. A creative team of social psychology researchers constructed unflattering (and flattering) portraits of liberal and conservative world-
views as a way of demonstrating the subjectivity in our evaluations of
one another's beliefs. These write-ups are too long to reproduce here
but offer a fascinating cross-ideological perspective: Tetlock et al.,
"Liberal and Conservative Approaches to Justice," 238–45.

87. Justin Naylor, "Why I Am a Conservative," *Better Angels* blog, March
13, 2019, better-angels.org/why-i-am-a-conservative/.

88. Jonathan Haidt, "What Is Wrong with Those Tea Partiers?" *Sabato's
Crystal Ball*, University of Virginia Center for Politics, February 4,
2010, centerforpolitics.org/crystalball/articles/jdh2010020402/.

89. Pew Research Center, "Religion in America: U.S. Religious Data,
Demographics and Statistics," Pew Research Center Religion &
Public Life, May 11, 2015, pewforum.org/religious-landscape-study
/political-ideology/conservative/.

Chapter 4: Curiosity—The Antidote to Contempt

1. Some material in this chapter originally appeared in Erica Etelson,
"How to Flip a Trump Voter Without Pushing Too Hard," *AlterNet*,
September 17, 2016, alternet.org/election-2016/how-flip-trump-voter
-without-pushing-too-hard.

2. Robin DiAngelo, *White Fragility: Why It's So Hard for White People
to Talk about Racism* (Boston: Beacon Press, 2019).

3. Working America, "Changing Minds. Bridging Divides. Winning
Elections," YouTube video, 3:06, October 3, 2017, youtube.com/watch
?v=WZKDxAqnFxs.

4. Thomas Frank, "Four More Years," *Harper's Magazine*, April 2018,
harpers.org/archive/2018/04/four-more-years-2/5/.

5. David Brookman and Joshua Kalla, "Durably Reducing Transphobia: A Field Experiment on Door-to-Door Canvassing," *Science*
352, no. 6282 (April 2016), 220–24, science.sciencemag.org/content
/352/6282/220; TEDx, "How We Can Reduce Prejudice with a Conversation, David Fleischer," YouTube video, 16:51, January 25, 2017,
youtu.be/xN6O5LTaGyg.

6. David Fleischer, interview by author, June 4, 2018.

7. TEDx, "How We Can Reduce."

8. Elizabeth Levy Paluck and Donald P. Green, "Prejudice Reduction:
What Works? A Review and Assessment of Research and Practice,"

The Annual Review of Psychology 60 (2009), 339–67, doi.org/ 10.1146 /annurev.psych.60.110707.163607.

9. Lisa Legault, Jennifer N. Gutsell, and Michael Inzlicht, "Ironic Effects of Antiprejudice Messages," *Psychological Science* 22, no. 12 (2011): 1472–477, doi.org/10.1177/0956797611427918.

10. Angela King, interview by author, June 15, 2018; Christian Picciolini, "Uniting Against Hate," Lecture, Berkeley City College, Berkeley, CA, June 15, 2018.

11. Denis Arp, "Getting to the Root of Racist Hate," Chapman University Newsroom blog, August 10, 2018, blogs.chapman.edu/news-and -stories/2018/08/10/getting-to-the-root-of-racist-hate/.

12. Sally Kohn, *The Opposite of Hate: A Field Guide to Repairing Our Humanity* (Chapel Hill: Algonquin Books of Chapel Hill, 2018), 99.

13. "Never" may, in fact, be too strong a word—AIDS Coalition to Unleash Power (ACT UP) shamed the federal government into responding to the AIDS epidemic by targeting NIH and FDA health professionals who were already highly sympathetic but trapped in bureaucratic complacency. It was a risky strategy, born of desperation as the number of dead mushroomed. It's not clear if all of the targeted federal officials and researchers were catalyzed due to shame or to being confronted with the urgent reality, but ACT UP undeniably activated the conscience of a nation. My takeaway is that shame can be a tactic of last resort when there's reason to believe the target would respond positively rather than with hostility or withdrawal. Anthony Fauci, interview by author, December 14, 2018; #MEAction, "Peter Staley: Lessons from the AIDS Movement," YouTube video, 70:00, May 14, 2014, meaction.net/tools/case-studies/how-to-survive -a-plague/peter-staley-transcript/; F. Diane Barth, "7 Ways to Respond When Someone Shames You," *Psychology Today*, October 29, 2017, psychologytoday.com/us/blog/the-couch/201710/7-ways -respond-when-someone-shames-you; Patrizia Velotti et al., "Faces of Shame: Implications for Self-Esteem, Emotion Regulation, Aggression and Well-Being," *The Journal of Psychology* 151:2 (2017), 171–84, doi.org/10.1080/00223980.2016.1248809.

14. Erika Hayasaki, "The Pathology of Prejudice," *The New Republic*, November 27, 2018, newrepublic.com/article/152299/white-suprem acists-learn-hate.

15. Manny Fernandez, "Lesson on Love, From a Rabbi Who Knows Hate and Forgiveness," *The New York Times*, January 4, 2009, nytimes.com /2009/01/05/nyregion/05rabbi.html.

16. Eli Saslow, *Rising Out of Hatred: The Awakening of a Former White Nationalist* (New York: Doubleday, 2018), 80.

17. Ibid., 266.

18. "Challenging White Supremacy Workshop," Institute for Global Communications, cwsworkshop.org/resources/ARAgenda.html.

19. The White Ally Toolkit Project, whiteallytoolkit.com/.

20. "Selected Quotes," Stanford University Libraries, accessed October 11, 2018, swap.stanford.edu/20141218230015/http://mlk-kpp01.stanford.edu/kingweb/popular_requests/quotes.htm.

21. The King Center, "The King Philosophy," accessed June 20, 2019, thekingcenter.org/king-philosophy/.

22. Van Jones, *Beyond the Messy Truth: How We Came Apart, How We Come Together* (New York: Ballantine, 2018), 27.

23. David Campt, "Listening Tips for Anti-Racism Allies," *The White Ally Toolkit*, static1.squarespace.com/static/58b4700803596efb0e7f6062/t/59da451dcf81e005db70faba/1507476769346/Listening Tips and Worksheet.pdf./Listening Tips and Worksheet.pdf.

24. Wochit News, "Portland Hotel Calls Cops On Black Guest In Lobby," YouTube video, 1:18, December 28, 2018, youtu.be/vpvzHIlajKg.

Chapter 5: Speaking Your Peace

1. Eve Ensler, "A Letter to White Women Who Support Brett Kavanaugh," *Time*, October 4, 2018, time.com/5415254/white-women-brett-kavanaugh-donald-trump/.

2. "Drop by Drop/While Rome Burns," *Towardanakedheart* blog, October 31, 2018, towardanakedheart.wordpress.com/2018/10/31/drop-by-drop-while-rome-burns/.

3. Ken Taylor and John Perry, "How to Humbly Disagree: Interview with Nathan Ballantyne," *Philosophy Talk* podcast, 0:30, March 11, 2018, philosophytalk.org/shows/how-humbly-disagree.

4. Lisa Friedman, "White House Tried to Stop Climate Science Testimony, Documents Show," *The New York Times*, June 8, 2019, nytimes.com/2019/06/08/climate/rod-schoonover-testimony.html.

5. Massimo Calabresi, "Donald Trump and Undocumented Workers at Trump Tower," *Time*, August 24, 2016, time.com/4465744/donald-trump-undocumented-workers/; Steve Reilly, "*USA Today* Exclusive: Hundreds Allege Donald Trump Doesn't Pay His Bills," *USA Today*, April 25, 2018, usatoday.com/story/news/politics/elections/2016/06/09/donald-trump-unpaid-bills-republican-president-lawsuits/85297274/.

6. Steven Brill, "What Donald Trump's University Reveals About His

Nature," *Time*, November 5, 2015, time.com/4101290/what-the-legal
-battle-over-trump-university-reveals-about-its-founder/.

7. Dave Fleischer, interview by author, June 14, 2018.

8. Erica Buist, interview by author, February 20, 2018. By February
2018, Erica's tweet had 6 million impressions plus viral Facebook and
Instagram exposure.

9. Fox News, "Florida Students Walk Out of Schools, Press Lawmakers
for Tougher Gun Laws," Fox News, February 21, 2018, foxnews.com
/us/2018/02/21/florida-students-walk-out-schools-press-lawmakers
-for-tougher-gun-laws.html.

10. David Brooks, "Respect First, Then Gun Control," *The New York
Times*, February 20, 2018, nytimes.com/2018/02/19/opinion/parkland
-gun-control-shootings.html?smid=tw-nytopinion&smtyp=cur.

11. Joseph Wulfsohn, "Twitter Blasts David Brooks for Suggesting the
Left Should 'Show Respect to Gun Owners,'" *Mediaite*, February
20, 2018. mediaite.com/online/twitter-blasts-david-brooks-for
-suggesting-the-left-should-show-respect-to-gun-owners/.

12. E.J. Dionne, Jr., "Why Is Only One Side in the Gun Culture War
Required to Show Respect?" *The Washington Post*, February 21, 2018,
washingtonpost.com/opinions/gun-owners-demand-respect-they
-just-arent-willing-to-give-it/2018/02/21/0d18397c-173d-11e8-92c9
-376b4fe57ff7_story.html?undefined=&utm_term=.c9b9dfa872d9
&wpisrc=nl_most&wpmm=1.

13. Eric Lipton and Alexander Burns, "The True Source of the NRA's
Clout: Mobilization, Not Donations," *The New York Times*, February 24, 2018, nytimes.com/2018/02/24/us/politics/nra-gun-control
-florida.html.

14. Ijeoma Olou, *So You Want to Talk About Race* (New York: Seal Press,
2018), 168.

15. Nazgol Ghandnoosh and Christopher Lewis, "Race and Punishment:
Racial Perceptions of Crime and Support for Punitive Policies," *The
Sentencing Project* (2014), 23, sentencingproject.org/wp-content
/uploads/2015/11/Race-and-Punishment.pdf.

16. For a powerful example of nonaccusatory, passionate anger, watch
Arkansas Senator Stephanie Flowers stand her ground against
stand-your-ground laws that have lethal consequences for black men
like her son. (The only part of Flowers's speech that may not have
been ideal was when she tells her colleague to go to hell.) THV11,
"Arkansas Sen. Flowers Makes Passionate Speech about 'Stand Your
Ground' Bill," YouTube video, 4:31, March 7, 2019, youtu.be/FNt
EiAu4mtE.

17. David Agren, "Migrant Caravan Members Unfazed by Trump: 'He'll Change His Thinking,'" *The Guardian*, October 26, 2018, theguardian.com/us-news/2018/oct/26/migrant-caravan-us-border-reaction-trump.

18. Chantal Da Silva, "Donald Trump Jokes about Shooting Migrants at the Border," *Newsweek*, May 9, 2019, newsweek.com/donald-trump-jokes-about-shooting-migrants-border-thats-only-panhandle-you-1420611.

19. Patricia J. Williams, "Our Toxic-Speech Epidemic," *The Nation*, April 15, 2019, thenation.com/article/new-zealand-speech-murder/.

20. Guardian News, "Trump Supporter Tells Man in Racist Rant That She Hates Him Because He Is Mexican," YouTube video, 0:35, June 26, 2018, m.youtube.com/watch?v=Lz3qobaxHpc.

21. CNN, "Alt-Right Leader: 'Hail Trump!,'" YouTube video, 2:10, November 21, 2016, youtube.com/watch?v=106-bi3jlxk.

22. David Campt, "Important Principles for Effective Engagement of Racism Skeptics," *The White Ally Toolkit*, static1.squarespace.com/static/58b4700803596efb0e7f6062/t/59da44d41f318d0de5daa57b/1507476695346/Principles for Effective Engagement.pdf./Principles for Effective Engagement.pdf.

23. David W. Campt, *The White Ally Toolkit Workbook*, ii.

24. DiAngelo, *White Fragility*, 151.

25. Nakagawa and Ramos, "What Time Is It?"

26. Mike DeBonis, "Pelosi Fills Role as Trump's Sparring Partner, Respecting the Office But Not the Man," *The Washington Post*, January 2, 2019, washingtonpost.com/powerpost/pelosi-fills-role-as-trumps-sparring-partner-respecting-the-office-but-not-the-man/2019/01/02/26680196-0d37-11e9-84fc-d58c33d6c8c7_story.html?utm_term=.52ca53011c09.

27. Allyson Chiu, "'Queen of Condescending Applause': Nancy Pelosi Clapped at Trump, and the Internet Lost It," *The Washington Post*, February 6, 2019, washingtonpost.com/nation/2019/02/06/queen-condescending-applause-nancy-pelosi-clapped-trump-internet-lost-it/?utm_term=.a06eea9013b1&wpisrc=nl_most&wpmm=1.

Chapter 6: Putting It All Together

1. Hoggan, *I'm Right*, 200.

2. Miki Meek, "Where Have You Gone, Barbara Jordan? Our Nation Turns Its Lonely Eyes to You," *This American Life* 665, podcast, 61:29, February 11, 2019, thisamericanlife.org/665/before-things-went-to-hell/act-one-0.

3. Julia Preston, "Immigrants Aren't Taking Americans' Jobs, New

Study Finds," *The New York Times*, September 21, 2016, nytimes.com /2016/09/22/us/immigrants-arent-taking-americans-jobs-new-study -finds.html.

4. Hunter Hallman, "How Do Undocumented Immigrants Pay Federal Taxes? An Explainer," *Bipartisan Policy Center* blog, March 28, 2018; bipartisanpolicy.org/blog/how-do-undocumented-immigrants -pay-federal-taxes-an-explainer.

5. Marco della Cava and Ricardo Lopez, "Could California Produce Soon Cost You More?" *USA Today*, March 1, 2019, usatoday.com /story/news/2019/01/27/could-california-produce-soon-cost-you -more/2594964002/; Madison Iszler, "Are Immigrants Taking Farm Jobs From U.S. Citizens? In NC, Farmers Say No," *Raleigh News & Observer*, July 2, 2017, newsobserver.com/news/business/article160 086719.html; Gary Wishnatzki, "Thanksgiving Without the Sides: Lack of Farm Labor Could Make Fruits, Vegetables Unaffordable," *USA Today*, November 20, 2018, usatoday.com/story/opinion/voices /2018/11/20/thanksgiving-food-agriculture-farming-farms-column /2053772002/; Mary Jo Dudley, "Why Care about Undocumented Immigrants? For One Thing, They've Become Vital to Key Sectors of the U.S. Economy," *The Conversation*, January 24, 2019, theconver sation.com/why-care-about-undocumented-immigrants-for-one -thing-theyve-become-vital-to-key-sectors-of-the-us-economy -98790.

6. Fox News, "Town Hall with Bernie Sanders, Part 1," YouTube video, 2:27, April 15, 2019, youtube.com/watch?v=p4ozAACcc8I.

7. Paul Gorski, "The Myth of the 'Culture of Poverty'," *Educational Leadership* 65 (April 2008), 32–36, researchgate.net/publication/228 620924_The_Myth_of_theCulture_of_Poverty".

8. Joe Berkowitz, "Behind 'Conversations with People Who Hate Me'," *Fast Company*, August 10, 2017, fastcompany.com/40448817/behind -conversations-with-people-who-hate-me-the-timeliest-podcast-of -2017.

9. Dylan Marron, "Empathy Is Not Endorsement," *TED2018* video, 10:46, April 2018 ted.com/talks/dylan_marron_how_i_turn_negative _online_comments_into_positive_offline_conversations/discussion ?language=en.

Conclusion: To Bridge or To Break

1. Allied Media Conference, "Alicia Garza Speaks on Building Power to the AMC2017 Opening Ceremony," Allied Media Projects, September 5, 2017, alliedmedia.org/news/2017/09/05/alicia-garza-speaks -building-power-amc2017-opening-ceremony.

2. Diana C. Mutz, *Hearing the Other Side* (Cambridge: Cambridge University Press, 2006), 41.

3. Mutz, *Hearing*, 107–08.

4. Hawkins et al., *Hidden Tribes*, 110–14.

5. Mutz, *Hearing*, 8.

6. James S. Fishkin, *Democracy When the People Are Thinking: Revitalizing Our Politics through Public Deliberation* (Oxford: Oxford University Press, 2018), 157–60.

7. Better Angels, "In Conversation: Black Lives Matter and the Tea Party," YouTube video, 1:31:41, June 21, 2019, youtube.com/watch?v=dnMTrKUnfPU.

8. Yascha Mounk, "Republicans Don't Understand Democrats—And Democrats Don't Understand Republicans," *The Atlantic*, June 23, 2019, theatlantic.com/ideas/archive/2019/06/republicans-and-democrats-dont-understand-each-other/592324/.

9. Mason, *Uncivil Agreement*, 127–28.

10. Jonathan Ladd, "Negative Partisanship May Be the Most Toxic Form of Polarization," *Vox*, June 2, 2017, vox.com/mischiefs-of-faction/2017/6/2/15730524/negative-partisanship-toxic-polarization.

11. Ifat Maoz, Andrew Ward, Michael Katz, and Lee Ross, "Reactive Devaluation of an 'Israeli' vs. 'Palestinian' Peace Proposal," *The Journal of Conflict Resolution* 46, no. 4 (August 2002): 515–46, journals.sagepub.com/doi/abs/10.1177/0022002702046004003.

12. Louis Jacobson, "Obama Says Heritage Foundation Is Source of Health Exchange Idea," *PolitiFact*, April 1, 2010. politifact.com/truth-o-meter/statements/2010/apr/01/barack-obama/obama-says-heritage-foundation-source-health-excha/.

13. Mason, *Uncivil Agreement*, 54.

14. Ibid., 54.

15. Desmond Meade, "The Urgency of Bridging," Lecture, at the *Othering & Belonging Conference*, from the Haas Institute for a Fair and Inclusive Society at UC–Berkeley, Oakland, CA, April 10, 2019.

16. Ralph Nader, *Unstoppable: The Emerging Left-Right Alliance to Dismantle the Corporate State* (New York: Nation Books, 2015).

17. Jesse Hellmann, "Cruz, Ocasio-Cortez Efforts on Birth Control Access Face Major Obstacles," *The Hill*, June 16, 2019, thehill.com/policy/healthcare/448682-cruz-ocasio-cortez-efforts-on-birth-control-access-face-major-obstacles; Kate Irby, "AOC and Ted Cruz Working Together?" *McClatchy DC Bureau*, May 31, 2019. mcclatchydc.com/news/politics-government/article231045408.html.

18. John Whitesides, "From Disputes to a Breakup: Wounds Still Raw after U.S. Election," *Reuters*, February 7, 2017, reuters.com/article

/us-usa-trump-relationships-insight/from-disputes-to-a-breakup
-wounds-still-raw-after-u-s-election-idUSKBN15M13L.

19. Amanda Ripley, "The Least Politically Prejudiced Place in America,"
The Atlantic, March 4, 2019, theatlantic.com/politics/archive/2019
/03/watertown-new-york-tops-scale-political-tolerance/582106/.

20. Kirk Schneider and Sayyed Mohsen Fatemi, "Today's Biggest Threat:
The Polarized Mind," *Scientific American* blog, April 16, 2019, blogs
.scientificamerican.com/observations/todays-biggest-threat-the
-polarized-mind/.

21. Paula Green, interview by author, February 12, 2019.

22. Daryl Johnson, "Return of the Violent Black Nationalist," *Intelligence
Report*, Southern Poverty Law Center, August 8, 2017, splcenter.
org/fighting-hate/intelligence-report/2017/return-violent-black
-nationalist; Greg Kocher, "'I Apologize for My Actions,' Machete
Attacker Is Sentenced for Transylvania Attack," *Lexington Herald
Leader*, December 16, 2018, kentucky.com/news/local/crime/article
223103120.html; Jennifer Williams, "Antifa Clashes with Police and
Journalists in Charlottesville and DC," *Vox*, August 13, 2018, vox.com
/identities/2018/8/12/17681986/antifa-leftist-violence-clashes-protests
-charlottesville-dc-unite-the-right.

23. Richie Davis, "Did Hands Across the Hills Fall Short?" *The Green-
field Recorder*, October 18, 2018, pulitzercenter.org/reporting/did
-hands-across-hills-fall-short.

24. Parker J. Palmer, *Healing the Heart of Democracy: The Courage to
Create a Politics Worthy of the Human Spirit* (San Francisco: Jossey-
Bass, 2014), 32.

25. Jacob S. Hacker and Paul Pierson, *Off Center: The Republican
Revolution and the Erosion of American Democracy* (New Haven:
Yale University Press, 2006). Drivers of asymmetric polarization
include Southern leadership of the GOP, the influence (and money)
of the Christian right and right-wing think tanks and lobbies, over-
representation of far-right voters in GOP primaries, income inequality (which prompts both parties to take their cues from their big
donors), and the decimation of organized labor as a counterbalance.

26. Dionne, Jr., *Why the Right Went Wrong*, 13.

27. Frances Lee, "Why I've Started to Fear My Fellow Social Justice
Activists," *YES! Magazine*, October 13, 2017, yesmagazine.org/people
-power/why-ive-started-to-fear-my-fellow-social-justice-activists
-20171013.

28. Trent Eady, "'Everything Is Problematic.' My Journey into the Centre
of a Dark Political World, and How I Escaped," *The McGill Daily*, November 24, 2014, mcgilldaily.com/2014/11/everything-problematic/.

29. Krista Tippett, "Sally Kohn and Erick Erickson—Relationship Across Rupture," *The On Being Project* podcast, 51:58, October 11, 2018, onbeing.org/programs/sally-kohn-and-erick-erickson-relationship -across-rupture-oct18/?fbclid=IwAR3vNXakDMh38jSiCmwoexH-c31 Q3KQlV9kmkuF_MKSjQSxFj1QjRCfxgjQ#transcript.

Index

A

Abramsky, Sasha, 81
accountability
  and decorum, 11
  and humility, 15
  impact of contempt on, 33
  and position statements, 125–126
  for self-righteousness, 141–142
AFL-CIO, 14, 106
Alexander, Michelle, 73
alienation
  of conservatives, 35–36
  and conspiracy media, 100
  prevalence of, 175
  of swing voters, 42
Altman, Sam, 34
alt-right, online targets of, 19
ambiguity, accepting, 164
America, as super-group, 100–101
The American Conservative, 32–34
"A Mighty Kindness," v
Andrew (commenter), 32–33
anger
  as element of contempt, 3, 19,
    40, 147
  as element of humiliation, 6
  expressing, 11, 12, 98, 125, 137,
    147, 177
anxiety, and health, 81
apologies, and communication, 150–151
Appalachia, resentment in, 56
Appalshop, 56
Arendt, Hannah, 170–171
argument, as style of question, 117
Arnade, Chris, 59
The Atlantic, 54
attribution error, 93–94
authoritarianism, 83–84

availability bias, 96
avoidance, as contempt, 130

B

backlash contempt, 36–37, 40
Bailey, Rev. Jennifer, 9
Barber, Rev. William, 7
Becca (Wisconsin), 126–127
Bee, Samantha, 27
Bell, Michael, 115–116
belongingness, 40, 85, 110
Berry, Jeffrey, 26, 34
Better Angels, 32, 78, 123, 167, 172
Beyond the Messy Truth (Jones), 66
bias, 92–93, 94–95, 96, 104
bigotry. *See* racism
biopolitics, factors in, 80
Black, Derek, 111–112
Blankenhorn, David, 32
Blasey Ford, Christine, 88, 126
Blow, Charles, 28
body language, as communication, 148
bonding, social, 38
Bordoloi, Satyen, 15
Borowitz, Andy, 5–6
brain, physical responses by, 22, 30–31,
    80–81, 94
Breitbart, 99
Bridge Alliance, 167
Brooks, David, 133–134
Brown, Brené, 170
Brown, Sherrod, 49–50
Brzezinski, Mika, 25
Buist, Erica, 130–132
Bundy, Ammon, 78
Buttigieg, Pete, 49
Byerley, Melinda, 23
bystander intervention training, 165

C

Cache Valley Daily, 29
"call-out culture," 35, 178
campaign spending, corporate, 51
Campt, David, 93–94, 112, 119, 145
Canada, antiprejudice study, 109
canvassing, 106–109, 122
capitalism, 58, 71, 76
Carlson, Tucker, 93
causation/correlation, 91–92
celebrities, contemptuous language
    of, 23
Center for Courage & Renewal, 177
Center for Deliberative Democracy, 171
Center for the Study of Race, Politics,
    and Culture, 110
Chait, Jonathan, 30
Challenging White Supremacy
    Workshop, 112
Charlie Hebdo, 3
Chicago Sun-Times, 57
Chicago Tribune, 29
Christina H. (*Cracked*), 35–36, 167
Chua, Amy, 100–101
civility, benefits of, 11
civil rights, goal of, 7–8
classism
    class structure, 50–51
    contempt based on, 49, 53
    and cultural icons, 52, 58
    dynamics of, 49–50
    response to, 165–166
    slurs, 54
    as strategy, 52
climate change, 92–93, 128–129
Clinton, Hillary
    alienation of swing voters by, 42
    coal mining comment by, 55–56
    "deplorables" comment by, 20–21, 28
CNN, 25, 28, 65, 98
cognitive errors, 90–91
    attribution error, 93–94
    availability bias, 96
    confirmation bias, 94–95, 104
    conformity bias, 92–93, 104
    correlation taken as causation, 91–92
    gullibility, 97–98
    headwind-tailwind asymmetry, 91
    intuitionism, 97

just-world bias, 95
    loss aversion, 96–97
    present bias, 92
common ground, in issues, 174–175
communication
    apologizing, as strategy for,
        150–151
    counterattack, as style of, 7, 8
    energy of, 149
    ignorance, admitting in, 150
    issue, as focus of, 150
    mockery, using in, 149
    objectivity as judgmental, 127
    open mind, needed for, 151
    "othering" as type of, 6, 8
    partisanship, effect on, 148–149
    PNDC techniques for, 10, 11–12
    political discourse, as style of, 5
    retaliation, as tactic for, 8
    styles of, 179
    techniques for effective, 148–149
    training for, 106–109, 116, 122
    war model of, 15
    "we," using in, 149–150
    winning, as strategy in, 150
compassion, 40, 103, 111, 112, 147
complicity, as effect of contempt, 44
confirmation bias, 94–95, 104
conformity bias, 92–93, 104
Conner, Alana, 145
Conscientious Objections (Naff), v
conservatism
    and authoritarianism, 84–85
    and disgust, 82
    entrenching, 35–36
    government, perception of by, 104
    and gullibility, 98
    and moral/economic interests,
        102–103
    and religion, 103–104
    and social mobility, 102
    and social programs, 102
    status quo favored by, 101
    and tribalism, 86
    values of, 15, 86–87, 102, 103–104
conservatives
    alienation of, 35–36
    engaging with, 114, 168, 169–170
conspiracy media, increase in, 100

contempt
  addictive quality of, 43
  avoidance as, 130
  as backlash, 36–37, 40
  brain, response to, 22
  curiosity as antidote to, 114
  dehumanization as effect of, 41
  effectiveness of, 10, 40–41, 42, 44, 45
  elements of, 19–20
  escalation of, 40
  goal of, 20
  and group cohesion, 43
  in media, 25–26
  physical manifestations of, 19
  as predictor of marriage failure, 17
  as revenge, 42
  as self-protection, 3, 38–39, 43
  society without, 179
  study on, 31
  as used by Donald Trump, 7, 20, 40
  as used by Nancy Pelosi, 7
Contemptor, 28
*Conversations With People Who Hate
    Me* (podcast), 168
Conway, Kellyanne, 25
Cooper, Anderson, 25, 27–28
"corporatized outrage," 28
correlation/causation, 91–92
"cosmopolitan elite," 69
Coulter, Ann, 49
counterattack, effectiveness of, 7, 8
Cracked, 35, 167
Cramer, Katherine, 67
Crooks and Liars, 28
cross-partisanship, 170–172, 174–175
Cullen, Art, 13
culture
  "call-out culture," 35, 178
  cultural elitism, 67
  icons of, as elements of classism, 52
  influences on, 51
Cuomo, Chris, 25
curiosity questions
  demonstrations of, 118
  effectiveness of, 114, 115–116
  examples of, 119–123
  for finding common ground, 162
  goal of, 116–117
  ground rules for, 123

  oral v. written, 119
  outcome of, 124
  for self-exploration, 123–124
  technique for, 118–119

D
Daily Kos, 28
decorum, effect on accountability of, 11
"deep canvassing," 107–109
deep stories, 78–79, 88, 89, 90
defensiveness
  contempt as, 38–39
  effect of, 30–31, 41
  overcoming, 106, 114, 127–128
dehumanization, 41
Deliberative Polling, 171–172
democracy, public discussion and, 169
Democratic Party
  and demographic projections, 63
  voter base of, 58–59, 62–63, 69,
    72–73
De Niro, Robert, 23
dialogue, respectful, 112, 133, 144–145,
    176, 177
DiAngelo, Robin, 105–106, 145
Dionne, E.J., 59
discontent, populist, 66, 70
disengagement, in politics, 13
disgust, 82, 83
disinformation, 51, 99, 100
Dow, Whitney, 65
Dream Corps, 7
Dreher, Rod, 15, 26
*Dying of Whiteness: How the Politics of
    Racial Resentment is Killing Amer-
    ica's Heartland* (Metzl), 65

E
economy
  contemporary disruptions in, 69
  declining wage prospects in, 70
  and racism, 71, 72
  and voter motivation, 60
  and white nationalism, 59–60
Eisenstein, Charles, 7
elections
  2016, 13, 50, 57, 72–73
  2020, Trump strategy for, 13–14
  corruption of, 51

effect of contempt on, 42
2018 midterm, outcome, 13
elitism
    cultural, 67
    effect of, 44
    and 2016 election, 73
    focus on as strategy, 37
    focus on by media, 36
    resentment caused by, 49–50
Ellison, Sharon Strand
    background of, 10, 113
    on curiosity questions, 115
    demonstrations by, 118, 148, 168
    on position statements, 136–137, 142
    on respect, 147
    on war model of communication, 15
empathy, 134–135
    effect of, 83
    "empathy wall," 89
    impairment of, 40–41
    racism, counteracting with, 68
Ensler, Eve, 126
entrapment, 117, 118
environment, PNDC techniques for,
    121–122, 128–129
equality, of opportunity v. of outcome,
    102
estate tax, position statement on, 139
estrangement, of voters, 58–59, 62,
    72–73
Etelson, Erica
    communication style preferred by, 9
    formative experiences of, 1–2
    reaction to Brett Kavanaugh by, 41
    reaction to Trump by, 2–3, 21–22
Exhausted Majority, 169–170

F
Faith Matters Network, 9
Fallows, James, 54
families, separation of, 137–138
Fatemi, Sayyed Mohsen, 175
fear, 80–83, 84
Fishkin, James, 171
Fiske, Susan, 22, 38, 40
Flanagan, Caitlin, 26–27
Fleischer, Ari, 13–14, 130
Fleischer, Dave, 108

The Flip Side, 168
Fox News, 36, 80, 99
Frank, Thomas, 32, 73, 74
Frank (ex-Marine), 132–133
Fraser, Steve, 70
Frum, David, 177–178
"future shock," 75

G
Galston, William, 62
Garza, Alicia, 8
Gawker, 29
genetics, and political beliefs, 79
gerrymandering, 51
Gibson, Alex, 56, 61
The Gilded Rage (Zaitchik), 60
globalization
    impact on economic classes of, 69
    nationalism as response to, 72
GOP. See Republican Party,
    strategies of
Gottman, John, 17
government, conservative view of, 104
Gray, Briahna Joy, 63–64, 71
Green, Paula, 176
Greenberg, Stanley, 73
Greenspan, Stephen, 97, 98
Guardian, 58, 59
gullibility, 97–98
guns, ownership of, 131, 134–135
gun violence, 130–134

H
Hacker, Jacob, 177
Haidt, Jonathan, 40
Hardisty, Jean, 67
Harrold, Kaitlyn, 14
Harry, Ed, 62
hate violence
    curiosity questions on, 120
    groups, 72, 110
headwind-tailwind asymmetry, 91
healthcare
    curiosity questions on, 122
    position statement on, 139
Heartland
    characterization of, 13
    Hillary Clinton on, 20–21

Heartland (Smarsh), 52
Hela, Paul, 48
Heritage Foundation, 173
Highlander Center, 68
Hochschild, Arlie, 54, 78, 88, 89, 90
Hollaback!, 165
homophobia, 82
Horzempa, Maggie, 35
Huffington Post, 29
humiliation, effectiveness of, 6, 7
humility, and accountability, 15

I
immigrants, fear of, 59
immigration
    complexity of issue, 154
    curiosity questions on, 119–120
    nativism backlash, 154
immigration, dialogue on, 154–161
incel, 19
income inequality, 121, 171
Infowars, 99
Ingraham, Laura, 36
The Intercept, 63
intuitionism, 91, 97
Israel-Palestine experiment, 173
issues, maintaining focus on, 150

J
Jardina, Ashley, 57–58
Johnson, Gwen, 56
Jones, Van, 65–66, 113
Jordan, Barbara, 154
judgmentalism, 127, 143
Jumping at Shadows (Abramsky), 81
just-world bias, 95

K
Kavanaugh, Brett, 40, 41, 87–88
King, Angela, 109–110
King, Martin Luther, Jr., 7–8, 12, 113
Kingwell, Mark, 11
Kiser, Cindy, 35, 144
knowledge gap, admitting, 150
Knox, Connie, 62
Kohn, Sally, 179
Kristof, Nicholas, 32
Krugman, Paul, 28

Kubota, Jeni, 110–111
Ku Klux Klan, 72

L
labeling, effectiveness of, 144–145
LaPierre, Wayne, 36–37
Leadership Lab, 107–109, 116
learning, safety as precondition for, 31
Lee, Frances, 178
Lewis, Josh, 106
liberals/progressives
    class based contempt by, 49
    communication style of, 4, 5, 23–24
    complicity of, 44
    and conformity bias, 93
    Deep South, characterization by, 57
    and economic/moral interests,
        102–103
    entrenchment of conservatism by, 35
    and gullibility, 98
    Heartland, characterization by, 13
    incivility among, 5, 178
    perception of white privilege by, 60
    treatment of Donald Trump by, 22
Life After Hate, 109
Limbaugh, Rush, 49
The Limousine Liberal (Fraser), 70
Lindner, Evelin, 6
Listen, Liberal (Frank), 73
listening
    effectiveness of, 67–68
    and position statements, 136–137
    technique of, 119
Living Room Conversations, 167
Los Angeles LGBTQ Center, 107
    See also Leadership Lab
loss aversion, and conservatives, 96–97
Louisiana, white planter culture, 90
loyalty
    as conservative value, 15
    as function of tribalism, 85, 86, 88
    v. open-mindedness, 173–174

M
MAGA ("Make America Great
    Again"), 100–101
Maher, Bill, 23
Mahler, Luke, 17–19

"Make America Great Again" (MAGA)
    meaning of, 100–101
"Make America Great Again"
    (podcast), 83–84
Malheur National Wildlife Refuge, 78
Malik, Kenan, 58
Malkin, Michelle, 36
Malloy, Mike, 25
"Man Gets Schooled by Anti-Fascism
    Sign" (video), 17, 18–19
Marcotte, Amanda, 39–40
marriage, impact of contempt on, 17
Marron, Dylan, 168
Maslow, Abraham, 85
Mason, Lilliana, 172–173
Massey, Donna, 35
Matsumoto, David, 26, 42
McBride, Rev. Ben, 8, 130
McGill Daily, 178
Meade, Desmond, 174
media
    conspiracy, increased focus on by, 11
    contempt expressed in, 25–26, 26
    elitism, as focus of, 36
    right-wing, 98, 99
"meeting people where they're at,"
    146
meritocracy, 69–70
#Metoo, curiosity questions on,
    120–121
Metzl, Jonathan, 65
Miami-Dade County, anti-
    discrimination law, 107–108
middle class
    deep story of, 89, 90
    financial and social status of, 50
    resentments of, 66
migrants, separation of families of,
    137–138
misogyny, 51
mockery, effect of, 149
Moore, Michael, 24, 73
Morning Joe, 25
Morrison, Matt, 62
Moulitsas, Markos, 28
MSNBC, 25, 28, 29
Murray, Pat, 73
Mutz, Diana, 57

N
Nader, Ralph, 174
Naff, Dr. Monza, vii
NAFTA, 72
Nakagawa, Scot, 146
nationalism, white
    and economic anxiety, 59–60
    as outcome of tribalism, 87
    as response to globalization, 72
    and Trump supporters, 87
National Rifle Association (NRA), 36,
    135
nativism, 154
neuroscience, physical responses of
    brain, 22, 30–31, 80–81, 94
Newsome, Hawk, 172
New York, 29
New York Times
    on gun violence, 133
    Pizzagate, 99
    on Trump supporters, 28, 29, 32, 88
Nolan, Hamilton, 29
NRA (National Rifle Association), 36,
    135
Nussbaum, Karen, 107

O
Obamacare, model for, 173
objectivity, and liberals, 127
Occupy Democrats, 99
Ojeda, Richard, 56
Olberman, Keith, 54
oligarchy, tendency to, 102
Oliver, Eric, 97
Oliver, John, 27
Oluo, Ijeoma, 136
Open Markets Institute, 73
open-mindedness, 151, 170, 173–174
Operation Ceasefire, 8
opportunity v. outcome, 102
opposition
    and Deliberative Polling, 171–172
    engaging with, 169–170
    tempering of, 177
    understanding, 170–171
"othering," 6, 8, 44, 87
Othering and Belonging Conference, 8
"outrage discourse," 26

P

Palestine-Israel experiment, 173
Palmer, Parker, 177
parenting style, and political beliefs,
    79–80
Parks, Tim, 3
partisanship
    and communication, 39–40, 148–149
    as function of tribalism, 85, 86, 88
    as Trump tactic, 173
The Patch, 53
Patriot Prayer, 17
Pelosi, Alexandra, 48
Pelosi, Nancy, 7, 22, 147–148
Pendergraft, Rachel, 72
Petri, Alexandra, 53–54
Picciolini, Christian, 109, 110, 111
PICO California, 8
Pierson, Paul, 177
Pizzagate, 99
PNDC (Powerful Non-Defensive
    Communication), 153
    applied to political discourse, 10, 11
    basis of, 113–114
    benefits of, 11–12, 167
    demonstration of, 118, 140, 148, 161,
        168
    effectiveness of, 166–167
    integrating techniques of, 167
    objective of, 166
    See also curiosity questions; PNDC
        (Powerful Non-Defensive
        Communication), techniques of;
        position statements
PNDC (Powerful Non-Defensive
    Communication), techniques of
    boundaries, setting, 162–163, 164
    ending a discussion, 164–165
    finding common ground, 162
    introducing new topic, 163
    key issues, focusing on, 162, 163–164
    safety, 165
    starting a discussion, 161–162
    voice, tone of, 164
    "whatabouts," responding to, 163
    See also curiosity questions; PNDC
        (Powerful Non-Defensive Com-
        munication); position statements

polarization, 173, 175–178
political beliefs, roots of, 30, 78–80
"political correctness," 34–35
Political Research Associates, 67
Political Tribes (Chua), 100
politics, culture of, 5, 12–13
The Politics of Resentment (Cramer), 67
population, demographic shifts in,
    63, 71
populism, right-wing, rise of, 70
populists, discontent of, 66
position statements
    demonstrations of, 140, 148
    on Donald Trump, 129, 139–140
    on estate tax, 139
    functions of, 125
    guidelines for, 135, 136–137
    on healthcare, 139
    and self-righteousness, 141
    on separation of families, 137–138
    storytelling, using in, 135–136
    subjectivity in, 127
    technique for, 130
    use of with elected officials, 138
    on wealth and greed, 129–130
Post, Charlie, 72–73
poverty
    antipoverty programs, 171
    and self-contempt, 52–53
    and white privilege, 60
Powerful Non-Defensive Commu-
    nication (PNDC). *See* PNDC
    (Powerful Non-Defensive Com-
    munication)
prejudice, reducing, 109, 111
present bias, 92
progressives. *See* liberals/progressives
psychological needs, and tribalism, 85
public support, increasing, 176–177
punishment, effectiveness of, 147

Q

questions, types of, 117–118
    See also curiosity questions

R

RACE (Reflect.Ask.Connect.Expand),
    112

racism
    counteracting, 64–65, 68, 144–145
    curiosity questions on, 120
    fostered by economic inequality,
        71, 72
    labeling as, 34, 144–145
    in mass culture, 51
    as misdirected class resentment, 58
    as moral failing, 106
    and political parties, 87
    prevalence of, 58, 61, 106
    shaming, effect of, 63–64
    as voter motivation, 57–58, 69
"radical civility," 167
Ramos, Tarso Luis, 146
reconciliation v. retribution, 113
Red for the Blue, 168
Reich, Robert, 60–61
relationships, 8, 9, 17
religion and conservatives, 103–104
Repairers of the Breach, 7
Republican Party, strategies of, 47, 84
respect, absence of, 147–148
respectful dialogue
    as antiprejudice technique, 112
    benefit of, 133
    effect of labeling on, 144–145
    importance of, 176, 177
retaliation, effectiveness of, 8
retribution, reconciliation v., 113
revenge, contempt as form of, 42
Revolutionary Love Project, 7
Roberts, Julia, 23
Rules for Resistance (Cole), 14–15
rural America, 54–55, 59, 62–63
Rust Belt, voter motivation in, 60–61

S
safety, 31, 165
Salon, 29, 39
satire, 3, 26, 27, 53–54
Saunders, George, 75
Scarborough, Joe, 25
Schiller, Daniela, 80
Schminke, Dennis, 21
Schneider, Kirk, 175
Schumer, Chuck, 62–63
self-contempt, and poverty, 52–53
self-esteem, 30, 85

self-exploration, questions for, 123–124
self-protection, and contempt, 43
self-righteousness, 141–142, 178
shame
    avoiding, author experience of, 1
    effectiveness of, 4, 31, 63–64, 108, 110
    inciting hostility with, 109
Shapiro, Ben, 95
Shenker-Osorio, Anat, 64–65
Shokraifard, Jodie, 4
Simi, Pete, 110
Smarsh, Sarah, 52–53
SMART Politics, 30, 167
Smicker, Dan, 54–55
Sobieraj, Sarah, 26, 34
social change, stress of, 75, 76
social conditions, 70, 71, 76
social inequality, preserving, 101
social justice, preconditions for, 7
social media, 36, 75, 98, 99, 167
Social Psychological Answers to
        Real-World Questions Center, 145
Socratic questions, 117–118
South, resentments in, 56–57
So You Want to Talk About Race
        (Oluo), 136
Starnes, Todd, 36
status
    as dynamic of contempt, 19
    perceived loss of, 31–32, 47–48
    threat to, 30
status quo, preserving, 101
stereotyping, and attribution error, 93
Stoller, Matt, 73–74
stories, deep
    creating, 78–79, 88
    of working class whites, 89, 90
storytelling
    and communication, 112, 135–136
    in position statements, 135–136
    power of, 107, 108, 110–111
Strangers in Their Own Land
        (Hochschild), 88, 89
Streep, Meryl, 23
stupidity, as accusation, 29, 30
subjectivity, in position statements, 127
submissiveness, roots of, 90
Sullivan, Margaret, 15
Summers, Lawrence, 69

superiority
  and belongingness, 40
  as dynamic of contempt, 19, 20, 114
  effect of, 3, 41, 57, 142
  shedding sense of, 123–124, 167

T
Taking the War Out of Our Words
  (Ellison), 168
Tamerius, Karin, 30
"thoughts and prayers" as response,
  130–133
threats, responses to, 22, 30–31, 80–81,
  94, 145
Toffler, Alvin, 75
trade deals, 72
training, bystander intervention, 165
Trans-Pacific Partnership, 72
transphobia, overcoming, 107–108
tribalism, 85, 86, 87, 173–174
Trump, Donald
  appeal of, 38, 47–48, 56, 75
  and compassion, 12
  as intuitionist, 97
  position statements on, 129, 139–140
  treatment of, 22
  use of contempt by, 7, 20, 40
"Trumpkin," 53
Trump supporters
  and authoritarianism, 84–85
  demographic makeup of, 61
  and loss of status, 31–32
  motives of, 66

U
understanding, and position statements, 125
University of Pennsylvania, study by, 31
upper class, attitudes of, 51

V
values
  altruistic, loss of, 70
  of conservatives, 103–104
  of liberals, 103
  shift in, under populism, 70
vibes, effective, 149
violence
  gun violence, 130–134

hate violence, 72, 110, 120
  against women, 126
voice, tone of, 118, 137, 146, 164, 167
voters
  discontent of, 66, 67, 70
  disengagement of, 51, 73
  motivations of, 57, 60–61, 66
voters, estrangement of, 58–59, 62,
  72–73
voters, swing
  alienation of, 42, 51, 178
  in 2020 election, 13, 56, 66
  motivation of, 14
  openness to voting Democratic, 62
  in Trump strategy, 14
voters, working class whites, 50, 62
voter suppression, 51
vulnerability, in relationship, 9

W
Walsh, Jamie, 60
war model, of communication, 15
Warrick, Ray, 172
Washington Post
  on disillusionment of voters, 59
  on gun violence, 134
  on motivations of Midwest voters, 61
  on Pelosi and respect for Trump, 147
  poll on oligarchy, 102
  on rural resentment, 54–55
  treatment of Trump by, 15, 28–29, 53
Wasserman, Edward, 5
"we," use of, 149–150
wealth and greed, position statement
  on, 129–130
Weisser, Rabbi Michael, 111
welfare, 121, 171
"whataboutism," 162–163
white allies
  role of in antiracism, 112, 145
  "tone policing" by, 146
White Ally Toolkit (Campt), 93
White Fragility (DiAngelo), 105
White Identity Politics (Jardina), 57
"whitelash," 66
white-male archetype, deconstruction
  of, 65
white nationalism
  and economic anxiety, 59–60

as outcome of tribalism, 87
as response to globalization, 72
and Trump supporters, 87
    (*See also* white supremacist
    groups)
white planter culture, legacy of, 90
white power, 68
white privilege, 60, 90
white supremacist groups
    antiprejudice techniques with,
    109–110
    dynamics of, 68
    shaming, effect on, 64
    (*See also* white nationalism)
White Working Class (Williams), 50
Williams, Joan, 50
Wilson, Theo E.J., 68–69
winning, and communication, 150
Wisconsin, voter resentments, 67
Wonkette, 28

Working America, 14, 62, 106–107
working class whites
    class based contempt by, 49
    deep story of, 89, 90
    economic situation of, 59
    engaging with, 63
    estrangement of, 58–59, 62, 73–74
    immigrants, fear of by, 59
    perception of party differences
        by, 62
    Republican Party appeal to, 47, 84
    trade deals, perception of by, 72
    voting record of, 50

Y
Younge, Gary, 59–60

Z
Zaitchik, Alexander, 60
Zapollo (commenter), 33–34

About the Author

ERICA ETELSON is a writer, community activist, and certified Powerful Non-Defensive Communication™ facilitator. A former human rights attorney, she has advocated in support of welfare recipients, prisoners, indigenous peoples, immigrants, and environmental activists. She has also organized for clean, community-owned energy as a solution to the climate crisis. Following the 2016 election, Etelson became active in the resistance movement and in red–blue dialogue initiatives. Her articles have appeared in the *San Francisco Chronicle*, *San Jose Mercury News*, *Truthout*, *The Progressive Populist*, and *Alternet*. She lives with her husband and son in Berkeley, California.

Book website: ericaetelson.com/beyondcontempt

ABOUT NEW SOCIETY PUBLISHERS

New Society Publishers is an activist, solutions-oriented publisher focused on publishing books for a world of change. Our books offer tips, tools, and insights from leading experts in sustainable building, homesteading, climate change, environment, conscientious commerce, renewable energy, and more—positive solutions for troubled times.

We're proud to hold to the highest environmental and social standards of any publisher in North America. This is why some of our books might cost a little more. We think it's worth it!

DON'T EAT THIS BOOK *(but you could)*

- We print all our books in North America, never overseas

- All our books are printed on **100% post-consumer recycled paper**, processed chlorine-free, with low-VOC vegetable-based inks (since 2002)

- Our corporate structure is an innovative employee shareholder agreement, so we're one-third employee-owned (since 2015)

- We're carbon-neutral (since 2006)

- We're certified as a B Corporation (since 2016)

At New Society Publishers, we care deeply about *what* we publish—but also about *how* we do business.

Download our catalog at https://newsociety.com/Our-Catalog or for a printed copy please email info@newsocietypub.com or call 1-800-567-6772 ext 111.

New Society Publishers
ENVIRONMENTAL BENEFITS STATEMENT

By using 100% post-consumer recycled paper vs virgin paper stock, New Society Publishers saves the following resources:[1] (per every 5,000 copies printed)

24	Trees
2,188	Pounds of Solid Waste
2,408	Gallons of Water
3,140	Kilowatt Hours of Electricity
3,978	Pounds of Greenhouse Gases
17	Pounds of HAPs, VOCs, and AOX Combined
6	Cubic Yards of Landfill Space

[1] Environmental benefits are calculated based on research done by the Environmental Defense Fund and other members of the Paper Task Force who study the environmental impacts of the paper industry.

Certified **B** **Corporation**

MIX
Paper from responsible sources
FSC
www.fsc.org
FSC® C016245

new society
PUBLISHERS
www.newsociety.com